MARGARET PAWLEY

Donald Coggan

SERVANT OF CHRIST

First published in Great Britain 1987
SPCK
Holy Trinity Church
Marylebone Road
London NW1 4DU

ACKNOWLEDGEMENTS

Thanks are due to the editor of the *York Journal of Convocation* for permission to
quote from the journal.

Thanks are also due to the following for permission to use the photographs
reproduced in this book:

11: Burdekin Photographic Library, Church Information Office;
12, 16: Keystone Press Agency Ltd;
13: *Yorkshire Post*;
14: Brian Duff, *Daily Express*;
15, 18, 19, 26: *Kentish Gazette* Photographic Service;
17: The Press Association Ltd;
20: J. H. Ray (Associates) Ltd;
23: Gopal Chitra Kuteer
25: John Miles, Church Information Office;
28: The Reverend Canon Degwel Thomas.

British Library Cataloguing in Publication Data

Pawley, Margaret
  Donald Coggan: Servant of Christ.
  1. Coggan, Donald   2. Church of England — Bishops — Biography
  I. Title
  283'.092'4   BX5199.C567

ISBN 0-281-04326-4

Typeset by York House Typographic
Printed in Great Britain at
The University Press, Cambridge

For B.

In memoriam amantissimus

Ministry — the work of the servant, the slave (doulos) *of Christ, the man or woman who has been laid hold of by Christ . . . the man who, to a greater or lesser extent is finding that slavery to be in fact his freedom . . . that is our theme.*

Donald Coggan, Archbishop of York,
on the opening day of the
1968 Lambeth Conference

There is only one title I am proud of, and that is the same as St Paul's — slave of Christ . . .
When you think of your Archbishop and, as I hope, pray for him sometimes, just think of him as the slave of Christ, and remember that is the title he loves best of all.

Donald Coggan, Archbishop of Canterbury,
in Accra, West Africa, March 1979

Contents

Preface

My intention in this work has been to present the results of my search for facts and opinions concerning the life of Donald Coggan, and to try, within my shortcomings, to interpret them. The limitations are two-fold: first, this book is written by one who is by trade a historian; those who look for specifically theological insights will look in vain; secondly, the events portrayed are so recent as to preclude any but a short-term appraisal of Donald Coggan's ministry at York and Canterbury against the backdrop of mid-twentieth century national and ecclesiastical affairs. His place in history may not become apparent until another three or four Archbishops have come and gone; when historians, looking back to the 1960s and 1970s, will be able to assess measures suggested, stands taken, in greater perspective. If Intercommunion, Covenanting, the ordination of women in the universal Church, should have come to pass, he will be regarded as having been something of a prophet. If some future Archbishop of Canterbury should happen to be able to discover effective means of evangelizing these islands, Donald Coggan will receive less sympathy. If not, he may be given the credit for trying, and for keeping the matter always before him.

There are a number of debts to acknowledge in the preparation of this book: my greatest is to Lord Coggan himself, for his expenditure of time and patience in relating many of his memories and experiences, and for the loan of books and papers; likewise to Lady Coggan whose guest I have been on many occasions. I record my thanks to numerous others, whom I have not mentioned by name, who have helped me by answering demanding questions. Two I should like to single out: the Hon. Ruth Coggan, FRCOG, OBE, for her kindness in lending me the letters to Pakistan written by her parents, 1969-80; also Mr Patrick Coggan of Stratford-sub-Castle, Wiltshire, a distant cousin, who led me through villages in Somerset, with an emphasis on graveyards. Hosts in various parts of the world have given me generous hospitality during the research period: the Reverend and Mrs Reginald Stackhouse, then of the Principal's House, Wycliffe College, Toronto, Miss Pamela Bird, Personal Assistant to the then Primate of Canada, Miss Peggy

Chisholm, who not only entertained me in America, but lent me her flat in London, the Right Reverend Colin Buchanan, then Principal of St John's College, Nottingham, and the Focolare movement in Rome; my thanks to them all.

I also wish to acknowledge my indebtedness to the librarians and archivists of many libraries and archive collections who have helped me in the provision of printed and written material: the British Library, the Bodleian, Canterbury Cathedral Library, Lambeth Palace Library, Library of Wycliffe College, Toronto, of St John's College, Nottingham, the Borthwick Institute in York, the Archive department of the General Synod, of Hackney Public Library, the Record Offices of Hampshire and Somerset, Racal-Chubb Ltd, the Guildhall Library, the Library of Sion College, the libraries of Christ Church and of St Augustine's College, Canterbury, the Ashford Branch of the Kent County Library. Mrs Deborah Webb has typed, with invariable cheerfulness, a manuscript written in handwriting wrecked by higher education. I am grateful to her and to the friends who have helped to read the proofs.

MARGARET PAWLEY

July 1987
Old Wives' Lees
Canterbury

CHAPTER ONE

Youth

During the summer months of the First World War a solitary, sensitive fair-haired boy walked along the beaches of his native Somerset. It became for him a crucial place, for on the hard flat sands of the estuary of the river Parrett at Burnham-on-Sea with their fringe of gorse-covered dunes, home of gulls, oyster catchers and shelduck, he heard a message of such clarity that its content and impact never left him.

Donald Coggan was born in Highgate on 9 October 1909 and he was therefore technically a Londoner and townsman. But his roots in the West Country were deep; far deeper than either he or his immediate kin were aware. The past has never held much interest for him; the present made instant and overwhelming demands. Such folk-memories as remained connected the Coggan family with Ireland. This was partly true, but its origins lay elsewhere. In the old Welsh language *cogan* meant a cup, bowl or depression in the land. A mile from Penarth in Glamorgan lies a small hamlet in a hollow; its name is still Cogan. There remain the ruins of a castle, a house by the name of Cogan Hall, and nearby, of more recent introduction, Cogan dock and Cogan station.

In the late eleventh century Rhys ap Tewdwr was recognized as the lord of South Wales, of the ancient Kingdom of Deheubarth, and was mentioned as such in Domesday. On his death in 1093 the Normans, who had not as yet been able to penetrate into southern and central Wales, were able to do so. Gerald of Windsor became Constable of Pembroke Castle and married Rhys ap Tewdwr's daughter Nesta whose beauty caused her to be known as the Helen of Wales. They had a numerous and illustrious progeny: one was Maurice, founder of the house of Fitz-Gerald, the Geraldines, later to take part in the Norman subjection of Ireland; another son was William of Barri father to a further Gerald, who as Silvester Giraldus Cambrensis achieved lasting fame for his spirited if partial historical and topographical accounts of the period. A daughter Gledewis also appears on the pedigree, whose marriage to Gwgan of Cogan Castle, Penarth, produced two sons, Miles and Richard of Cogan.

William Rufus had boasted that he would make himself master of

Ireland. It was not however until the reign of his third successor that a move was made: Henry II acquired a Bull from Pope Adrian IV approving a plan of conquest; concern for the isolated Irish Church may well have been responsible for the sanction. The first of Henry's barons to take advantage of the position was Richard, Earl of Striguil and Pembroke, commonly known as Strongbow. In 1170 he set out for Ireland accompanied, among others, by a number of Welsh/Norman knights; Maurice Fitz-Gerald and Miles of Cogan were of the company. Miles of Cogan distinguished himself in the storming of Dublin and was left by Strongbow as governor of the city; an epic poem survives to describe the event[1]. Assuming the kingship of Cork and Desmond, he met his death in 1182 at the hands of Mac Tire, King of Cork. His place in Ireland, by command of Henry II, was taken by his brother Richard.

Richard of Cogan's descendants settled not in Wales, but in Devon and Somerset; the knightly seat in the thirteenth and fourteenth centuries was at Huntspill, only three miles from Burnham. During the seventeenth century members of the Cogan family moved to London, Nottingham, Northants and Hull; the surname carried the variation Coggan, awareness of kinship being maintained by an attachment to the original coat of arms – a red shield charged with silver oak leaves and the motto *Constans Fidei*. For example, William Cogan[2] or (as it was often written) Coggan, apprenticed as an apothecary, became a prosperous Alderman and twice Mayor of Hull in the eighteenth century. Among his other charitable works was the foundation and endowment of a school for twenty poor girls in July 1753. The pupils were taught to read, to know the catechism and attend church regularly, and be trained to work in a household; a Bible and twenty shillings were provided as they left the school and upon marriage a dowry of six pounds. Their distinctive dress with white starched cap and large apron earned them the name *Coggy's dollys*. The school after a series of changed guises, with numbers greatly increased, endured until 1950 and a new Education Act, when a modern secondary school took its place; but the name the Alderman Cogan School survived, as also has its badge, the coat of arms from earlier times.

Many Cogans/Coggans (the varied spelling can be found within even close relations) remained in Somerset. A survey of the lands of

---

[1] 'De Cogan led the way' (Anglo-Norman Poems, ed. F.P. Barnard, Maurice Regan, *Strongbow's Conquest of Ireland*, 1166-86, David Nutt 1888).
[2] 1677-1774.

William, first Earl of Pembroke, in the sixteenth century lists five or six Cogans as tenants in the Chedzoy area, the wetlands of Sedgemoor. In more recent times, Donald Coggan's immediate ancestors lived for three hundred years in an area contained within a triangle drawn between Bridgwater in the west to Somerton in the east and Ilminster in the south. During this period both sides of each family were locally born: Coggan menfolk courted their wives within a distance which could be covered on horseback. At the end of the seventeenth century his forebears had settled at Somerton, a distinguished small market town with grey stone houses and tree-lined streets. John Coggan, born about 1670 was a husbandman who died there in 1733: his son Francis and grandson John were baptized and died there also. The latter's wife, Mary Bisgrove, came from Muchelney where the marriage took place in 1762. Their son Henry (1768-1843) was born in Somerton but died in Oath in Aller, five miles to the northwest, where, so his will discloses, he owned land on Aller Moor in addition to three acres at Ashen Cross to the south. He bequeathed to his wife, the former Mary Locke, some cottages in Somerton 'near the Ponpoole' (where stray animals came to drink) which can still be identified. Mary Coggan (1766-1852) left property and a will also, though she could not write her name to sign it. Her husband and sons were described as yeomen and their increased prosperity is clear to see. With their son George (1795-1870) came the first overt connection with the cattle dealing and meat trading that was to be the family's avocation for the next four generations.

George Coggan's success in his career is revealed by his choice of home. In 1819 he married Sarah Yarde from Martock, five miles south of Somerton, and they acquired a house at Curry Rivel, a village on a wooded bluff overlooking the wetlands, south east of West Sedge Moor. The Yews is a sizeable seventeenth-century building with later additions, enclosed within a large garden full of trees. There are stables, a separate coachhouse and a burial ground for dogs where the headstones date back to George Coggan's day. All his children were born there; his and most of their graves are in the churchyard. Frederick James Coggan (1820-1901) the eldest son, farmer and cattle dealer, married Ann Gristock from North Petherton in 1844. Their son William, born at Creech St Michael on 19 July 1851, was Donald Coggan's grandfather.

Clearly a man of considerable ability, it was doubtless because he felt the constraints of working within a confined geographical area, with limited authority, that he decided in 1875 to move to London.

In the previous year he had married Elizabeth Clothier, daughter of a farming family from Chilton Trinity near Bridgwater; Donald Coggan's father was the second son, Cornish Arthur, born in 1876. In London William Coggan joined the head office of the meat trading company of Lidstone (of which he became chairman) based on Smithfield market. Soon he assumed wider responsibilities; in 1900-2 he was President of the National Association of Meat Traders and in 1902-6 President of the London Association. Speeches at a public banquet given in his honour at the Hotel Cecil on 13 May 1901 described his activities: he had concerned himself with various Meat Marketing Bills before Parliament, and had suggested changes which saved his colleagues from the effects of unwise legislation; he had represented his field of work in municipal assemblies, courts of law and trade societies. He was thanked for his 'untiring industry, consummate tact and inflexible integrity' and honoured with a series of handsome silver gifts: a salver, tea set and candelabra, together with a bound volume which contained four hundred and fifty signatures.

William Coggan's greatest single contribution to the well-being of his fellows, for which he was awarded the OBE, was in breaking the price ring operated by leather and hide merchants against the interests of meat traders. A trifling sum (about sixpence) was all that was offered to cattle farmers for the hides of animals. William Coggan founded his own hide and leather company: with fleets of carts farms were visited and the hides collected, sprinkled with saltpetre and transported to warehouses in Bermondsey. There the leather was auctioned each Tuesday, and on the following Friday farmers received their cheques for pounds rather than pence: goodwill was created by this courage and initiative.

Cornish Arthur Coggan followed his father into the firm of Lidstone, and for many years was company secretary. In 1901, at the age of twenty-five, he married at the parish church of Weston-super-Mare Fanny Sarah Chubb who was four years his senior. They had three children, of whom Donald Coggan was the youngest. His Coggan inheritance held enterprise, application and capacity for hard work. His Chubb grandfather was also possessed of just such qualities.

Augustus Chubb was born in Fordingbridge in Hampshire in 1829, the son of John Chubb, a tick maker turned farmer, and his wife Martha. There were seven children; Augustus was the fifth. The harsh nature of the period is shown in the census returns of 1841 and 1851: many hand-loom and power-loom weavers were without work. Fanny Coggan passed on to her children the impression that she was related to the family of Chubb the famous locksmith. This was very likely, in view of the proximity of their origins. Although no connection can be traced in the late eighteenth and the nineteenth centuries, it may well have occurred before 1730, when the company's records begin to operate. What is significant is that both Augustus Chubb and Charles Chubb, founder of the locksmithing business, showed a similar genius for developing their own resources at times of great hardship.

Charles Chubb, born 1744, third son of a tick weaver of Fordingbridge, moved to Winchester at the end of the eighteenth century to set up his home and a hardware business. In 1802 he and his family moved to Portsea and became ship's chandlers. After the invention of the Chubb detector lock in 1818, lock manufacturing became their main concern; the basis of the empire had been laid.

Augustus Chubb left Fordingbridge for Taunton in Somerset to become apprenticed to Francis Wookey, a large linen-draper at 5 Fore Street. By 1851 he had become the most senior of Wookey's seven assistants. On 27 August 1856 he married at St Mary Magdalene's Church nineteen-year-old Elizabeth Ann Chibbett. Soon after his marriage Augustus Chubb established his own linen-drapery at 14/15 North Street where he and his wife with their large staff of four assistants and seven apprentices, and a maid, shared the two houses. A daughter Florence was born there in 1861.

Notice of the failure of several Taunton businesses occurs in the local press throughout the 1850s and 1860s, including a number of tailors and linen-drapers. But that of Augustus Chubb flourished to such an extent that by the astonishingly early age of thirty-seven he was able to retire and move to Porlock. On 13 June 1870, at an auction at the Nag's Head Hotel in Taunton, he bought a house in Rowbarton, the northern part of the town in the parish of St James. From the sale notice and in an old drawing, Rowbarton House appeared a property of size and distinction (it was pulled down in the 1930s): there were three reception rooms, domestic offices, five bedrooms, servants' rooms, attics, a lawn, garden, coachhouse, cider house and cellar. The new owner's flair and industry had served him well. His son Frederick was born there in 1870 and Donald Coggan's mother, Fanny, on 29 March 1872. Rowbarton House remained their home until the early 1890s, when a move was made to Weston-super-Mare: the place from which Fanny was married.

She and her husband went to live in North London, at 32

Croftdown Road, off Highgate Hill. There Norah their first child was born in December 1902 and was followed by a second daughter, Beatrice, in September 1906. Donald, three years younger, was only five at the outbreak of the First World War, but certain memories of it were vivid: his father in the uniform of a special constable, told him that his responsibilities lay in Smithfield Market, which would be particularly dangerous in the event of an air-raid because of the extent of the overhead glass. The boy and his mother were walking along York Rise, Highgate, which he assumed was written 'Your Prize' (a prophetic error), when a German plane appeared in the cloudless sky; greatly alarmed, they took refuge in a nearby house and he received milk and biscuits. Perhaps it was this incident that precipitated the move to Burnham-on-Sea of Fanny Coggan and her three children for the remainder of the war. They lived in a guest house; Fanny was thereby near her mother and sister at Weston (Augustus Chubb died in 1912), but maintained some independence. Arthur Coggan (as he was known) made isolated visits.

Among the salient events of the Burnham period was the beginning of Donald's formal education. He entered the kindergarten of Oakover School in Berrow Road, parallel to and in close proximity to the beach. The grey stone, double fronted, Victorian premises were created by joining a pair of adjoining semi-detached houses, with characteristic bay windows and steep-pitched tile roofs ornamented with wooden scroll-work giving an appearance of solidity and security. Donald certainly was happy there, and remembered the experience with affection. The school was in the hands of Mrs Archer (who acted as matron-housekeeper) and her three daughters. Miss Ruth, the youngest, ran the kindergarten classes. Now Mrs Mugliston, in her late nineties, from a retirement home in Guildford she recalled the young Donald Coggan as a bright child who did not cause trouble. She devised a game for wet days which gave a great deal of pleasure: she would draw a large map of England in chalk on the floor of the classrooms cleared of desks; then as Miss Ruth called out the name of an English town, the children were expected to take up their positions on the map; those who made mistakes were sent to the Scilly Islands. Donald Coggan was the only child in her entire experience who had the initiative to ask whether he might go to a place of his own choosing. Geography was clearly a dramatically taught subject: Donald himself remembered for over seventy years that Miss Ruth would give a jump to illustrate Start Point.

Oakover was technically a girls' school; Norah and Beatrice

Coggan were also pupils. Male presence was restricted to the lower forms; around 1915 there were three boys: Donald, Peter Johnson, and Richard Daunton-Fear whose memory of his contemporaries is distinct. He well recalled Donald because he was so clean, so able and so zealous over his home-work; already the beginnings of musical competence had begun to show: he would withdraw from lessons to go and learn to play the piano with Miss Marion, second of the Archer sisters. The only sign of revolt (which the other boys shared) was towards attempts to teach them to knit: they thought it unmanly.

All three boys were later ordained into the ministry of the Church of England. Peter Johnson became vicar of St Mary's Islington, Richard Daunton-Fear an archdeacon and Donald Archbishop of Canterbury. The foundation of their Christian commitment was laid at Burnham, for it was there that they encountered Ashley King and the Childrens' Special Service Missions.

Ashley King was considered by many to have been a saint. Born on 8 September 1885 in Oxfordshire, the youngest of eight children, he attended Dean Close School in Cheltenham and Clifton Theological College. He decided against ordination, but became a lay missionary, as were both his sisters. He offered himself to the Egypt General Mission and went abroad in 1911, where his first post was head of the Boys' School at Ismailia. A fluent Arabic speaker with a deep love for the Egyptian poor, he married in Egypt and spent forty-five years in the service of the Mission. It was an interdenominational association (Ashley King was an Anglican) founded about the turn of the century by seven young men in Belfast: a so-called 'faith mission' modelled on the lines of the China Inland Mission; missionaries were given an allowance, rather than a fixed salary, which varied according to the money available each month.

Ashley King's parents moved to Burnham-on-Sea before the First World War; on his furloughs from Egypt he and his family lived a few yards from Oakover School, and he continued his evangelistic work by conducting missions for children on the beach. The power of his conversation, his godly outlook, his sense of humour and the warmth of his personality affected many who met him. Though he suffered from a pronounced limp from a childhood illness, he would take young people for walks and expound to them the basis of his faith. All three Coggan children were moved by what they heard, and returned to London bearing its impact with them. It was a first-century apostolic message based on the Scriptures; clear and strong and uncompromising; asking for commitment and prayer and acceptance of Jesus of Nazareth as Lord, without the theological overtones of succeeding ages. It was how Ashley King saw his religion. He was once in trouble[3] with the CSSM Council because he invited a Roman Catholic priest to speak to a meeting of children on the beach. His times were not ready for a prophet such as he. Ashley King died in 1984, aged 98, having a few days before his death recited the twenty-third psalm without mistake, to the amazement of those around him in the hospital.

Donald Coggan's youthful experiences had effects of two kinds: some he treasured so much that he continued to value their elements for the rest of his life. His attitude towards missions was of this type. Because of his own personal gain, he later persisted in rating this method of evangelism highly when some of his contemporaries had come to consider it outdated. In regard to his experience of family life, however, he took the opposite course. When he came to be a husband and parent he was able to jettison the example that he was set by his own father (no mean feat this), and establish relationships of quite a different sort.

The return to London was the herald of some painful years. Contained within the family was a degree of tension and strain. For the daughters it was an area that is still too sensitive to be much discussed; as for Donald, it was serious enough to make him ill. Photographs of him demonstrate changes that took place: the cheerful, fat child with merry eyes gave way to a thin-faced youth of nervous aspect. He developed asthma, so serious that his family were much alarmed by the severity of the attacks. Vapourizers were lit; breathing exercises prescribed. Donald was helped by his siblings, by an osteopath who tried to develop his lung power, and most of all by the magnitude of his own efforts to overcome his disability. The discipline that he adopted was to stand him in good stead in the future. It was one that he needed to extend not only over his physical self, but over his emotions also; his extreme sensibility worried his sisters; passages of music, especially on the organ, reduced him to tears. Donald's state of health made formal schooling impossible, but it was his musical ability that led to the solution. Helen Gardner, a gifted musician who lived in the neighbourhood, on becoming a widow began to give music lessons, and Donald was one of her pupils. The arrangement was so successful that she became his tutor for school subjects also for the next four

---

[3] Recalled by R. Daunton-Fear.

years. Her daughter[4] recalled the delicate boy for whom her mother provided a life-line.

Donald's father, Arthur Coggan, was probably the most able of his parents' seven sons. No concession was made to his father's position; Arthur as a boy of fifteen after only two years at Dulwich was required to enter the family company at the bottom of the ladder. At seventeen he began to learn the wholesale side of the business with two successive firms in Smithfield Market; by twenty-one years old he was Company Secretary of Lidstones. In November 1906 he was elected a member of the St Pancras Borough Council and immediately made Deputy Chairman of the Finance Committee (he soon became Chairman) and Chairman of the Rating Sub-Committee; later he was required to chair three further types of meetings. In 1912, he became the unanimous selection of the Council to be Mayor. Precise and formal in his manner and appearance (he wore pince-nez spectacles, striped trousers, a black jacket and high starched white collar all his life) he was at thirty-six the youngest occupant of that office in one of the London Boroughs to date. The Requisition inviting him to accept the mayorality spoke of his talents:

> . . . we have recognized that your business capacity, your powers of exposition and other high qualities which you possess, would in a short time entitle you to appointment to those official positions which the Council is able to offer to its members . . . In the office of Chairman of the Finance Committee, your half-yearly statements when submitting the estimates of revenue and expenditure were models of conciseness and clearness, and your excellent grasp of the Finances generally of the Borough was especially noticeable. Your gifts in this direction were also brought to bear in the performance of the duties of all the other offices held by you, with similar success.

Many of these qualities of good chairmanship and succinct reporting were passed to his son; but his record within the family circle was less happy. For one thing, he was hardly ever there; apart from his business at Lidstones on six days each week, and local government work (for which he attended all but twenty meetings out of a possible 752 in the first six years in office), he was a founder member of the Rotary Club of London in 1911 and a prominent Mason. (All the work was voluntary; not even expenses were given at the time). For some years he served on the LCC Hospitals

---

[4] Dame Helen Gardner, lately Merton Professor of English Literature, Oxford University.

Committee; when he retired from the force of Special Constables in 1935, he had the rank of Chief Inspector. His wife and children had meals, holidays and went to church without him; and it seems that the separate nature of their existences tended to increase as the years passed, leaving each to their own loneliness.

During the early years of the century, Arthur Coggan was a member of the congregation of Kentish Town parish church; his children were baptized there. A correspondent remembers a period when he would arrive to sit in the pew in front of her, accompanied by Donald and his sisters. After the Burnham experiences, the children began to take the initiative in religious matters; there were difficulties in finding a church where they felt at home. They attended St Anne's, Brookfield, for a time, a graceful, neo-gothic building with tall spire and carriage entrance.

> But awe and mystery were everywhere,
> Most in the purple dark of thin St Anne's.

wrote John Betjeman, who was born a stone's throw from Donald and in the same year, in his *Summoned by Bells*[5]. The Gardner family were there also, but the young people never spoke. Donald and his sisters were a small, self-contained unit. Few visits were made and there was no entertaining. Their ten first cousins were unknown to them.

Around 1922 the children with their mother began to worship at St Peter's, Upper Holloway. Arthur Coggan transferred his allegiance to the church of St Martin, Gospel Oak, where he became a churchwarden and friend of Thomas Henry Russell, vicar there for thirty-seven years. He remained a faithful member of the congregation for the rest of his life.

Awe and mystery were not the hallmarks of St Peter's, Upper Holloway; they were not intended to be, for it embraced a different emphasis in worship and teaching within the comprehensive nature of the Anglican Church. The great gaunt edifice of red brick was like a fortress, the *feste Burg* of Luther's poem. St Peter's was a Conservative Evangelical stronghold; the word can be used advisedly. From it emanated a powerful message, which called for repentance and proclaimed the certainty of grace available to all who believed in Jesus as Son of God, and followed him as their Lord and Saviour. His sacrificial act upon the cross had paid for all time the price of sin; the substitutional nature of the atonement was central;

[5] John Murray 1960.

other aspects of the gospel were seen as subordinate to it. Since the Scriptures provided affirmation of the doctrine, biblical exposition occupied an important place.

The Evangelical wing in the Church of England had undergone various transitions since its rise in the late eighteenth century, with John Wesley as its chief agent, as a reaction to spiritual turpitude and current low moral standards. By the twenties of the present century, Evangelical strength lay in particular parishes rather than among the leaders of the Church, and was nurtured by clergy whose convictions lay within its distinctive outlook. They in turn influenced lay people who rated high as part of their commitment carrying the message to the next generation; thereby the tradition was preserved. Throughout the nineteen-twenties young Evangelicals would teach Crusader groups, or during the summer lead the activities of the CSSM in various popular seaside towns. The friendship and sincerity of the organizers, their sacrifice of time and energy, and the intensity of the appeal that was made, produced a rich harvest. Donald Coggan was one of many[6] of his time who came to Christian belief by this path. He had been drawn, as they were, not by a system or institution, but to following a Master; hence his natural progression, for the initial stages of his spiritual development at any rate, towards a Conservative Evangelical parish.

Such parishes were maintained by trusts; in the case of St Peter's the Church Pastoral Aid Society, which by their patronage assured the provision of acceptable incumbents. When Donald Coggan joined the congregation the vicar was Edmund Dunn; he left in 1923 after a term of twelve years. 'A wonderful man and priest . . . He gave me a fine example of Christ's ministry in action'[7]. The parish contained 8,000 inhabitants, most of whom lived in the rows of modest terraced houses and small shops of the neighbourhood. Those whose memories stretch to the 1920s suggest that there was no great poverty nor great wealth within the parish boundaries, although it was less prosperous than Highgate to the north west where the Coggans had their home. The parish magazine reflects intermittent difficulty in raising money for running expenses; the weekly programme of worship and activities was extensive.

[6] Among them Max Warren (1904-77), General Secretary of the Church Missionary Society 1942-63 and Canon of Westminster; also Joseph Edward Fison (1906-72), Bishop of Salisbury. See Max Warren, *Crowded Canvas*, Hodder & Stoughton 1974 and F.W. Dillistone's two books: *Into All the World*, Hodder & Stoughton 1980 and *The Life of Joe Fison*, Amate Press 1983.

[7] Robin Daniels *Conversations with Coggan* (Hodder and Stoughton 1983), p.19.

Each Sunday there was a celebration of the Holy Communion at 8 am; on the first and third Sundays also at midday, and on the fourth Sunday after Evening Prayer, which was at 6.30 pm; and on major saints' days. Sunday Morning Prayer was at 11 am. Prayer meetings each Saturday evening were well attended. A service for men on Sunday afternoons, a women's guild, Band of Hope, sewing parties, Bible classes in various grades for men and women, boys and girls, scouting and guiding, all formed part of the pattern. Segregation of the sexes was a general practice, reflecting the principle of exclusiveness which permeated the Evangelical outlook of the twenties. Christian commitment was of a primarily spiritual kind: intellect and imagination were not greatly engaged and few attempts were made to grapple with current social and political problems or the implications of the gospel in this respect. The general strike and high unemployment figures went unrecorded in the parish magazine. Before the Second World War, Evangelical congregations, in the world but not of it, tended to live in isolation from their contemporaries. The stress on personal holiness of living made social activities, parties, dances, entertainment, particularly the theatre, somewhat suspect.

Lack of interest and appreciation in cultural and artistic fields was a further source of division in these times. The interior of St Peter's was as forbidding as the exterior, without concession to grace of line or decoration. The great high brick walls were red, as was the marble of the east end and pulpit, relieved only by brass rails. Stone pillars were bare except for the flags of parish associations; the floor bore a pattern of red and black tiles in between fixed pews of varnished pitch-pine. Gas lighting was replaced by electricity in 1927. But as a contrast to the stark surroundings, the leadership at St Peter's evoked an atmosphere of warmth, loyalty and enthusiasm, though it was of a confined sort and little was done to relate to other members of the world-wide Church. Missionary thrust would seem to have been concentrated towards the Jews, with speakers, collections and prayers in this interest.

Edward Hewlett Gladstone Sargent[8], a graduate, which Edmund Dunn was not, succeeded him as vicar in 1923. Gladstone Sargent had a radiant personality and was a powerful preacher. His considerable musical talent made him a good pianist and composer of hymns and choruses, and his gift for identifying with young people produced respect, admiration and a desire to imitate.

[8] St John's College, Cambridge 1906-9.

The Coggan children were happy to worship in this environment. The outcome was prodigious: Donald was led towards ordination, Norah towards training as a parish worker, Beatrice became a nurse in the mission field. Did they fit in well because it reflected their outlook; or because they allowed its outlook to affect them? This is a relevant question; and no doubt there is some truth in both propositions. They lived in a world of their own; almost the only outsiders with whom they had dealings were Fanny Coggan's family at Weston: her mother, much older sister Florence and brother, 'tall' Uncle Fred who would take the three children to a sweet-shop and give each half-a-crown to spend. It is a measure of their circumstances and lack of sophistication that this was a treat remembered for fifty years. The enjoyment of beach missions continued: Francis Noel Palmer[9] (nicknamed Tiny because he was six foot seven inches tall) recalls Donald Coggan's presence (aged about twelve) at one such held in Weston in 1922, and his 'unfailing and active help in all sorts of ways'. Cecil Cullingford[10] remembers him at a CSSM there two years later: 'a very pleasant, obviously Christian lad' whom he asked to read the Scripture Union portions at the beach services, which he did very well; 'a mature Christian for his age'.

There was an Uncle Fred also among the Coggan uncles, of whom Donald knew almost nothing except to register his size as 'little' Uncle Fred. The Coggan grandparents lived on Herne Hill in comparative affluence: William Coggan had a large black Ford (a rarity at the time) and driver; his wife was a martinet and dedicated teetotaller, of whom all seemed afraid. Donald saw little of them, and apparently did not attend his grandfather's funeral in 1926, when hundreds of those whom he had benefited followed on foot the horse-drawn funeral procession as it made its way through the streets of London to a mausoleum in Brompton cemetery.

By the summer of 1923 it was decided that Donald's health had improved sufficiently for him to go to school. It was a decision not without trauma. His had been a secluded, protected, protracted childhood, spent in the more recent years mainly in the company of his mother, his tutor and his sisters. As the result of their excursion to the St Pancras Town Hall when their parents were mayor and mayoress, the children played out their brief experience of local government with a game in which 'Hear, hear, Mr Mayor' was a

---

[9] b.1897; badly wounded in Great War; after some years as a lay missioner, ordained 1931.
[10] 1904 -; Headmaster Monmouth School 1946-56.

recurrent theme. Norah, Beatrice and Donald all clearly adored their mother and, with perhaps some degree of understanding of her isolated existence, did what they could to please her. Home-made banners were constructed for her birthdays, and on one such occasion, bearing the motto 'Land of Hope and Glory, Mother of the Three', they marched singing round the house. Strangers who met Fanny Coggan remarked on her grave beauty and considerable reserve.

The choice of school was in the hands of Donald's father who made what was, on the face of it, a strange choice, but which later proved heaven-sent. He decided to send his son to Merchant Taylors'. Donald felt that it was partly on account of its location near Smithfield Market, the scene of many of his father's own activities; clearly it was anticipated that he would follow the family tradition and enter the world of commerce; many London business mens' sons were at the school, and moreover, Arthur Coggan and the headmaster were fellow Freemasons. Donald sat the entrance examination; he had been well taught by Mrs Gardner in a routine that had included lessons on Boxing Day. There had sometimes been tears in achieving it, but the required standard was reached; Donald passed the test.

Since its foundation in the reign of Elizabeth I in 1560-1 the school had established a mainly sound reputation, and sent many boys to the universities, some of whom were later to hold places of responsibility in Church and state. There was a particularly strong connection with St John's College, Oxford. But in 1923 when Donald Coggan made his appearance, the school was at a low ebb.

For the first three hundred and sixteen years of its existence, the school was located in Suffolk Lane, in a part of the City of London later demolished. When Charterhouse School went out to Godalming in 1877, Merchant Taylors' acquired the more spacious buildings in Charterhouse Square, EC1, and was able to expand. A games field at Catford led to a tradition of sporting successes. With the tendency for the inhabitants of inner London to move further into the suburbs, many of the pupils (all of whom were day-boys) endured long and tiring journeys to school.

John Arbuthnot Nairn had been headmaster since 1900. He was a classical scholar of great distinction, but during his reign several weaknesses became accentuated: the buildings and furniture (already shabby) deteriorated; boys were exhausted by travelling; the distance from the games pitches was an additional burden. Most important of all, much of the curriculum was considered unsatisfactory by inspectors, and no longer suited to the current need; five particularly valuable schoolmasters had been killed in the war and had not been adequately replaced. Donald Coggan's accounts of some of the teaching he received in his first two years are not impressive.

The headmaster was known as Pongo: perhaps because he was round and bouncy. Donald recalls trying to conjugate the familiarity: *Pongo, Pongere, Ponxi, Ponctum.* Dr Nairn was short, with a tremendous voice, dressed always in cap and gown, and can be remembered sweeping into the great hall to rattle through identical prayers day after day at speed; or he would roar through the entrance lobby, driving all loiterers before him, shouting 'outside is good' as he ejected boys into the pea-soup fogs frequent in the London of the 1920s. From his secluded background Donald Coggan found the school environment full of shocks. Standards of integrity were low: the behaviour of some of the staff seemed no better than that of many of the boys. His form master, remembered by all contemporaries as a particular tyrant, often failed to arrive until five or ten minutes before the end of a lesson; he would creep stealthily into a form room and accost a victim with particular ferocity; beating was a frequent occurrence with seemingly little justification except as a show of authority.

The early terms at Merchant Taylors' were painful for Donald. First came the journey: a tram ride from the bottom of Highgate Hill to King's Cross; then an underground train to Aldersgate, and a rush to Charterhouse Square if the transport was at all delayed, to arrive panting for breath at morning assembly. A day of fog worsened his condition. How much easier it would have been for him at the then much more benign Highgate School (with John Betjeman) on the doorstep of his home. For one unaccustomed to the company of others, to be pitched into association with scores of rowdy boys was clearly an assault on his personality. He became a target for bullying as a consequence of his inability to attain the accepted norms of prowess at games and membership of the School Cadet Corps. He was excused both on account of his health. At his father's wish he had entered the school on the Modern side, as the best training for his future in commerce. Donald's lack of interest and achievement in French and German was a further problem; he was older than many boys in his set, but his performance was barely average. He withstood these disadvantages with the courage and resilience with which he had earlier faced his asthma, though the inferiority he felt in relation to his peers stayed with him.

In the winter of 1924/1925, Donald joined a group of eight in Gladstone Sargent's confirmation class at St Peter's, Upper Holloway. He was confirmed by the Bishop of Stepney on 25 March 1925. One of the girls, Florence Good[11], who was fourteen at the time, has a clear picture of the candidates: Donald Coggan, pale and delicate, did nothing energetic, but sat down and stood up with care: 'you instinctively felt he was clever'. Frederick Guy Thompson, one of the other two young men, left a written testimony of his years at St Peter's which has been preserved. A large gulf separated their educational attainments, but his tribute to the efforts of successive vicars to bring him to a knowledge of Christ and the Scriptures would doubtless have been echoed by Donald.

The conviction that he should be preparing himself for ordination became increasingly strong at Donald Coggan's confirmation; so much so that he braced himself for the greatest ordeal so far. He needed to tell his father and ask to be allowed to change from the Modern side of the school, and begin to study the classics. His father was still a remote figure, and there was an element of fear in the relationship. The problem seems to have been not so much a matter of possible disapproval of the proposed step (Arthur Coggan was in no way anti-clerical and went regularly to a place of worship), as the idea of the confrontation itself, with the absence of communication over the years. However, Donald need not have been so anxious: in the event all passed off easily; Arthur Coggan offered no objection, for which his son was profoundly thankful.

At the beginning of the spring term of 1926, he changed to the classical side. A transformed life was to follow. Merchant Taylors' was the only public school of the day which still retained Hebrew as a classroom subject; as a result it claimed the bulk of the scholarships at Oxford and Cambridge. The Semites, as the Hebrew class was named, had a sanctum from which other boys were banned; a punishment book recorded the names of transgressors from outside the select circle. The group of around ten boys was closely knit under the benign tuition of F.J. Padfield[12], who became friend as well as schoolmaster; his own son was one of the Hebrew class of 1926-8, and he became a father-figure to the remainder also. His influence upon Donald Coggan was considerable. The study of Hebrew gripped him from the start, and he made rapid progress; his newly-found confidence spilled over into other school subjects; he

[11] Later a Deaconess, and still living in the parish.
[12] The Reverend Francis John Padfield, Scholar of Caius College, Cambridge.

applied himself diligently to the new discipline of Greek. There were barely two years left before university entrance and much ground to be covered. One day his father came home with a present of a Greek New Testament, a gesture that was greatly appreciated.

An important new source of benefit came to Donald in the spring of 1927 in the form of a new headmaster. Spencer Leeson[13] was then thirty-five, and still a layman. Described by one of his pupils at Winchester as 'one of the most vivid personalities I have ever met', he spent only three years as a master at what was the school of his own youth before his appointment at Merchant Taylors' as head. He was clearly an excellent teacher who had high standards and demanded as much from his pupils.

> Spencer was in the habit of setting more prep than anyone else . . . it was more an inward than outward compulsion that drove one to do it. He himself took infinite trouble to prepare his side of a lesson and put such intellectual enthusiasm into the way he dealt with it that one would not wish to be ill-prepared for it. His sense of the wonder of men's history and achievements communicated itself . . . But it was more a sense of intellectual force that he communicated. I recall one day when the impediment in his speech was bad, he apologized to the class for it. Boys are cruel creatures, but I don't remember any of my contemporaries wanting to laugh at him for his affliction, or that it in any way affected his ability to keep order or get his lesson across . . . it taught me something of what humility is[14].

Many years later Donald Coggan, as Archbishop of York, recorded on the radio his own indebtedness to his former headmaster. The passage of time gave proportion to the measure of obligation; he could see the more clearly what had been the narrowness of his position and the extent to which the fresh influence helped to broaden his views:

> Quiet of bearing, walking often with his massive head bowed, afflicted by a very pronounced stutter which persisted to the end of his life, gifted with a tremendous capacity for enjoying a joke and the good things in life, he came to my school like a breath, no, a gale, of fresh air. In spite of his youthfulness . . . he brought considerable experience to his task – Winchester, Oxford, service in the First World War, administrative work in the Board of Education, call to the Bar and so on. . . . He brought humility, a love of the beautiful in music, art, architecture, an impatience with the stuffy, a passion for education in the broadest and fullest meaning of that word. A school that had been drab and rather

[13] 1892-1956; Headmaster Winchester 1935; ordained 1940; Bishop of Peterborough 1949.
[14] *Spencer Leeson. A Memoir by some of his friends* (SPCK 1958), p.41.

uninteresting 'came alive' under his touch. Music flourished, clubs sprang up. After-school activities proliferated. Many a boy began to put new meaning into the word 'life', and it was Spencer Leeson who whetted their appetite for full and gracious living.

Donald Coggan's academic spurt was achieved with help and encouragement from his new mentor. The fact that he secured an Open Exhibition to St John's College, Cambridge, for the Michaelmas term of 1928 is a measure of his diligence. Also the Simmond's Memorial Prize for Hebrew came his way in the school prize list at the end of his last term. He did not neglect his religious studies, for every year he won the Hussey divinity prize given in each form of the school. He helped to found a Christian Union, at times the cause of derision among his schoolfellows; one of the monitors, who was especially antagonistic, beat him for daring to use the school badge on a programme of meetings without permission. Some contemporaries have provided their memories of Donald Coggan in the happier period towards the end of his schooldays. The only master who survives, S.G. Charrett, writes:

> In 1927 I was a young, enthusiastic schoolmaster of twenty-two, fresh from Cambridge, in my second year at Merchant Taylors', and much encouraged by the arrival of Spencer Leeson . . . as a reforming and revivifying headmaster, who engineered the move of the school to its present site at Northwood after Donald Coggan had left. It is a trick of old age . . . to remember almost every individual of those early days . . . Donald Coggan at the age of sixteen was tall, slim, rather serious in manner, but not lacking a quiet sense of humour. He had an unusually deep and resonant voice for a boy of his age, and could read a Shakespeare part at sight remarkably well. I can still remember the mock solemnity he put into the part of Dogberry in *Much Ado about Nothing*, or his stirring tones as Henry V . . . In his slightly aloof way, as older than many of them, he appeared quite popular with his fellows . . . I am sure he was influenced by Spencer Leeson.

Donald Coggan's unaggressive manner is recalled: 'more a presence than an extrovert character', from a member of the same form; 'he was always a quiet, cheerful person . . . a very able academic would have been our estimation of his future then'. He began to teach Greek in the lunch hour to another boy, who was on the science side; many years later they met at the London College of Divinity; Donald was Principal, his pupil an ordination candidate. With a member of the Hebrew class Donald made a visit to the Hendon air display, where in the crowd they noticed a man with a placard bearing a Bible text. His companion did not altogether approve of the method of proselytizing; Donald, however, much admired the openness of the witness. It was typical of him.

None of his schoolfellows appear to have received an invitation to visit the Coggan home; it remained very secluded, although Donald's own horizons had broadened as the result of his new fields of learning and more sympathetic, more inspiring teachers. He became fond of his own neighbourhood of Highgate and Hampstead, walking on the Heath and to the Spaniards, though the tomb of Karl Marx in Highgate Cemetery, and the large Passionist church on West Hill remained unknown territory. Music was an important interest. By eighteen Donald was an accomplished pianist. His relationship with his father remained distant; it was a surprise, therefore, when it was announced that a course of organ lessons at St Martin's Church, Gospel Oak, had been arranged and paid for. A series of impulses on the part of Arthur Coggan to reach out towards his son he clearly found difficult to articulate; they could only take material form.

Loyalty to St Peter's, Upper Holloway, and Gladstone Sargent remained throughout Donald's school days, although the ethos there was more fundamentally conservative than the principles adumbrated by the new leadership at Merchant Taylors'. The years 1927-1928 were crucial ones for Conservative Evangelicals. A revised Prayer Book had been presented to the Convocations of Canterbury and York in 1927 and was approved by large majorities. The voting in the Church Assembly was 'For' 517, and 'Against' 133. Parliamentary sanction was at that time required for any change. Although the House of Lords recorded a favourable vote, this was not the case in the House of Commons. A greater dependence on the Prayer Book of Edward VI of 1549 as a pattern for the revised Eucharistic rite alarmed Evangelicals, who were apprehensive of moves towards pre-Reformation forms, and they were sufficiently well represented and led in the House of Commons to defeat the Bill. Minor changes were made in the revised Book, and in 1928 it was presented once more. Its rejection by an even larger majority of 266 against, 220 in favour, was a considerable victory for lay opinion.

In what he conceived the interests of doctrinal purity, Gladstone Sargent added his voice in St Peter's parish magazine in April 1927: While there was much that was desirable in the revised Prayer Book 'there is a great deal which involves a definite slide Romewards'. There were changes which strike at the very heart of the Bible doctrine of Justification by Faith which is the very kernel of the Gospel, and blaspheme Christ's *finished* work of Atonement on the Cross. Let us continue to pray that our beloved Church may be preserved from sanctioning the false and poisonous teaching . . .

It was with such exhortation as this as part of his endowment, that Donald Coggan went up to Cambridge in the autumn of 1928.

CHAPTER TWO *Cambridge*

The University of Cambridge represented a number of challenges and hazards. Donald Coggan at nineteen (his birthday was during the first week of the new life) had never lived away from his parents and had not travelled further than Somerset and Frinton, and then only for family holidays. He had attended a school of comparative antiquity (1560), but the buildings were Victorian. Pressures were three-fold: first, an experience faced him of living in association with strangers where no one was responsible for him in detail, only in the broadest sense; he was required to arrange his programme and make his own decisions. He would be part of a system and among buildings that stretched back to the middle ages: customs and taboos of which he had no knowledge faced him on all sides. Secondly, academic expectations were high: he held an Exhibition (a type of lesser Scholarship) and therefore it was presumed that he could be relied upon to perform well in his studies. Thirdly, his interior life was to be tested. Donald had so far been given, and accepted, religious teaching of a fairly conservative sort. Would he adhere to this pattern, develop within its structure, or react against it and associate with a religious clique of a different ethos; these were all possibilities.

The indications are that he stood up well to the exposure that was involved. No doubt his belief in the divine purpose that had led him to Cambridge sustained him; his faith gave him courage, as also his experience of previous struggles against adversity, fought and won. It has been a matter of comment that Donald Coggan has never been called upon to face serious personal tragedy, hardship or prolonged deprivation. But these are relative terms; none can measure the extent of suffering endured in another man's heart. The situation in which Donald found himself in his early days at Cambridge was of the kind that not infrequently created casualties among undergraduates. But though shy and diffident, he was not one of them. His faith and strong sense of personal identity helped him to survive without psychological injury, and his academic and social development became rapid.

The college of St John the Evangelist is not the oldest of the Cambridge Colleges, but it was the largest until the end of the eighteenth century when it was overtaken by Trinity; it still retains this position of size and distinction. It was founded in April 1511, through the Will of Lady Margaret Beaufort, Countess of Richmond and Derby, mother of Henry VI, who also founded Christ's College, and at the time of her death in 1509 was turning her mind towards Oxford. John Fisher, Bishop of Rochester, persuaded her instead to endow a further College at Cambridge and the last of her many charitable acts was to make the necessary provision. A site had been chosen on the river Cam where a hospital dedicated to St John, and maintained by Canons regular, had been established since the middle ages. It was suspended and the monks went to Ely.

The first buildings of the new College, consisting of one court (an architectural term for what at Oxford is named a quadrangle), were finished in 1520. Most of the east front towards St John's Street survives as then built. It was in First Court that Donald Coggan lived for his second and third years at Cambridge. The original chapel (along the north side of this court) was demolished in the nineteenth century, and rebuilt on the same site in 1864-9 to a design by Sir Giles Gilbert Scott. Donald's near neighbour was this large edifice in the style of the thirteenth century early decorated period, with apse reminiscent of the Sainte Chapelle in Paris. The tower, 163 feet high, would have soared directly above him. During subsequent centuries three further courts and numerous other buildings were added to the west and straddling the river, till the College achieved its extensive and impressive twentieth-century aspect: grey stone, water and splendid formal gardens.

The broad heading for the course followed by Donald Coggan was Oriental Languages. In order to sit for the examinations for Honours leading to the degree of Bachelor of Arts (known as Tripos examinations) in this subject, candidates were required to study either one oriental language or two related languages. The emphasis was upon the attainment of sufficient proficiency to lead to a grasp of the original source material, and thereby to an understanding of one or two of the major oriental civilizations which existed in Asia over the past 5,000 years. Donald made Hebrew his first choice and his second, which he proceeded to learn *ab initio*, Aramaic, another of the Semitic languages, belonging to the North-west group. Originally spoken by Aramaeans in Northern Syria and Mesopotamia, it gradually became the *lingua franca* of the Near East at the time of Christ. A third pursuit was the study of Syriac, an important dialect of late Aramaic developed round Edessa, which persists as the liturgical and literary language of several of the Eastern Churches, and which has left a particularly rich heritage of manuscripts.

The Tripos examinations were taken in two parts: Part I after two years and Part II after a third; both were classed. A rigorous study of a large number of texts was called for. Examination questions would be set partly on material that had been prescribed and where some measure of preparation was possible, and partly on unspecified texts which were more elusive; the only way to success lay along a thorough knowledge of the languages. Sources included the books of the Old Testament in classical Hebrew; also in Rabbinical Hebrew the Talmud which embodied the Mishnah, a Jewish set of writings setting down oral teachings, and Gemara, or discussions on the Mishnah; Targums, Aramaic translations or paraphrases of the Old Testament made when the Jews ceased to speak Hebrew, and so on.

Both the content of the course and the discipline it exacted were to have a profound effect. Donald's interest and respect for the Jewish people, their religion and culture did not diminish, but increased over the years, and it was to take a variety of positive forms in the future. Likewise, the ability to sustain concentrated, accurate, detailed effort upon the mastery of ancient scripts had its impact on the training of Donald's mind and habits. He received immediate rewards for his industry.

During his first term he was selected for a John Stewart of Rannoch University Scholarship in Hebrew (in company with a contemporary among the Semites at Merchant Taylors', I.E.S. Edwards[1], who had come up to Caius on a College Scholarship). At the end of his first year, Donald came out with a high first class in his Inter-Collegiate examination, (called the Mays) on the strength of which St John's made him a Scholar of the College. This entitled him to the rooms in First Court for the next two years and a Scholar's gown; he was also given a prize of books.

In the summer of 1930 he sat Part I of the Tripos. A three-hour paper on unspecified Hebrew texts on the morning of 2 June was followed by eighteen compulsory questions on the books of Genesis, Judges, 2 Samuel, Isaiah, Amos and Zechariah in Hebrew for three hours in the afternoon. A second gruelling day followed with a requirement to 'translate into Syriac with Jacobite vowels' an extract of the works of the Shepherd of Hermas, a second-century Christian slave, and two other passages; there was a three-hour paper on

[1] 1909- ; Keeper of Egyptian Antiquities, British Museum 1955-74.

Aramaic texts in the afternoon. Finally on 4 June a general essay ended the examination; a choice of eight topics was offered, all concerned with Semitic religion, literature and culture. On 19 June Donald heard that he had been placed in the First Class.

Congratulations from distinguished sources flowed in to him at home (which was now 58 Ashbourne Avenue, off the Finchley Road, in London; Fanny Coggan's health had deteriorated and this was a more convenient house). There was at this time no teacher in Hebrew or Aramaic at St John's. Donald's tutor (a purely supervisory role) was Martin Charlesworth[2], a classicist and editor of the Cambridge Ancient History. Teaching, both formal and informal, was given by members of the Oriental Languages Faculty. Donald's main teachers were Stanley Arthur Cook[3] of Caius; Professor Anthony Ashley Bevan, then Lord Almoner's Professor of Arabic; A. Lukyn-Williams, Hon. Canon of Ely; and Herbert Loewe, of Queens', a practising Jew whose encouragement and interest were enduring qualities. A letter from Professor Robert Kennett, holder of the Chair of Hebrew, expressed the hope that a similar success awaited Donald in Part II; Norman McLean[4], a great Orientalist and University lecturer in Aramaic, wrote, 'You have completely fulfilled my expectations. I know how well you have worked and how thoroughly you have earned your distinction'. From Professor Bevan, on holiday in the Isle of Wight, came, 'I had confidently expected it from what I have seen of your work'. A card from Pongo, then an incumbent near Maidenhead, has survived; Edwards had obtained a First Class also and the results therefore reflected great credit upon Merchant Taylors'. The Dean of St John's reported that it was a very good First Class; a Wright's prize of books for performance in the Tripos accompanied the news.

Like most universities, Cambridge provided a range of Societies to cater for the interests and tastes of undergraduates. For some, these activities and the resulting companionship counted for more than the academic courses. Despite Donald Coggan's determination to give most of himself to his studies, he was immediately drawn into the Cambridge Inter-Collegiate Christian Union, known as CICCU, and became an enthusiastic member. It would not be an exaggeration to say that any leisure he was able to create beyond his work, was devoted to this circle. (He still played no games.)

[2] 1895-1950; ordained 1940; President and Classical Lecturer.
[3] 1873-1949; Regius Professor of Hebrew 1932-38.
[4] 1865-1947; Master of Christ's College 1927-1936.

Probably all his Cambridge friendships were contained within it; his participation and responsibilities made him grow. It is a cause of amazement that he was able to achieve such a full programme; a state of affairs that has not ceased.

Donald was drawn to CICCU for two reasons; first on account of his personal commitment to Christ. Upon membership he signed a declaration that was customary: 'In joining this Union I declare my faith in Jesus Christ as my Saviour, my Lord and my God': it exactly explained his position. There have been great Christians who have come and kept to the faith after and through periods of agnosticism. Donald did not know this state; herein lay one of the most constant factors of his life. Secondly, in CICCU he was on familiar territory. Its doctrinal stance matched his own background from St Peter's, Upper Holloway.

CICCU adopted a Conservative Evangelical base and an evangelistic outlook. A short outline of its history is not out of place here, for it explains the position that it held within University circles (which affected its members). But more importantly, the originator of this Evangelicalism in Cambridge was a man much after Donald Coggan's heart, and if there was a single priest in the Church of England upon whom Donald modelled himself during his ministry, this was he.

Charles Simeon[5] went to King's College, Cambridge as a Scholar from Eton in 1779. He had only been there a few days when he learnt that a corporate Communion would take place during the term and he would be required to take the Sacrament. 'Conscience told me,' he confided later to a friend, 'that Satan was as fit to go there, as I; and that if I *must* go, I *must* repent, and turn to God'. After a period of spiritual difficulty, of reading, fasting and prayer, he came upon a passage on the meaning of Old Testament sacrifices. It occurred to him that it was possible for guilt to be transferred. And God had provided an offering for him. 'I sought to lay my sins on the sacred head of Jesus,' he wrote. On Easter day he awoke with an overwhelming sense that Christ had risen: 'From that hour peace flowed in rich abundance into my soul; and at the Lord's table in our chapel I had the sweetest access to God through my Blessed Saviour.' Here was the source of the emphasis placed on the atonement, and upon assurance, by the Cambridge Evangelicals.

[5] 1759-1836; Much of the material contained here is taken from Donald Coggan's essay on Charles Simeon in *These were his Gifts*, the substance of the Bishop John Prideaux Lectures, University of Exeter 1974.

Certain features of what Donald Coggan has written on Simeon reveal as much about himself as his subject. This is particularly true of the paragraph on discipline[6].

> . . . very soon after his conversion, Simeon formed a habit which was to prove, above all other things, effective in forming a pattern of character which was strong, saintly and controlled. He rose at 4 am, lit his fire and spent four hours in Bible study, meditation and prayer, before calling in a friend and his college servant, praying with them and embarking on the tasks of the day. There can be no doubt of the influence of this habit.

These were prophetic words about rules of life which Donald himself absorbed through his membership of CICCU. Though he was later to depart from some of the dogmatism of its doctrinal stand, the practices of Bible study, meditation, prayer, self-control and stewardship of time learnt in the Cambridge days have lasted a life-time.

Likewise, Donald was attracted to Simeon as Churchman; Simeon's refusal to be labelled as the representative of any one party (he disliked controversy) was noted and increasingly adopted, particularly in the days as Archbishop, first at York and then at Canterbury. Simeon's recognition of the corporate nature of the Church, his love for the Church of England and its liturgy, the need for regular reception of Holy Communion, were features to which Donald drew attention[7]. His own passion for order and decency in the conduct of services, which not infrequently was to strike terror in the casual and faint-hearted in the future, may well have had some of their origins here. Both men disliked indiscipline and were fussy about attention to detail. Both based their lives on the revelation of God in the Scriptures. Praise for Simeon as a preacher and missionary strategist gave promise of where Donald's own emphases were likely to appear. For a period of some twenty years, Simeon held sermon classes on alternate Fridays in term. It is not fanciful to see the correlation between this practice and the schools of preaching that Donald held in the Maritimes and North-Western Canada in the 1940s in search of the same goal: to improve the manner in which the word of God was presented to the world.

Simeon was ordained priest in 1783 and worked at Holy Trinity in Cambridge (a church with which Donald Coggan was to be closely associated); he continued his ministry in it for fifty-four years, combining this with his Fellowship at King's. Despite opposition to

[6] ibid. pp.14-15.
[7] ibid. p.16.

some of his emphases, Simeon's influence grew: an Evangelical sermon in Holy Trinity each Sunday in term, a Sunday School in Jesus Lane, and a daily prayer meeting in term time (which began in 1862) were some of the results. A call for personal holiness, for study of the Scriptures and for missionary activity both at home and abroad, was heard in Cambridge in the 1870s. Groups of Christians in the Colleges were endeavouring to respond to it. A mission by Sholto Douglas[8] in November 1876 was the catalyst. He preached with great zeal that nothing was more urgent than immediate decision for Christ. On the final day, 18 November, sixty undergraduates had breakfast with him at the Hoop Inn. Sholto Douglas convinced them that a structured organization which would harness the efforts of the individual Christian Unions in the Colleges, could arrange combined evangelistic campaigns and allow continuity. The Cambridge Inter-Collegiate Christian Union was born.

It was the product of a biblical theology. The authority and inspiration of the Bible were totally accepted; its truth wholly independent of change in human thought and philosophy. God had spoken to men; he had acted in Christ to save men. The Cross was central; Christ's death was nothing less than substitutionary and to accept it as the only ground of forgiveness was the way of man's reconciliation with God. The necessity of a new birth, as a gift from God to sinners who were justified by faith in Christ, was seen as essential: without such new birth no true life was possible. A powerful sense of responsibility existed within those justified sinners towards any who were as yet without personal faith in Christ. This missionary spirit was one of the hallmarks of CICCU for the next fifty years. Donald Coggan joined it shortly after its Jubilee.

CICCU membership in the intervening years produced many remarkable and changed lives. The claim of the gospel, to leave all and follow, was often taken quite literally: men left their families, their studies and the University, abandoned a distinguished career or athletic promise; some gave up their incomes to show that 'God's work in God's way will never lack supplies'. China drew many Cambridge members of the Christian Union; others went with the Church Missionary Society to Africa, still disease-ridden for Europeans.

[8] 1839-1916; The Reverend Sholto Douglas Campbell-Douglas; 2nd Lord Blythswood 1908.

Handley Moule[9], for many years Principal of Ridley Hall Theological College, characterized the CICCU standpoint when he wrote[10] in 1886 on the sacrifice that was required of the Christian disciple: utter surrender of heart, emotions, will and ambition. Christ dwelling in power in the trusting heart would sustain such a man; his life cultivated by study of the Scriptures, by worship and Breaking of Bread and above all by prayer. Donald Coggan would have been made aware of the spiritual giants who had passed through the CICCU.

These attitudes were not achieved without outside criticism of neglect of University work for Christian activity; nor of lack of respect for the intellect and the needs of the world. Two events exacerbated the disparagement of CICCU a year before Donald Coggan's arrival. The first was a statement of a somewhat uncompromising and conservative nature put out for the Jubilee celebrations of 1927[11] which rejected a liberal view of Scripture, attempts at social improvement and an evolutionary attitude towards creation; and was less than enthusiastic on schemes for achieving world peace by political means. These were not considered part of the faith which would support men by the shores of the Nile or Yangtze.

Cambridge, home of Darwinism and scientific experiment, where biblical textual criticism and modernism were taken seriously, was not impressed, though sincerity and dedication were recognized. 'They thought us fools,' was a comment of Norman Anderson[12], President of CICCU in 1930, who added that in his year of office, all the officers of CICCU gained First Class degrees (Donald Coggan was one of them).

Secondly, there was the episode of the Mission to the University of 1927, an event that took place about every three years. The various emphases contained in the theology of the Christian Societies in the University were reflected among the missioners: William Temple[13], then Bishop of Manchester, was the principal Anglican; Dr Cyril Norwood of the City Temple, was the Free Churchman; CICCU had chosen John Stuart Holden, vicar of St Paul's, Portman

[9] 1841-1920; Bishop of Durham 1902.
[10] *Thoughts on Christian Sanctity.*
[11] T.E.B. Howarth, *Cambridge between the two wars* (Collins 1978), p.49.
[12] 1908- ; Professor of Oriental Laws and Director of the Institute of Advanced Legal Studies, University of London; Chairman of House of Laity, General Synod, 1970-1975; Kt 1975.
[13] 1881-1944; Archbishop of York 1928-42; Canterbury 1942-4.

Square. At the last moment Stuart Holden was unable to come, on medical grounds. Anxious that its distinctive message should be heard, William Nicolson from Northern Ireland, of whom great things had been heard as a powerful evangelist, was invited by CICCU.

His impassioned oratory, anecdotal approach, rough-spun humour and uninhibited talk of hell, proved somewhat of an embarrassment. Those members of CICCU who took him to dine at High Table were faced with a delicate problem. Conversions were undoubtedly made by Nicolson's blunt, forceful and dramatic methods, but there can be no doubt that the gulf between CICCU and the rest of Christian opinion in the University was widened by the emergence of this more aggressive type of evangelism. This was the situation when Donald Coggan appeared on the Cambridge scene.

The disdain of fellow-undergraduates increased the sense that CICCU members had of needing to endure the mockery of men to obey the Lord. The paramount importance of gaining souls demanded this sacrifice. Donald, whose experience of mission had changed his life, now began to win others: to evangelize the world, beginning with the University. He accepted the call to put aside his shyness, reserve and self-consciousness. It was a hard lesson, but the effects were enduring: a life-long capacity to stand against the tide for conscience sake. Looking forward to his later ministry, it is remarkable to find the extent to which his habits and cast of mind were formed during this period. His training ground lay in the CICCU.

Donald managed nevertheless not to neglect his academic studies for his religious interests (in the Mays, he and I.E.S. Edwards were told that they had set a new standard for the examination). His pattern for this intense level of performance was set during the Cambridge days. First came a determination, which persisted all his life, to be the master not servant of time (although this discipline often failed to endear itself to his subordinates, and reduced opportunity for reflection). He worked always at full pressure, absorbed material fast, and could produce clear, accurate and succinct answers at speed.

Some of Donald's CICCU associates have provided an outline of the strenuous weekly programme in term time, in which he took a full part. After a morning of lectures, they would hurry on their bicycles to the daily prayer meeting at five past one till one twenty-five, held in the Henry Martyn Hall attached to Holy Trinity Church. Christian Union groups in Colleges met frequently for

Bible study and prayer; at St John's often in Donald's room, where he had a piano and 'could play anything'. On Saturday evenings, until examinations became close in the spring, there was a Bible Reading, with large numbers attending in the Debating Hall of the Union, and prayers were held elsewhere for what was to happen on Sunday. Some CICCU members would attend their College chapels, Holy Trinity Church or St Paul's, Hills Road; Donald went rather more than others to his chapel at St John's. The Director of Music, Dr. C.B. Rootham, had developed a method of singing the psalms called speech-rhythm, which Donald, who had a great affection for the psalms[14], greatly admired. During the week he would examine the psalms in Hebrew as part of a course led by the Professor, who amended them so radically, according to Donald, that they seemed more according to Kennett than David[15]. Although not an organ scholar, he was permitted to use the instrument in the chapel as a special concession, because he played well.

Most members of CICCU had regular Sunday assignments, such as leading a Bible class or Sunday School in a Cambridgeshire village. Bible Reading in the Henry Martyn Hall at midday and an evangelistic sermon in Holy Trinity Church at eight-thirty pm were part of the Sunday pattern. In the summer, open-air missions were held instead of the sermon. One was always in the Market Place, where CICCU members would hire a cart upon which Donald played a harmonium; or he would be called on to lead a mission at Royston, fourteen miles away; or with CICCU members of St John's on Parker's Piece.

Chief among the lasting experiences of Cambridge for Donald Coggan were these efforts at evangelism. Max Warren, in an earlier generation, acknowledged a similar debt[16]:

> The CICCU taught me never to forget that being a Christian meant being a disciple and not a fellow traveller. A disciple has other responsibilities for people in addition to enjoying them.

Years later he was to write, 'from the evangelistic task of the Church in loyalty to the Church's Lord there can be no retreat'[17]. The words could equally well have been spoken by Donald Coggan. His exposure to the work of lay evangelists at this period was equally significant for the future.

---

[14] He was to head a Commission for a new translation in 1958.
[15] *York Journal of Convocation*, 1 Oct. 1957 (CIO) p.19.
[16] Max Warren, *Crowded Canvas* (Hodder and Stoughton 1974), p.40.
[17] F.W. Dillistone, *Into all the World* (Hodder and Stoughton 1980), p.22.

CICCU placed a high value on ordination; it was a calling second to none. (Donald continued to reflect this attitude, corroborated by his call to the full-time ordained ministry of the Church, as the subject of his enthronement sermon at Canterbury.) But missionary responsibility was entrusted to lay men and women also. In 1929 the *Maréchale* was invited to come for ten successive evenings to lead a Mission in the Cambridge Guildhall. Donald was much involved in the arrangements. She was the mother-in-law of his mentor from the Weston days, Noel Palmer. Catherine Booth-Clibborn was one of the daughters of the Salvation Army General, William Booth. 'You are not in this world for yourself. You have been sent for others' were her mother's words as in 1881, at the age of twenty-two, she was sent to France in her navy-blue uniform with a crimson ribbon round her bonnet, to the alleys and slums, 'wherever there are lost and perishing souls'. Among scenes of depravity and degradation, armed with a Bible and French dictionary, she began to preach. At first she was named *La Capitaine*; soon she became renowned as the Field Marshal or *La Maréchale*.

In 1887 she married a fellow-evangelist, Arthur Sydney Clibborn[18]. They left the Salvation Army on a point of doctrine in order to have liberty to preach what they spoke of as 'a full Gospel', and were still preaching it all over the world into old age. At the time of the Cambridge Mission, the *Maréchale* was seventy-one and had borne ten children. She had relinquished her Salvation Army bonnet for exotic headgear of her own choosing. Her eloquence, power of making Jesus real, love for souls, her watchwords '*Aimez toujours et malgré tout*' had earned her the title from a previous generation of undergraduates, of the 'Heavenly Witch'.[19] Alfred Owen[20] of Emmanuel changed his life-style as the result of the Mission. His father's large engineering businesses became run on Christian lines. Donald Coggan later considered her message to have been thin on intellectual content, but that the *Maréchale's* gifts were being used was certain. He began to think it wasteful to exclude women from the ministry of the Church.

In a series of interviews published in 1983,[21] Donald spoke of his debt while a student to experiences in one of the poorest areas in the

[18] 1858-1955.
[19] Carolyn Scott. *The Heavenly Witch. The story of the Maréchale* (Hamish Hamilton 1981).
[20] 1908-75; Kt 1961.
[21] Robin Daniels, *Conversations with Coggan* (Hodder and Stoughton 1983), p.16.

East End of London. The Hoxton Market Christian Mission and Institute was in the hands of Lewis Burtt[22], a layman of genius who for half a century gave hope, food, boots and holidays by the sea to Hoxton children. After an illness, he wrote to Donald, who helped with the Mission in his holidays: 'How can one go slow for such a Master. I love the term *labourer* for God, and must live up to the privilege'. Donald felt humbled in the presence of such a man, and saw his own gifts of the intellect in proportion. Likewise, he often referred with gratitude to what he had learnt from Charles Hodges, a former torpedo-boat wireless telegraphist in the Royal Navy, who became an evangelist with the Open Air Mission[23]. During several summers at Teignmouth, Donald played the harmonium at gatherings where he was pupil rather than teacher.

During his student days Donald first met the Church Army, whose work he came greatly to admire. Men from Cambridge would assemble at the Headquarters behind the Cumberland Hotel near Marble Arch in London, for week-ends spent in evangelism at Speakers' Corner and elsewhere in Hyde Park. Donald Coggan joined such on several occasions; he learnt to respond to heckling and abuse and to care for vagrants and the drunken who came to the lantern services at night. Hugh Evans Hopkins, President of CICCU in 1929-30, has remarked on Donald's ability to contend with these situations, and the associations he created in spite of his sheltered background. Without a shred of cynicism in his nature, he continued throughout his ministry to be successful in relationships with the unsophisticated in all walks of life. Encounters with the cynical and worldly-wise he found more difficult.

Canon John S. Boys Smith[24], who was chaplain at St John's from 1927 and later a Research Fellow, Tutor and Master, remembers the young man that Donald was. A good head, covered with close cropped light reddish hair, pleasant, studious, with warm evangelical sympathies, are his recollections. Donald's contemporaries fill out the picture, and tell of his unassuming manner, his sense of humour and powers of mimicry which are still with him. The inferiority complex which dogged his schooldays still lingered despite his academic successes; it was probably not until his marriage that it left him. One of his more discerning friends thought

---

[22] 1860-1935; Hackney Archives Department has details of the work of this remarkable man.
[23] Founded in 1853 for evangelistic work in holiday towns and sporting events.
[24] 1901- ; Master of St John's College 1959-69.

that the strong clear voice he had despite his reserved nature, and somewhat deliberate and heavy gait, were a pose of strength that he did not feel.

In 1929 Donald was asked to join the CICCU Executive, and became its Treasurer. The CICCU was about 200-250 members strong during these years, and entirely composed of men. A Women's Christian Union had been started in 1920, but there was little or no joint activity; women did not attend the daily prayer meetings, and sat in the last four rows at Holy Trinity for the evangelistic sermon on Sunday evenings. Most of the men were Anglicans and had been to public school. Few, with the important exceptions of Max Warren and Falkner Allison[25], read theology, but were followers of other disciplines. The Theology Faculty encompassed attitudes which were historical, liberal and critical; CICCU men feared for their faith. There were no dons associated with the Christian Union; the only senior member who took a leading role was Basil Atkinson of the University Library, who held spirited Bible Readings. Donald was not above mimicking his idiosyncracies.

The main rival to CICCU was the broader based Student Christian Movement, with its much larger membership of men and women. CICCU men had joined with the SCM in the Missions to the University with some misgivings for a number of years, anxious lest what they regarded as the supremely important witness to their interpretation of God's way of salvation through Christ, might not be made. The SCM, it was felt, had a rather 'social service' theological outlook. In 1929 the issue came up again and it is important here in that Donald Coggan took part in making the decision to withdraw from the combined Mission.

Thirty-six members of CICCU wrote to say that although they agreed with standing by principle, the Executive had been high-handed. Donald was one of those who shared the personal interviews that were made with each of the thirty-six, to explain the Executive's motives. Unlike instances where his development followed earlier indications, this marked an attitude from which he later departed in the years of his maturity; his instincts turned to favour reconciliation of outlook wherever possible, rather than exclusion. He loved the word Evangelical, he was to say in 1983:[26]

[25] 1907- ; Bishop of Winchester 1961-74.
[26] *Conversations with Coggan*, op.cit. p.30

It has a good New Testament pedigree: *evangelion* meaning 'the gospel', 'good news'. I don't mind being called an Evangelical, provided the word is allowed to stand on its own without another word being hyphenated to it; and provided it is not given any nuance of exclusiveness.

Exclusiveness was certainly the hall-mark of the Christian Union of his day. Members joined in all forms of sport in the University, but otherwise kept apart. Their social habits were particular, innocent of the issues that affected other coteries: Marxism, Pacifism, egalitarianism and so on. They did not dance, drink, nor go to the cinema. Whether they should play cards was debated, as was the whole matter of sanctification[27]: how it could be achieved.

In 1930 Donald became a vice-president of CICCU during the Presidency of Norman Anderson, and he was asked to become a member of the Executive of the Inter-Varsity Fellowship, an organization which bound together the Christian Unions of all the British Universities. He agreed, with consequences that were profound. That summer he went to the Keswick Convention in the Cambridge Camp. This was an annual event of great significance to Evangelicals, where spirituality was deepened and decisions made; Donald played the piano on occasions in a big (circus) tent when nearly 5,000 were present, and laid the foundations of his belief in the inspirational value of corporate holidays.

In the spring of 1931, in anticipation of another triumph in Part II of the Tripos, Donald received a letter from the University of Manchester. The Committee responsible for the appointment of an Assistant Lecturer in Semitic Languages and Literature asked him to appear before them. He did so, and subject to a satisfactory outcome in the Tripos, was offered the post. The fact that he had been accepted for ordination by the London diocese three years earlier made him feel he might have to refuse; but in the event his advisers, Spencer Leeson and the Chaplain of St John's, were united in telling him to go to Manchester. In the circumstances the London Diocesan Ordination Candidates' Council 'had no hesitation' in allowing him to postpone ordination for three years since the experience would be a valuable help 'against the time when you are a parish priest in the diocese'. It was his former schoolmaster, Francis Padfield, who had the most prophetic voice. He was glad of the prospects of Manchester:

[27] See Norman Anderson, *An Adopted Son* (Inter-Varsity Press 1985), Chapter 9; George S. Ingram, *The Fulness of the Holy Spirit* (Thynne and Co.), p.26.

I believe that teaching is a splendid training. It trains a man to be simple and lucid and to understand the other man's point of view and difficulties. I don't anticipate the possibility of your degeneration into a *mere* lecturer all your life. I feel that your life's work is as an Evangelist and for this a year or so at teaching will be an invaluable preparation.

On 8, 9 and 10 June 1931, Donald sat the six three-hour papers of Part II of the Tripos examination in Old Testament Hebrew, Rabbinics, Aramaic and Syriac. On the 17th came the news that he had secured another First Class. Dr Cook wrote him a donnish letter:

We examiners were very pleased with your papers, for although your Syriac was far from faultless and your comp. grammar was like the curate's egg, you got your first easily. It is a splendid conclusion to your three years because from the first you have showed promise and you have always worked well.

He urged Donald not to rest on his laurels but to try for various prizes and scholarships in Hebrew: the Tyrwhitt, Mason and the Jeremie Septuagint (he was to win them all).

It was on this note that Donald left Cambridge; before him was the prospect of being pitched, without training or practice, into University teaching in Manchester.

CHAPTER THREE

Manchester, Oxford, Islington

Despite his inexperience, Donald Coggan soon became a useful university teacher; according to his students he was thorough, painstaking and friendly. Hebrew became a kind of code language between them for the rest of their lives. One who became a bishop in the Northern Province recalls that communications from his Primate invariably carried a personal message in the Hebrew script. Donald based his methods, so it is revealed in the letters they exchanged, on the sound individual attention he had received from his tutors at Cambridge. 'I am glad you like your work,' wrote Dr Cook 'and gratified that you recall our hours together. I think we all had a good time, didn't we?'

Founded as a university college in 1846, opened in 1851, the Victoria University of Manchester achieved full university status in 1903. It soon enjoyed a high reputation and drew to itself distinguished scholars: Walter Hamilton Moberly[1] had the Philosophy of Religion Chair during Donald's years, and the celebrated Charles Harold Dodd[2] with whom he was to work on the New English Bible from 1956 was Rylands Professor of Biblical Criticism and Exegesis.

A Chair in Hebrew had been in existence since 1851, which title was altered to Oriental Languages in 1866 and Semitic Languages and Literature in 1903. Maurice Canney, who was Professor in Donald's time, had been so since 1912 and was close to retirement. There was one other lecturer in the department.

Associated with the University were a number of denominational Colleges for the training of clergy: Methodist, Baptist, Moravian and so on; their students attended University classes; many studied Hebrew. Donald was thereby given the opportunity of mixing with men who were other than members of the Church of England. He was on particularly good terms with Jewish students destined for the

---

[1] 1881-1974; Kt 1934; KCB 1944; GBE 1949, Chairman of University Grants Committee 1935-49.
[2] 1884-1973; CH 1961; Norris-Hulse Professor of Divinity, Cambridge 1935-49.

rabbinate. One of them, a graduate reading for a doctorate in Cuneiform studies, met Donald often in the Semitic languages department and they would talk together. Fifty years later he comments that Donald

> . . . stood out in a crowd and like King Saul, he was head and shoulders over the rest of the people. His love for music was unqualified and he would give a musical illustration to clarify a text . . . He was dignified, impressive, gentle, scholarly and lovable. He was especially happy when reminded of his ability to speak Hebrew, a language which he spoke and wrote beautifully. Most of his Jewish students, are, alas, no longer in our midst, but there can be no doubt that some of them afterwards became rabbis and indebted to him for their inspiration.

These relationships were not without a certain amount of residual tension, for Donald, while he deplored anti-semitism and was disposed to be sympathetic, was after all a member of a missionary Church. It was probably not until towards the end of his ministry as Archbishop, that he resolved this conflict[3].

Teaching was far from being the only call on Donald's time at Manchester. Professor Canney had made it clear on his appointment that he would be expected to do some research. Donald's interest in Syriac received considerable stimulus from the presence in the city of the remarkable John Rylands Library, filled with manuscripts and early printed works: a papyrus roll of AD 29, a Syriac version of the Gospels of AD 550, an eighth-century Coptic version of St Luke, and so on. He was soon at work on a Syriac document. He joined the Manchester Egyptian and Oriental Society, and his first published work was a short monograph, printed under its auspices, on the use of a certain Hebrew term in Job 5.24.

Donald continued to sit for Cambridge prizes. Dr Cook, writing in the autumn of 1931, described some of the opposition for the Jeremie Septuagint Prize on the Greek version of the Hebrew Old Testament. 'I cannot see that they are necessarily formidable. Your *general* learning will be your strength, for the two men know a tidy lot of Hebrew, but that alone won't score'. He spoke advisedly; he had won the prize himself in 1896. In December Donald heard he had won this prize. I.E.S. Edwards, his school contemporary, also a competitor, sent him a generously worded telegram. 'And next year "the Crosse", I hope,' wrote one of his other teachers.

In March he sat for the Tyrwhitt Hebrew Scholarship at

---

[3] *When Christian meets Jew*, 1985 St Paul's Lecture, delivered at the Sir John Cass Foundation School on 14 November 1985.

Cambridge, which had been Professor Bevan's in 1888; the standard of the award is so high that in some years no candidate reaches it. Donald did so, and came first; he also received a Mason Hebrew Prize on the examination. All seemed set for a distinguished academic career. But his call to ordination remained strong; so that when the Registrar to the University of Manchester wrote in January 1934 to tell him of his reappointment for a further period of three years, he sent his resignation.

He had by no means restricted himself to purely academic work at Manchester. With his extraordinary capacity for creating the time that he needed, Donald continued his efforts in evangelism; since God had visited and redeemed his people, such must be proclaimed. Donald also accepted new responsibilities with the Inter-Varsity Fellowship. His belief in his vocation became reinforced by these activities.

On arrival in October 1931, he joined the interdenominational Manchester City Mission, and despite his youth became a member of the board of management. It was an energetic evangelistic organization of ninety-five years' standing, with forty mission halls, three Gospel caravans, a wide programme and many missionaries of whom seventy-five were full time. Donald became President of one of the Mission Halls (Charlestown, Salford); he supported the missionary, his wife and local helpers, and preached there and at other Halls. Inevitably he played the piano at services; he spoke at Crusader meetings of young men and inspired the opening up of Crusader work in a new housing estate at Wythenshawe. 'He left his mark,' is how one of his contemporaries put it.

When Donald came to leave Manchester members of the Mission urged him to think seriously before committing himself to ordination: his influence in the academic world might be more important, and one of them writes:

> Dare I now admit that when I first heard that Donald was to take Orders I was deeply disappointed. He had been of great help to young people in the Manchester area and . . . I thought he would be lost in some sleepy country parish and a most promising evangelical voice lost from the wider Church.

The Mission's Annual report for 1934 carried a warm tribute to this 'devoted and deeply taught servant of Our Lord' who had 'delighted in the work and gave us unreservedly his time and talents'.

This was not all; throughout the Manchester years Donald had acted as Editor of the IVF magazine *Varsity*, which circulated among the Christian Unions of the British Universities. Frequent journeys were made to London, and elsewhere, to meet the General Secretary (1924-64), the indefatigable Douglas Johnson, to plan and compile issues. Assignations to hand over copy and discuss future editions took place in all weathers at various railway stations between London and Manchester, or at Sion College on the Embankment, where Donald often went to write or read.

Douglas Johnson, who was a doctor, combined medical commitments with his IVF work, and was a man of the Coggan pattern: he never stopped working. Donald was particularly helpful because he thought and wrote quickly and accurately. He could produce a piece for the magazine in a few hours which would take others several days. One of their joint efforts was the compilation of a history[4] of the Inter-Varsity Fellowship and account of its activity.

There seems to have been a compulsion on Donald's part at this period to push himself to his limits. In one instance he pushed himself beyond them. Spurred on by encouragement from Cambridge, he decided to enter for the most exacting Scholarship so far, the Crosse, 'intended to test knowledge of the Old and New Testaments, Church History and the history of Christian Doctrine' beyond the stage required for the full theological Tripos. Early in December 1933 he sat six stiff examination papers; a fortnight later it was announced that the Scholarship had been awarded to C.F.D. Moule[5]. Dr Cook offered his sympathy. Donald had done well in Old and New Testament papers, but those on Doctrine and Church History, which he had to cram on his own, were less good. The competition had been severe. His rival was on the spot in Cambridge for lectures and reading. 'It was felt that you had made a very good performance considering the difference as regards previous experience . . . and when I recall how keenly you are working away at Semitics'. Donald was obviously disappointed, for he wrote at the top of Dr Cook's letter, 'On not getting the Crosse after six months' work'.

But the result may well have been salutary: it showed him that self-taught methods of learning Doctrine may not be the best; here was a further cause which pushed him towards entering a theological college. The eventual catalyst was a letter from James Hewitt[6],

---

[4] F.D. Coggan, ed., *Christ and the Colleges.* IVF 1934.
[5] Later Lady Margaret's Professor of Divinity in the University of Cambridge.
[6] 1881-1967; Educated Trinity College, Dublin; Prebendary of St Paul's.

vicar of St Mary's, Islington, early in 1934, asking him to be his curate, should the Bishop of London be willing to ordain him in September.

> I am looking for one who will come with the old Gospel message, and a zeal for soul-winning. The fact that you have been ready to consider a parish such as this, with its multitude of poor, is sufficient proof that you answer this test.

The two men had met briefly, and Donald's academic record had come to Hewitt's notice:

> In making choice of a fit person to invite to join me as a colleague I have always desired not only the spiritual and intellectual qualifications which are needful, but also a certain 'affinity' so that our association in the ministry may be a really brotherly one. In you I find all these desiderata, and I should be very happy in the prospect of having you as my colleague.

There was a brief period when Donald considered going for training at Cheshunt, but a visit confirmed that it was not for him. In June 1934 he entered Wycliffe Hall, a theological college with an Evangelical tradition, at Oxford. There followed an intensive few months. In view of his past experience, academic background and the immediate suitable niche for him at Islington, it was conceded that Donald should be ordained after a period of training much shorter than the norm. It was a fruitful time, for his main teachers had gifts in addition to the intellect that had won them first-class degrees. John Ralph Strickland (usually known as Puffy) Taylor[7], who came to Wycliffe after nine years as Headmaster of St Lawrence College, a public school for boys at Ramsgate, was Principal. He had as Vice-Principal Douglas Harrison[8], originally a scientist, and a particularly good teacher. The third was Joe Fison, fresh from the Middle East and Abyssinia, an inspired man with qualities of imagination and originality beyond the ordinary. He had come from much the same background as Donald and was in the process of broadening his horizons. Still before him was the experience, as chaplain, of riveting members of the desert army by his idiosyncratic preaching. His influence at Wycliffe was no less powerful. A student wrote of him many years later[9]:

> I have always ministered with the inspiration which he engendered. He had the great gift under the Holy Spirit of showing us our true selves but

---

[7] 1883-1961; Bishop of Sodor and Man 1942-54.
[8] 1903-1974; Archdeacon of Sheffield 1943; Dean of Bristol 1957-72.
[9] F.W. Dillistone, *The Life of Joe Fison* (Amate Press 1983), p.30.

not leaving us there in bewilderment; but showing us clearly what we must do and the power in Christ that was available to us.

Donald continually acknowledged his debt to them all.

Notice that he had passed the Bishop of London's examination[10] came in mid-September, together with the request that he should present himself on the 27th at Fulham Palace for the ordination retreat. The Bishop of London, Arthur Foley Winnington-Ingram[11], was a prelate of the old school. He had been a bishop since the last days of the nineteenth century and was within five years of his retirement at the age of eighty-one. In no way did his new deacon reflect his style when his own turn came and he was consecrated to episcopal orders in 1956. The ordination took place in St Paul's Cathedral on Sunday 30 September 1934; there were twenty-three priests and thirty deacons for the London diocese. One of Donald's CICCU contemporaries, also awaiting ordination, wrote to ask him whether he would be wearing a stole. Some Evangelical candidates chose not to do so (much to Bishop Winnington-Ingram's annoyance), since they felt it smacked of sacerdotalism, which implication they wished to avoid. Donald replied that he did not like discord; no principle needed to be upheld and he had therefore decided to conform (which his friend did not). It was the beginning of some parting of the ways. His mother and sisters came to the ordination, but his father, for some reason, was not present.

The parish of Islington had two connotations: one was a neighbourhood, the other a particular ecclesiastical tradition. The parish boundaries of St Mary's Church contained a few square miles of densely populated North London streets, immediately beyond and adjacent to the City. Now the homes of prosperous stockbrokers and consultants, some of the tall, gracious eighteenth-century homes, set in neat squares, had become in the early twentieth little better than broken-down tenements. In many of these lived at least one family on each floor, sometimes in one room. Sanitation, water supply, methods of heating, cooking and washing, were for the greater part hopelessly inadequate. The district was poor in economic terms; there was much unemployment, and those who worked had low incomes; hence the over-crowding to reduce the rent. But although there was some violence, particularly in the form of street fighting, it was a relatively safe neighbourhood in which to move

[10] His marks were: Prayer Book beta; Doctrine alpha minus; OT alpha plus; NT alpha plus; Pastoralia alpha.
[11] 1858-1946; Bishop of Stepney 1897-1901; of London 1901-39.

about at night and the inhabitants were reasonably law-abiding. There was little sign of the vicious elements that accompanied the squalor and degradation of certain other areas of contemporary London.

The church that Donald knew (it was bombed in the war and later reconstructed) was built in the 1750s. Twenty years before, John and Charles Wesley had preached in an earlier building, and some of Charles Wesley's famous hymns may have been composed in the parish. George Whitefield was a visitor in April 1739, but having no licence, preached only in the churchyard. In 1821 the appointment of Daniel Wilson[12] as vicar set the Evangelical seal upon the parish. On 4 January 1827 he met with twelve friends at his vicarage to discuss the subject of prayer. It was the first meeting of what was to become the Islington Clerical Conference, which has endured until the present.

As the Conference developed and became well-known as the focus of Evangelical outreach, no hall in the neighbourhood was large enough to contain all who came (some hundreds of clergy), and so the Conference was moved to Church House, Westminster. But the firm connection with the parish of St Mary's Islington remained; it became almost a national centre of the Evangelical tradition. The establishment of several Evangelical theological colleges had its origins by way of this co-operation; prominent among them St John's College, Highbury, later the London College of Divinity, of which Donald Coggan was Principal from 1944-56.

It is reasonable to consider to what extent Donald was equipped for his Islington assignment, far from the detailed examination of texts in the Syriac script. The exactness and care which he had learnt to give to the study of oriental languages he now devoted to the study of the Bible; here his CICCU training stood him in good stead, as also did his grounding in the practice of prayer. He became a remarkably effective exponent of the Scriptures, for which he is remembered in Islington. He was not allowed to preach much, but when he did, his injunctions were Bible-based.

A source of strength was awareness of his call. 'I do pray that you will go to Islington with the certainty that God has answered your deepest prayers,' Douglas Harrison had written to Donald on the eve of his ordination; of this he was assured. Though still shy and reserved, he was friendly, compassionate, humorous and humble, and most remarkable of all, lacking in intellectual snobbery and

[12] 1779-1858; Bishop of Calcutta 1832-58.

élitism. He obviously regarded his particular kind of brain as an endowment for which he could claim no credit; it tied up with the doctrine of grace he had been taught. His evangelistic experiences in market-places in Hoxton, with the Open Air Mission, the Church Army and elsewhere, had brought him in touch with men and women who had gifts superior to his in practical fields, which he was wise enough to recognize.

His knowledge of the world was limited, which brought a certain lack of perception of the complexity of the human condition, psychological, social and economic. A letter survives from a family grateful for having been found new living space; Donald had written to the London County Council on their behalf. It would seem he felt he had cured their problems. To his contemporaries he appeared to see life in particularly simple terms; hence his unsophisticated, sometimes innocent message. It was often appreciated by those who came to listen; but there were many in the parish of nearly twelve thousand souls who did not.

Donald's reactions to his first curacy survive in a source that reveals many of his early activities. At Cambridge he had joined a Missionary Fellowship of CICCU friends who contracted to keep in touch with each other through prayers and biannual letters; also to support a missionary. The original membership numbered about thirty men, most of whom went at some time or other to the mission field. (Those who survive still write and meet, fifty-seven years later.) The missionary sponsored in the early days was Oliver Allison[13], later Bishop in the Sudan. Letters were addressed in the first place to the Secretary (at the beginning Joost de Blank[14]) who collated and distributed them. The early letters in particular were almost all written in the phraseology then common to Evangelical Christians. Reaching back over the long span of years from all over the world, they are of considerable interest. Donald wrote to his friends early in 1935 of his arrival at Islington:

> Parish life is a great contrast after university work – a strange mixture of the comic and the sad. One does not realize the dense heathenism of London till one gets to grips with it, visiting the homes of the people.

His vicar, James Hewitt, was a somewhat fey, vague Irishman whom his new curate found to be a poor organizer of his time. Donald was in the main indulgent, and sought to explain away the

[13] 1908- ; CMS missionary Juba 1938-47; Bishop in the Sudan 1948-53.
[14] 1908-68; Bishop of Stepney 1952; Archbishop of Cape Town 1957-63.

shortcomings of his superiors, but this was an issue where he had strong views. The parish had recently been in the hands of Prebendary Herbert Hinde[15], an austere, stiff man who was not warm in sermon or speech; the Hewitt era was fortunately more relaxed. The fellow curate for the first nine months was Oscar Keith de Berry[16], a St John's and CICCU contemporary. Donald preached his first sermon in Islington parish church on 14 October 1934, a fortnight after his ordination. On the 23rd there appeared in the *Times* newspaper the notice of his engagement to be married.

He had continued to act as Editor of *Varsity* during the months at Wycliffe Hall and was intending to continue to help Douglas Johnson, the honorary General Secretary of the IVF, from his Islington base. The enterprise had become more enjoyable, since an interesting young woman had joined the Executive Committee.

Jean Braithwaite Strain was the fourth daughter and seventh child of a surgeon, William Loudon Strain; there were eventually ten children. After training at Glasgow University where he became a gold medallist, Jean's father began his medical career in 1884 in Brazil, at St Paulo, where he organized one of the first modern hospitals, and established himself. During a furlough in England he married Dorothy Savory, the daughter of the Rector of Palgrave in Norfolk, and a relation of the poet Wordsworth. They returned to Brazil, where their first five children were born; the need for an English education brought them back again. In 1905 William Strain became a London surgeon and they all moved into 'The Plaisance', a large family house in Wimbledon.

Although Jean's life at home had been less secluded than Donald's because of the larger number of children, there were similarities in the restraints that were placed upon her, for her father was a member of the strict exclusive sect, the Plymouth Brethren. Moreover, he suffered two grievous personal tragedies: his eldest son, to whom he was particularly devoted, and to whose future as a doctor he looked forward, was killed at Ypres in 1917; he had committed the boy to God's keeping and it was to him inconceivable that he would not be protected from bodily harm. A few years later another son was drowned when aged sixteen, swept away by the current while swimming in Cornwall. Jean was with him on the beach. The tensions caused by the family life-style were heightened by William Strain's darkness of spirit.

[15] 1877-1955; Principal of Oak Hill Theological College 1932-45.
[16] 1907- ; Rector of St Aldate's, Oxford 1952-74.

The Meeting of the Brethren for the Breaking of Bread claimed the family on Sundays. As she grew older Jean began to recognize that although there was much in her parents' outlook that impressed her, she had never felt at home with its foundations. As a young child she had been seriously alarmed by the threat of eternal punishment for the infringement of rules, and the memory of her fear was deeply implanted. She ceased to attend the Meeting, and after some years of searching she became an Anglican.

Jean Strain's early education took place at Wimbledon High School, during which time she considered studying medicine, perhaps to be a medical missionary, but her father would not hear of it. Eventually, as a compromise, she entered Bedford College, London, to take a two-year course in Social Studies; the practical side of it interested her particularly. Her diploma recorded distinction in all subjects. At college, Jean had been drawn into the Inter-Varsity Fellowship of Christian Unions, and when she came to leave she agreed to give temporary help with the Central organization at the London office. It was due to Donald Coggan that the London office existed at all.

All that comprised the headquarters of the IVF had had its base since 1924 in the various lodgings, student hostels, medical missions and so on, lived in by Douglas Johnson. He and Donald had often discussed the need to find better and permanent premises. The Executive Committee hung back on grounds of expense. After one of their meetings to discuss the magazine, the two friends passed an estate agent in Southampton Row; they decided to ask whether any modest offices were vacant and to let. The clerk, son of an Islington parishioner, produced one in Russell Square which was suitable; the rent was £50 a year with a deposit also of £50. Donald offered to pay the rent if Douglas Johnson found the deposit in anticipation of agreement from the Committee. It was in this small office that Jean Strain came to give voluntary assistance: she also helped Douglas Johnson in a medical mission he had started in Lansdowne Place in the Borough, near Tower Bridge. Later, when her efficiency and capacity to speak to groups of girls made itself known, she became Travelling Secretary for Women Students. Her work took her to universities all over England, to Keswick and elsewhere to arrange conferences and CSSM House Parties, but in between commitments she returned to the Russell Square office.

Douglas Johnson took note that each conference and House Party brought her a new crop of suitors. Jean was intelligent, godly, cheerful and good-looking. He was impressed by her straightforwardness, an abiding characteristic. When he looked like making a mistake, she would preface her suggestions with the remark 'If you were one of my brothers'. In the early autumn of 1934, Douglas Johnson became engaged to be married to a student at Holloway College in the University of London. He and his fiancée thought they perceived an increased interest by the Editor of *Varsity* in the Travelling Secretary for Women Students. On 17 October Douglas Johnson invited them both to lunch in the dining-room of the headquarters of the British Medical Association in Tavistock Square. He arranged to be called away at the end of the meal and left Donald and Jean on their own. In the courtyard of the building, beside the fountains and the statues of Hygiene and Aesculapus, he proposed to her and was accepted. They made their way back to the office to which Douglas Johnson had already returned. He gathered that the indications had been correct when his astonished typist brought him the remarkable news that Mr Coggan had come in with his arm round Miss Strain.

A wish to show Jean his new surroundings led them up to Islington. Donald assured her that she would be recognized by nobody. It is a mark of the formality of the times that this should have been important. Keith de Berry, walking along Upper Street, was surprised to see Jean Strain, whose family in Wimbledon he knew well, on the steps of St Mary's. Even more surprising was to realize the identity of her companion as his fellow-curate. There seemed no option but to apprise Keith de Berry of the new relationship and to ask him to keep it to himself. From the vantage point of the present day, the courage and determination that went into the step which Donald Coggan had taken can hardly be appreciated. His twenty-fifth birthday, his ordination and his arrival in the parish were only a couple of weeks past; his stipend was £250 per annum[17]; he had dropped a sixth of his income on leaving Manchester; he lived in lodgings in one room. It was not usual for clergy of the Church of England to marry until they had become vicar or rector of a parish.

Certain of the probity of his aspirations, aware no doubt that otherwise he might miss this prize, Donald had decided to act promptly. It was one of the most felicitous decisions of his life. Only he can calculate what the partnership with Jean brought him in personal terms during the next fifty years. From the point of view of the world at large, her support and identification with all that

---

[17] Paid quarterly in arrears.

concerned him seem to have been immeasurable, at times at great cost to herself.

There were three immediate hurdles for Donald to surmount: telling his vicar, his family, and Jean's. Their opinions carried more weight than in the present climate of greater independence. O.K. de Berry was a witness to the encounter with Prebendary Hewitt, and recalls the incident. When Donald asked what he would say if one of his curates told him he wanted to be married, the audacity of the question made the vicar speechless — 'But he got used to the idea.'

Donald's family produced no opposition; their chief reaction seems to have been that of surprise. Until the announcement of the engagement, his sisters were unaware of Jean's existence; but she was made welcome and the curious ban on visitors was lifted in her regard. Few had been so privileged. Douglas Johnson was three times in the house in six years; another friend twice. In the Cambridge days, a contemporary who had a small car and collected Donald on his way to the University from north of London, would find him waiting outside the house on the pavement with his trunk. After the restricted circumstances of his upbringing it was remarkable that Donald was so outward-going towards all whom he met, so persistently humorous and optimistic, and that he wanted to form a close personal relationship of his own. In spite of the delicate physical health which had dogged him as a boy, his psychological strength was considerable and remained so. Donald and Jean went reasonably frequently to his parents' home for meals during the year of their engagement, although she only met Donald's father once before her marriage.

Her own father's reservations about the clergy of the established Church filled Jean with apprehension. She told her elder sister Evelyn of her engagement to marry Donald; Evelyn's response 'Why him?' became a stock Coggan family joke in the decades that followed, years which provided a more than adequate answer. Donald's appearance without a clerical collar and with his customary interest in the doings of others, in this case William Strain's exploits in Brazil, paved the way to his acceptance as a future son-in-law.

The year before his marriage Donald spent in lodgings at 101 Calabria Road, in a row of terraced houses later condemned and demolished, which he shared with the curate of a neighbouring parish. His landlady, fat and inquisitive (she had a reputation for listening at keyholes), he named 'the Feather Bed'.

The worst years of the Depression of the 1930s were over; the soup kitchen in the churchyard of St Mary's, which had given nourishment daily to those without food or means, no longer operated. But a Bread Service when loaves were distributed still took place on Saturday afternoons, and a medical mission provided a rudimentary health service. A formula whereby to bring the poorest into Church functions had not been discovered, though since they were still parishioners they needed to be visited and cared for; here the curates were busy. The regular members of the congregation were for the most part clerks in offices, small shop-keepers, skilled workers and a few professional people.

Donald had a good relationship with a flourishing Christian Endeavour group of about eighty young people who joined the Bible studies on Wednesday evenings. Remnants of the group, now in their late sixties, recall that it was particularly enjoyable when Donald's turn came to be the leader. On summer evenings, outdoor services in the courtyard outside the Church drew members of the parish who were loath to come inside. Donald noticed without envy the ease with which the London City Missioner, a layman attached to St Mary's, moved among the more destitute.

The interior of the Church was austere, with galleries, very large high pulpit reached by a long flight of steps, and lectern which had a more than life-sized eagle to hold the Bible. Services were formal, with ceremonial that included a preacher being conducted to and from the pulpit by a verger who carried a sceptre-like wand before him and opened and closed the door. Little concession was made to the sensibilities of the unlettered, or those without proper shoes, so it was hardly surprising they were not there. Donald was much occupied with the sick, with a special care for those who had tuberculosis. His ministry to a particular dying girl is still remembered. His post-ordination training was well placed in the hands of Allan John Macdonald[18], vicar of St Dunstan's-in-the-West in Fleet Street, to whom he submitted his sermons for comment and talked with profit.

Donald's examination for priest's orders took place on 10 September 1935. The month of October was one of the most memorable of his life; on 6 October he was ordained priest in St Paul's Cathedral by the Bishop of London; the 9th was his twenty-sixth birthday; on the 17th he was married to Jean in Wimbledon Parish Church. Prebendary Hewitt, all qualms resolved, preached the sermon with the text 'Heirs together of the grace of life'. There

[18] DD (Cantab) 1930: F.R. Hist.C; author of *Lanfranc* 1926 and *Hildebrand* 1932, etc.

had been some doubt as to whether Arthur Coggan would come to the wedding; one of Donald's sisters now thinks he did not, but she is mistaken: a photograph shows his presence, a source of pleasure. Moreover, he provided a handsome canteen of cutlery. A reception in a marquee in the garden of The Plaisance followed, before the couple left for a honeymoon in Buckinghamshire and Devon.

Back in Islington they made their home at 21 Highbury Park Road, a street of tall Victorian houses now largely destroyed to make space for the huge Highbury Grove Comprehensive School. Their flat on the first floor comprised a sitting room, bedroom and kitchen, part of which had been made into a bathroom; the bath doubled-up as refrigerator in hot weather. It was hardly luxurious except by the standards of a number of their neighbours. In Jean's home in the 1930s cooking and cleaning were not done by members of the family. In the new circumstances she did much of it herself, but did not intend to allow her life to be dominated by chores.

From the first Jean Coggan established a pattern for herself which was to endure: she set out to provide support to enable Donald to pursue his ministry to the best of his ability, but at the same time she wanted to share as much of it as appropriate. From the Islington days onwards they became known as a combination; one partner was seldom thought of without the other. The relationship was built more upon similarities than upon the attraction of opposite qualities, although obviously there were some differences. Jean could relax and do nothing; Donald worked on unremittingly. Many interests and standards were held in common, without straining in order to achieve a *modus vivendi*. Some later critics of their unassuming life-style were to feel they were too alike; had they not reinforced each other's opinions, it might have led them to be more adventurous.

Their main mutual preoccupation in Islington, as for the rest of their lives, was a concern for the people who lived in their neighbourhood. A particular friend was Katie Hazzard, old, deaf, poor, partially sighted and alone in one room filled with smoke from a faulty chimney. The Coggans saw her often, invited her for Christmas. In heaven, Katie Hazzard would be in the front row, Donald told his fellow curate; she had a strong and lasting influence upon him. It came more easily to Donald and Jean to relate to the cheerful survivor, by reason of the circumstances of their own backgrounds, than (though they were both compassionate) to the feeble or feckless whom others might find more attractive. Two early sermons that survive corroborate this tendency: the text of the first was 'The fruit of the Spirit is . . . self control,' and the other spoke of the metaphor of the broken reed.

The vicar of Islington's wife, Evadne Hewitt, was kind and understanding to the newly-married couple; she provided furniture, and each Sunday evening invited them for supper at the vicarage. Moyra[19] her daughter, then a child at school, recalls lying in bed and hearing the sounds of laughter from the ground floor of the house. Her mother brewed barm-beer with a mixture of yeast and sugar which she fondly imagined to be non-alcoholic, for they were all teetotallers: no doubt it had a relaxing effect at the end of a long day.

Shortly after his priesting, Donald was asked to read a paper to the 109th Islington Conference, probably the youngest speaker ever to do so; a considerable honour. His essay *Grace and Merit* was an exposition of the doctrine of Justification (declared righteous by God) by faith, in its post-Reformation form. The theme of the Conference was the Gospel of Grace, defined by an earlier speaker as 'love in the mind of God as exhibited towards sinners'. It had been explained that it was a love due entirely to God's good-will and spontaneous favour, and not to any possible merit on the part of those towards whom it was exhibited; a theme much chosen by Evangelicals. Donald's paper drew attention to the tendency towards 'moralistic' religion, or the doing of things by rule for some outside end, i.e. to gain merit, which, he argued, was not possible within the Christian dispensation. He showed evidence of wide reading for which he was commended both by Dr Macdonald, who read the essay before it was delivered, and by members of the Conference who obviously considered that the young man had acquitted himself well.

The future was an open question. A discussion between Donald and his fellow curate had brought them to the conclusion that there were few opportunities of ministry then open to Evangelicals, particularly in the diocese of London. Requests for his services began to come from beyond the Church of England, from the wider bounds of the Anglican Communion. He was a comparatively rare phenomenon, a good Evangelical pastoral priest with teaching experience and high academic record.

In 1936 came a pressing invitation to go as Vice-Principal to Moore College, Sydney, a theological college in that Australian diocese which had a strong Evangelical ethos. Donald did not

---

[19] Now Mrs Charles Smith, married to a surgeon in York.

consider the call one that must be accepted, despite an even more persuasive letter which followed his refusal, from the Archbishop of Sydney[20]. Another request followed the same year from the Anglican Church in Canada. Robert Benjamin McElheran[21], Principal of Wycliffe College, Toronto, a theological college of Evangelical outlook, arrived in England to search for a member of staff who fulfilled certain requirements. Donald Coggan he considered to do so, and he invited him to Canada. The fact that he had only completed two years of his first curacy made Donald hesitate, and the Canadian authorities in question agreed to wait a year for one whom they considered the right candidate.

For the Coggans the decision was not without conflicting issues: they were happy in the parochial scene; here was a proposed return to the academic world which Donald had already once decided to forsake. Moreover, both of them had deep feelings of affection for their mothers in which protective instincts were prominent. In the years before air-travel, Toronto was far away. But the vocational pull was strong. Donald was well qualified for this opportunity in the service of the gospel. The decision was made to accept the offer and go to Canada.

A holiday in Switzerland in the company of Jean's mother, Dorothy Strain, and sister, Evelyn, preceded their departure from England for Canada on 24 August 1937 by the Canadian Pacific liner 'Empress of Australia'. Donald did not see his mother again; Fanny Coggan died on 26 January 1938.[22]

---

[20] Howard Mowll, a former enthusiastic member of CICCU.
[21] 1877-1939; Rector of St Matthew's, Winnipeg 1907-30; Principal of Wycliffe College 1930-39.
[22] She had been suffering from Bright's disease for some years, and was only 66.

Anglican Province of Canada 1937

CHAPTER FOUR *Canada*

News of the Coggans' safe arrival in Canada came in the autumn from 99 Madison Avenue, Toronto, to the members of the Cambridge Missionary Fellowship. After a six-day passage across the Atlantic, two of rough seas, they had reached Quebec and the Heights of Abraham. A train then took them alongside the St Lawrence river for the 162 miles to Montreal, where they spent the night, and then another 323 miles to Toronto, on the shores of Lake Ontario; a short distance by Canadian standards. 'The world's clammiest heatwave' greeted them, and the news that the opening of the new term at Wycliffe College was being delayed by an 'outbreak of infantile paralysis'. But Donald's letter[1] went on to say that the students had eventually reassembled and he was teaching the New Testament to sixty-five of them.

The designation of the post to which he had been appointed was a somewhat ambiguous one from a British point of view; in fact the scope of his duties, which were many and varied, could not accurately be deduced on the eastern side of the Atlantic from his title as Professor of New Testament. It derived from the particular nature and history of the establishment he was to serve, which he did with energy and dedication for the next seven years.

At the early age of twenty-eight, Donald was not the occupant of a university Chair in the British sense, concerned largely with administration and the supervision of a department. There was no faculty of theology in the University of Toronto; teaching of this discipline was carried out in the constituent theological colleges of which Wycliffe was one. Donald's main responsibility was to teach the New Testament as a whole, and in particular the Greek language in which it was written, so that men might be able to read the original text. He did so by means of class-room tuition, lectures and seminars. He also taught women students of a training college for deaconesses, situated in Toronto. It was a heavy load to lay on one pair of young shoulders, particularly as this was not the total sum of

[1] 4 October 1937.

his duties. He visited Wycliffe graduates[2] in their parishes and missions throughout the huge country in which many dioceses were larger than the whole of the United Kingdom; he conducted Schools of Preaching in several far-flung areas before the development of air travel. Some of this work was his by nature of the appointment; some he initiated himself. As time went on there were pastoral aspects also, in addition to academic ones, after he had been appointed Dean of Residence.

A further bulletin[3] to the Fellowship giving an account of himself which followed in the Spring, showed that even by his own exacting standards a great deal was demanded of him. There had been so much of 'the midnight hour and after, for me lately' that he had not written earlier; an afternoon's invigilating gave him the present opportunity. The first six months at Wycliffe had been heavy going, but abundantly worth-while, 'for the foundation of many of the men's thinking and preaching is laid during their time here'. He referred to the death of his mother in January; although he had not intended to leave Canada that year, he felt he should see his father and sisters, and was therefore returning briefly to England.

He sailed on the *Queen Mary*, spent a fortnight with his family in London and preached twice; on one occasion at the familiar St Mary's, Islington. He achieved a somewhat closer acquaintance with his father, whom he did not see again. His grief at the death of his mother was deep. To have left her in England when she was obviously not in good health was without doubt one of the greatest sacrifices of his life. He poured his feelings into the preparation of new courses for Wycliffe men.

The cause of Donald Coggan's heavy programme was a national economic crisis of great severity which had affected the Church as seriously as it had the country as a whole. The recession of the early 1930s hit the entire North American continent, Canada as well as the United States. One million men were unemployed in a population of only 11,045,000. Wycliffe College depended materially on endowments for its survival; when the value of investments dropped sharply, cutbacks were inevitable. The number of students fell also, which prevented a situation of intolerable strain, but a constant and untiring performance was still required by the reduced staff.

---

[2] This term has a different connotation in North America from that in England where it involves degree status; in Canada and the USA it implies passing a final examination.
[3] 1 April 1938.

There had been a change of Principal at Wycliffe at the onset of the straightened circumstances. T.R. O'Meara[4] who had been its leader through a heyday when it had been the largest single theological college in the Anglican Communion, sending scores of missionaries to the ends of the earth, died on 10 January 1930. The new Principal, R.B. McElheran, faced a challenging future. First, he had to retrench in order to remain solvent; he cut down the staff, appointed a number of part-time men and carried out some of the tuition himself. In addition to the administrative burden, he was Professor of Homiletics and Pastoral Theology at the time of Donald's arrival, and shared the teaching of Liturgics. Secondly, he had to find new sources of revenue. As the sparsity of staff inevitably led to a lowering of standards, Principal McElheran's third and subsequent move was to redress the balance. The appointment of Donald Coggan was one of his attempts to do so. He reported to his Council[5] on his return from England: 'Both he and his wife are charming, capable, consecrated Christian workers, whose influence will immediately be felt in the College and in the Church at large.'

It was in later years considered to have been a master stroke of McElheran's ministry at Wycliffe and one that helped to save the reputation of the College. The arrival of Frederick William Dillistone[6] the following year as Professor of Systematic Theology had the same intention and a like effect. All these changes required to be made within the framework of the ideology under which the College had been founded.

When members of the Church of England came as settlers to Canada, they carried with them the traditions which had been brought together to form the synthesis considered so important a basis of their Church: at the same time catholic and reformed. There were those who favoured one ethos more than the other. Thus it was that when Trinity College, Toronto, was set up in 1852 and included the teaching of theology in its programme, with an emphasis upon patristics and the Greek and Latin Fathers, there was a sharp reaction from some Evangelical Churchmen in Canada whose theology was more strictly Bible-based and who took their lead more directly from the insights of the German and English Reformers. Various attempts were made to reconcile the two aspects and to

[4] Principal 1906-1930.
[5] Minutes of Meeting of 7 December 1936.
[6] 1903- ; Dean of Liverpool 1956-63; Fellow and Chaplain, Oriel College, Oxford 1964-70.

accommodate both at Trinity. But the spirit of controversy proved too strong.

Wycliffe College was founded in 1877 to train men for the ministry of the Church who would teach and perpetuate what was regarded as the pure gospel message derived from the Bible, with a particular emphasis on the death of Christ on the Cross as 'the one perfect and sufficient sacrifice' for the sins of men. The call to the mission field, which was answered so readily and in such numbers, was a direct response to the Scriptures, to the Saviour's words: 'Go and make all nations my disciples'.[7] Wycliffe men were to endure isolation, danger, ice, snow, tropical heat, disease, privations and premature old age, as a measure of their obedience.

At first the new divinity school was temporarily housed near St James' Church (the present cathedral). Affiliation was granted in 1885, and in 1889 Wycliffe became a constituent part of the University of Toronto. The Wycliffe trustees recognized that this fact must become a visible reality. They were able to purchase the present site in Queen's Park and the foundation stone of the future college was laid in 1890. Students moved in during the following year. Wycliffe College was from now on at the heart of the University, part of the Campus, on the south side of Hoskins Avenue (Trinity College stood opposite on the north). Extensions followed: a new hall and library with hammer-beam roof, both of considerable size, were added in 1893; then the present chapel and houses for members of staff. In 1916 the trustees of Wycliffe College were authorised to grant degrees, including honorary degrees, in theology. It was Wycliffe's parting gift to Donald to give him the first of his many honorary doctorates in 1944.

The maintenance of these prestigious buildings, well used during the days of expansion and prosperity, was a further burden to the new Principal in 1930. (Shortly after Donald's arrival, McElheran solved a portion of this problem by moving him and Jean into the College in the Spring of 1938 and reducing his salary as payment of rent for the flat.) It was doubtless on account of R.B. McElheran's record as a man of considerable practical ability and pastoral gifts that he was selected during this critical period. His referees pointed out that 'he was no brilliant student'.

Robert McElheran's life is worth examining in detail because it leads to a greater understanding of the particular character of Wycliffe. Though born in south-eastern Canada, he migrated to the

---

[7] Matthew 28.19.

west, to Winnipeg, as a boy of thirteen, on the death of his mother. He supported himself by working for a newspaper, the *Farmer's Advocate*. After some years as a Lay Reader, when he helped to form the mission of St Matthew's, he became aware of the call to ordination. He went back to the east at the age of twenty-three to take his matriculation, and in 1902 entered Wycliffe College, simultaneously earning his living as a bookkeeper for several Toronto firms. He returned to St Matthew's, Winnipeg, as curate in 1906; from 1907 until 1930 he was Rector of what was to become, under his leadership, the largest and wealthiest church in the North-West; his Sunday School was the most immense in Canada, with nearly two thousand children. Though he had a warm pastoral heart, he was authoritative and paternalistic and found delegation difficult.

The extent to which Donald Coggan was influenced by his first Principal, and whether in any way inclined to repeat the pattern when he himself came to lead a theological college, is not easy to assess. Donald was to be authoritative also, at St John's College, Highbury, but probably more on account of circumstances rather than example. He did not need to emulate McElheran's dedication to his work; he possessed it already. The Principal's main thrust was towards loyalty to the Wycliffe tradition: to produce men who would uphold Church, Prayer Book and Bible, and whose faith would survive the worst that the world had to offer; a more catholic approach, he thought, led to disbelief. He did not have the intellectual equipment to hammer out the possibilities of reconciling traditions, nor the recognition that there are different philosophical terms with which the same gospel can be interpreted. Neither could Donald have attempted the exercise during the Canadian days: what he had been taught was still stronger than his experience. But there were changes in his thinking. As a result of his detailed study of the New Testament, although he continued to see the Scriptures as divinely inspired and entirely trustworthy records of God's revelation, nevertheless he thought he saw evidence of errors of copying and transmission which rendered them less than infallible. This attitude was to have repercussions in the future.

An area where McElheran may have left a mark on his young colleague was that he held the sinfulness of men responsible for the economic crisis of the 1930s. Donald inclined towards this attitude in that of the 1970s.

In August 1938, Donald and Jean's first child was born in a Toronto hospital, a daughter Dorothy (named for Jean's mother)

Ann. Parenthood brought him much joy and, since he had exemplary children (Ruth was born two years later), no sorrow except that of separation. He poured upon his daughters all that had been missing in his own relationship with his father, continuing expressions of love, interest and support.

Principal McElheran suffered a serious coronary thrombosis early in 1938; largely, it was thought, brought on by strain and overwork. It was no warning to Donald who was getting into his stride; he had been appointed Dean of Residence of the College which involved him in greater pastoral oversight of the students and responsibilities for chapel services; moreover, he had decided to work for a BD to provide an extra theological qualification. Then there was the extra load which had to be shared out on account of the Principal's illness. The arrival of F.W. Dillistone was a great help academically and his company a source of pleasure.

That summer came the news that Arthur Coggan had remarried at St Martin's, Gospel Oak, in July. His second wife, the former Norah Booth, was forty-five (he was sixty-two) and single, the daughter of a London auctioneer and surveyor. Donald's younger sister thought the relationship a success and reported that the second Mrs Coggan 'persuaded him out of his fads and fancies'. Beatrice was now free, at the age of 32, to pursue her career. She visited Donald and Jean for two months in Canada and then took up training as a nurse at St Mary's Hospital, Paddington. Arthur Coggan died on 24 November 1942, following an operation.

The students who passed through Wycliffe College in the 1930s duly found their way, as their predecessors had done, to foreign missions or Evangelical parishes throughout Canada. A feature of this generation[8] was that a high proportion remained faithful to their vocation. Many former students now serve in the Toronto diocese, which has made it possible to record a certain number of earlier impressions. Memories of the young teacher of New Testament are in nearly all cases happy: his exuberance was infectious; he was almost bouncy, said one. His youthfulness was a feature generally recollected. It endured; there never was a man less jaundiced with the passing of time. Donald's habit of twirling the hem of his gown in his enthusiasm for the imparting of Greek, was commented upon, as also his tendency to fling open windows in

[8] Arnold Edinburgh, ed., *A Centennial History of Wycliffe College, Toronto*. University of Toronto Press 1978.

what was considered cool weather in North America, to bring in more fresh air to a sluggish class-room.

There is no doubt that he was a most successful teacher; men learnt a great deal from him. His scholarship gained respect. Although a certain reserve was noted, it was attributed to his English origins, and he was nevertheless regarded as a man who was capable of acts of considerable personal kindness. One former student recalls that when he was ill in the infirmary, Donald was the sole member of staff who came to visit, and brought him books to read of a light and humorous kind. He could be sharp with students who did not exert themselves. A home-spun doggerel rhyme survives in a student magazine which makes this plain:

In teaching the New Testament Prof. Coggan's quite a wizard.
Tho' Revelation's stormy, he's a guide through any blizzard.
He wants his essays short and sweet, and served red hot on time.
And if you *miss* the deadline, boys, for you the bells will chime.

Another Wycliffe rhyme written once the war had started and practice blackouts were held in Toronto, tells of Donald's 'Let's study Greek' as a siren blew and students filed into the basement, and his 'Someone help him quickly' when mistakes were made. Not a moment was wasted. The students for whom Donald reserved the severest censure were those who failed to attend services regularly in chapel.

Criticism of him comes, in the main, from those former students who are now migrants from the Evangelical tradition, who profess to detect a certain lack of depth and breadth in what Donald had to offer in his Wycliffe days. A gap in acquaintance with Christian thinking between the second and sixteenth centuries was doubtless present. But it would seem to have been over-optimistic to have expected to find knowledge and experience of patristics and philosophy of religion in someone so young who had been exposed largely to the emphases of the Reformation, initially a linguist, engaged in the teaching of another field. It may well be that his pursuit of a Bachelor of Divinity degree was the result of his recognition of some of his deficiencies.

During 1939 Donald's experience broadened considerably. His knowledge of the physical world which had been so limited in England, was extended, as also his familiarity with the wider Church. There was a deliberate policy at Wycliffe not only to keep in touch with its own graduates to maintain their morale and their faithfulness, but also to try to influence the Canadian Church as a whole. Members of staff made regular tours of the enormous dioceses that made up the Province. With the illness of the Principal, it was now Donald's turn.

The Anglican Province of Canada was in 1939 only forty-six years old. Individual dioceses, especially those on the East Coast, had been established a good deal earlier, but had remained for many years under the jurisdiction of the Province of Canterbury. On 13 September 1893 the first General Synod of the Church of England in Canada met in Toronto; the Metropolitan of Rupertsland, Archbishop Robert Machray, was elected by the Upper House as Primate. By 1939 the number of dioceses had grown to twenty-seven; they stretched from the 500,000-square-mile diocese of Caledonia in the West, to Quebec, 280,000 square miles, in the East; from the diocese of the Arctic, a total of over 2 million square miles (of which one million square miles were of land), to Keewatin, 111,000 square miles, to the South.

The courage and endurance that had gone into the spread of the gospel across the vast largely empty spaces, with their difficult terrain, lack of communications and extremes of temperature, was of a high order[9]. Parishes and missions, schools for Indians, had been established in mountainous regions, beside frozen lakes and plains alike. Donald's visit in June 1939 was to Wycliffe men in the Maritimes, a name given to the areas of the eastern seaboard of Canada, facing the Atlantic ocean. On his return he reported on the isolation still endured.

A holiday in the Muskoka[10] Lakes district in a wooded area of great natural beauty in Ontario, 120 miles north of Toronto, had preceded Ann's birth the year before; Donald was being introduced to the infinite variety of the Canadian scene. Now in Nova Scotia he met countryside of greater cultivation, reminiscent of the English home counties. He began in Halifax, went to Prince Edward Island and then to Saint John's; he preached four times in the churches of Wycliffe graduates, conducted two Quiet Days and held meetings; then he moved on to the dioceses of Quebec and Montreal. An ingenious system of pick-up points, pooling of cars and petrol made it possible for him to see thirty active and retired Wycliffe men, and six present members of the College who were living on summer

---

[9] Archibald Lang Fleming *Archibald the Arctic*. (Hodder & Stoughton 1957), gives a graphic account of what was involved.
[10] Named after the Indian Chief Musqua Ukee (or Yellowhead) whose band once hunted each summer in the area.

missions. He also interviewed a number of young men who were contemplating ordination: all this in three weeks.

The sense of isolation of which Donald wrote was of two kinds: the first was the loneliness of those who were far away from colleagues and friends; the other was 'their sense of ostracism by their ecclesiastical leaders. Wycliffe men are sometimes ostracized because they are Wycliffe men'. Donald did not appear to have been in sympathy with criticism of his College. Although he eschewed fundamentalism, Wycliffe's strong Christocentric biblical orthodoxy and rigorous moral regulation matched his own. Solely by training men of faith by these exacting standards could 'the Gospel of Christ be led to victory in the world'[11].

Wycliffe's reputation in the 1930s was uneven. The stock of the College was high in Toronto itself due to the presence of its staff and some powerful men of the Evangelical tradition in the city. Donald played no small part in this process, of which the number of invitations to preach, and so on, gave evidence. In the Easter season of 1939 he had been invited to take part in a broadcast on Good Friday which was relayed from coast to coast. Toronto might not be the capital but was still a most important business centre of the country, strategically placed, and its influence was considerable. Nevertheless, leadership of the Canadian Province in the 1930s was no longer in the hands of Wycliffe men as it had been earlier when pioneer missionaries had become bishops of new dioceses.

In 1937 only four diocesan bishops of a total of twenty-seven had been through Wycliffe College. Of these only two had completed their entire theological education there: Archibald Fleming of the Arctic and Arthur Henry Sovereign of Athabasca; two others, William Archibald Geddes of Yukon and William T.T. Hallam of Saskatoon, had completed their training at Wycliffe, though they took initial degrees elsewhere. In spite of the lack of Evangelical leadership, defence of the principles for which Wycliffe stood continued to be made on conscientious grounds throughout the Province; to prevent the Church moving in a more catholic direction, seen as a distortion of the faith, was the intention. There was some success in this stand.

Donald commented in his report of the summer of 1939 that the East of Canada needed more men with a positive message and a spiritual life; critics of Wycliffe implied, on the other hand, that it was narrow and sectarian. One cause without doubt was the clea-

[11] A. Edinburgh, *A Centennial History of Wycliffe College*, op. cit.

vage, in the Evangelical circles of the 1930s, between sacred and secular. It was not considered part of holy living to be much involved in secular affairs. Wycliffe men did not drink or dance, play cards or go to the theatre. They were seldom seen at football matches, or meetings for social justice. The History of the College points out that its men were considered identifiable negatively by what they disapproved.

Liturgical practices were circumscribed: there were no Christian symbols in the chapel; no cross or candlesticks upon the holy table; clergy, who celebrated from the north end, did not wear stoles through fear of idolatry and lest it be thought that some form of continuing sacrifice was offered there. Christ's sacrifice had been made once and for all; rigorism set in to protect this revelation.

In the 1960s, a broadening of attitudes took place within Canadian Evangelicalism, as in England. It had already done so within the heart of Donald Coggan. At the Anglican Congress in Toronto of 1963 when Donald, as Archbishop of York, also delivered a powerful new message[12], Max Warren caused a sensation in Wycliffe circles[13]. Speaking on the theme *The Church's Mission to the World*, he articulated change in the setting-up of limits.

> All life is religious. For the Christian there can be in the central citadel of his faith no religious frontier. The Christian must refuse every pressure, however subtle, to divide men's experience of living under the separating titles of 'sacred' and 'secular'[14].

Particularly as Archbishop of Canterbury, Donald associated himself wholeheartedly with a wide range of causes that would have been regarded as 'secular', and therefore beyond his scope, in his Canadian days.

The death of Robert McElheran came in August 1939, with Donald in constant watch over the last few days. It was he who said prayers with the Principal as he died sending a last message to the people of Winnipeg whom he had served with such dedication. The Coggans' much needed holiday later that summer was in uncultivated lumber and hunting country, some sixty miles north of Ottawa and four hundred miles from Toronto; the place-names reveal the origins of the inhabitants as French Canadians, so *Poisson-Blanc Lake, Lac Gatineau, St-Aimé-du-Lac-des-Iles*. Here

---

[12] On Mutual Responsibility and Interdependence.
[13] Recalled by Dr Reginald Stockhouse, Principal of Wycliffe College 1975-84.
[14] Eugene Fairweather, ed., *Anglican Congress 1963-Report of Proceedings 13-23 August* (Toronto Canada p.20).

Donald and Jean swam in the river, walked and slept in the open air of a veranda. One fishing expedition produced over thirty pounds of pike. An incident recorded in Donald's diary gives an insight into one of his methods, even on holiday, of providing illustrations for sermons. The sight of timber floating down the river made him note the silent strength of the water, the clash of logs without noise, and that groups of wood moved faster than single units. (Another brief outline for a sermon on Nehemiah 6. 3,11, in his diary for July 1939, did not reach fruition until he was Archbishop of Canterbury at Easter 1976).

A holiday in England was contemplated, to take place the following summer, after three years in Canada, but the war which broke out in September cancelled all such plans. The appointment of a new Principal was made in the Autumn, but it was some months before he was free to move into the College. In the meantime the pace became even greater for Donald and his colleagues by the illness, followed by the death, of Frank Blodgett[15], the Field and Financial Secretary at Wycliffe College. A former missionary, he raised donations and arranged the placement of students. Another problem was the parlous state of the former Principal's affairs. R.B. McElheran had reduced his stipend by leaving his large Winnipeg parish. A generous man, he had helped several students financially. The College archives reveal Donald Coggan's pastoral sensitivity towards his widow. He tried to recover some of the debts owed, and if this proved unsuccessful, repaid them himself. Hours were spent sorting through McElheran's books so that some might be sold to advantage. On the first anniversary of his death, an entry in Donald's diary read 'order flowers for Mrs McElheran'.

There was an equal pastoral concern, as Dean, in Donald's letters to other correspondents. A former student had been heard to say he was trying to find Law's *The Tests of Life*. Donald wrote to tell him he had seen a second-hand copy in a book-shop and would send it, if required. He also wrote to men in the forces and prospective ordination candidates offering the loan of books by post. A contribution to the work of the College sent by a benefactor was on one occasion translated by Donald into fur-lined overcoats for two clergy on their posting to far north mission stations.

The new Principal was William Ramsay Armitage[16], born in Nova Scotia, son of a Wycliffe graduate. He attended Dalhousie

[15] 1876-1939.
[16] 1889-1984.

University where he read classics which he proceeded to teach in Western Canada as a layman from 1909. After a call to ordination, he entered Wycliffe College and was ordained in 1913. On the outbreak of the First World War he became a chaplain in the army and accompanied a Canadian expeditionary force to France, where he won the Military Cross. The greater part of his ministry was of a pastoral kind, as curate and Rector of the Church of the Messiah, Toronto; but he was also much seen in Wycliffe College as a part-time member of the teaching staff with a special responsibility for Greek from 1921-1936. In that year he was preferred to the Deanery of Christ Church Cathedral, Vancouver.

Ramsay Armitage had greater academic qualities with his classical background than had his predecessor, but he was a pastor also. Donald welcomed a leader of such all-round gifts whose particular aspiration was to bring all Canada to a knowledge of the Bible. On his arrival at the College the new Principal outlined in three talks how he conceived his task and that of Wycliffe. The adage 'God's Conquering Word' he made particularly his own.

In this way he gave encouragement to the development of a new project of Donald's; of profound significance in his future ministry for its subject was preaching. In the autumn of 1940 he delivered three lectures under the title of *The Preacher as a Biblical Student*, as a concomitant of the Principal's earlier words. The first of many such talks and writings on Donald's part, they had wide repercussions both for him and the College.

At times of crisis the Church depended most particularly, he said, on the preacher as 'a man sent from God to persuade men to put Jesus Christ at the centre of their relationships'. Such a man's preaching must be three-fold: prophetic, positive with the note of one who knows the coming Lord of whom he speaks, and thirdly 'the speaker must be so well acquainted with the Bible as to be able to show that the New Testament lies hidden in the Old, and the Old Testament is made clear in the New.' So well received were the lectures that the Executive Committee resolved[17]

> that Professor Coggan should attend the short course in the Spring at the College of Preachers in Washington, in order that he might give direction to something of the same kind in a modified form for our own Graduates at an early date.

Before this took place there were two further claims on his time

---

[17] At the Meeting of 17 December 1940.

beyond the ordinary. The first was a series of radio programmes in January 1941 which were relayed across the country by the Canadian Broadcasting Corporation on four Sunday afternoons; Donald shared the series under the title *God, Christ and Man* with another speaker. His own contribution *Christ in Man* he based on a poem, 'The Inn of Life' by John Oxenham. The first talk spoke of Christ within the imagery of the light of the world. He referred to the picture of this name by Holman Hunt with the Christ-figure knocking at the door which personified the human soul, asking to come in. The second talk spoke of the activity of God and the Cross as God's call. It described the message of the Cross; the Resurrection as God's ratification of all that Jesus was and did and as guarantee of the final triumph of good over evil. The meaning of Sonship was the subject of the third address, which spoke of the life which is lived by faith; a virtue he examined in some detail by reference to St Paul's Epistle to the Romans. The series was completed by a talk entitled the Life of Power which described the fellowship within the Church and the impossibility of solitary religion; it ended with a vigorous call[18].

Secondly, late in March 1941 Donald, accompanied by Jean, left for Winnipeg in the 28,000 square-mile diocese of Rupertsland for an intensive few days. It was their first experience of Western Canada, and involved a railway journey of around 1,260 miles each way. They left Toronto on Friday the 28th and were in Winnipeg early on the following Sunday morning the 30th, whereupon Donald preached three times: at 11 at St George's, at 4.15 at All Saints and at 7 pm at St Jude's. Supper was with Mrs. McElheran. The week was packed with addresses: each day at Holy Trinity at 12.15 and several others at St Matthew's, two of which were broadcast; one each at St Anne's and St Margaret's. They left Winnipeg for Toronto on 4 April and after the long journey across the prairies 'whose vast grain towers rose like cathedrals against the sky line'[19], arrived home on the 6th. The children had been under the care of a Scottish nurse.

In June, Donald left for Washington and the five-day course at the College of Preachers. It was an institution that was to become very close to his heart; not only did he make frequent return visits, but he later became associated with the establishment of a similar organiza-

---

[18] The talks were later published by the National Religious Advisory Council of the CBC under their overall title.

[19] F.D. Coggan *Convictions* (op. cit.), p.20.

tion in England. This was not his first time in America. He had boarded the Queen Mary from New York for his brief trip to England in 1939 and in the spring of 1940 he and F.W. Dillistone had made a short tour of the East Coast American theological Colleges. Later, with Jean, there was a holiday in Virginia, the Shenandoah National Park and 100-mile Sky Line Drive, whilst awaiting the birth of Ruth their second daughter in the summer of 1940. There was no other country to which he responded so warmly or returned so gladly.

A North American Ecumenical Conference took place in Toronto in June 1941, when Wycliffe College was host for several sessions and Donald had the company of theologians of a wide range of interests and from far afield. In July he received his Bachelor of Divinity degree which was awarded by a Council of General Synod composed of theological College principals. He was placed in the First Class with a percentage of 89. That year's holiday was close at hand, a mere hundred and fifty miles from Toronto at Parry Sound in the Georgian Bay of Lake Huron.

The proposed School of Preaching with Donald as Dean, took place at Wycliffe College in April 1942, with twenty graduates from parishes as the first students in the new enterprise. Others joined the open lectures to observe the experiment. Those who were accepted for the School were required to submit a written sermon and come prepared to preach another. The three-day course was a mixture of worship and devotional addresses; material to provide inspiration, content and shape to the creation of sermons; individual criticism of voice, diction, and use of language. F.W. Dillistone, teacher of Systematic Theology, gave a series of lectures on 'Preaching the Atonement'. G. Campbell Innes, an Englishman and singer of remarkable appearance and personality, with his broad-brimmed black floppy hat, velvet collar and silver-knobbed cane, had been a member of staff since the McElheran days, in charge of voice production. He was much in evidence at the School with a recording machine, by which means he attempted to help men to be more audible and intelligible.

The first School of Preaching in Canada was a notable success and a personal triumph for Donald Coggan who had been its prime instigator and mainstay. The only criticism received was that so few students could benefit at any one time. The College therefore decided not only to hold a further session in Toronto, but also to offer the opportunity of holding such events *in situ* to dioceses in the Canadian Province. It was accepted with enthusiasm and a programme for a travelling School of Preaching, to cover centres in North and North Western Canada with Donald Coggan as leader, was arranged for the spring of 1943.

Meanwhile a second tour of the Maritimes in June 1942 took Donald back to Eastern Canada three years after his earlier visit. To meet and encourage Wycliffe men was the prime object, since their ministry as Evangelicals held certain difficulties in the region; the stipends were meagre and travelling to alumni reunions in Toronto often impossible. Jean joined Donald at Halifax in Nova Scotia for a busy week-end there of preaching and meetings. A rail journey to Sydney Mines on Cape Breton Island gave them further experience of the Gulf of St Lawrence and a week's holiday together before the relentless programme began again in Fredericton, and a clergy summer school under the title *Qualifications for Ambassadorship*, in Saint John, New Brunswick.

Letters to friends in England and to the Cambridge Missionary Fellowship in particular, revealed how great was the Coggans' anxiety for those exposed to danger and hardship at home in time of war, when their own circumstances were safe and more comfortable. St Mary's, Islington, had been bombed and little remained standing of the original structure; houses of former parishioners were in ruins.

Though far removed from scenes of hostility, Canada was deeply committed to the war against Nazism; a large number of men and women joined the forces and many were posted overseas. Donald contributed towards two religious pamphlets designed for them; 160,000 of each were printed. Under an Air Training Scheme men from other parts of the Commonwealth joined with Canadians and were trained as pilots and navigators. Airmen assembled on the large open space of the University Campus at Toronto next to Wycliffe College; the Coggans' apartment, which was on the west side of the building, faced this drilling area. Ann and Ruth, four and two years old in 1942, spent happy hours as they watched the marching and military bands.

Taxes increased; a victory loan campaign was raised; tea, coffee and sugar were rationed. The effect of the war which impinged most directly on life at Wycliffe College was the shortage of clergy due to the number who had gone to be chaplains to the forces. Because of the distances students needed to travel, terms at Wycliffe were two per year, in the autumn and from January through the spring, rather than three, as in England; the summer months were spent on missions and in camps rather than on academic studies. Members of the staff served then in parishes which lacked a resident Rector. Donald and his family passed weeks of every summer in this way at the churches along the shore of Lake Ontario, or on the islands.

It was during such an interlude in 1942 that Donald wrote his *Story of the English Bible illustrated in the memorial windows of Wycliffe College Chapel*. Not a work of any great length, scholarship, or profundity, it described in sixty-three pages, and five chapters, the growth of the Bible in the English language as personified by the emblems and figures of the stained glass windows put up to the memory of past Principals. The aspects covered John Wycliffe, William Tyndale, Miles Coverdale, the authorized and modern versions. The whole was painstakingly compiled and showed, above all, Donald's own love for the Bible; his desire that it should be read and understood; particularly that the Scriptures should be presented in a contemporary, living tongue. This was to become a major personal crusade in the future and one to which he would devote a good deal of his time. Since it was published in Canada and not under restricted conditions in England, the book was well printed, pleasingly produced on thick paper and illustrated by large photographs of the windows concerned. Donald dedicated his work to William Eddington Taylor[20] who as vice-principal had seen the College through two difficult periods without a head, and to whom the Coggan family owed much for his support and kindness.

The Story of the English Bible was widely distributed in Canada and copies also reached England in spite of the war. The Council of Wycliffe in gratitude for Donald's writing during what should have been College holidays, voted that during his projected tour of the North and West of Canada the following Spring, so that Schools of Preaching might be held in localities other than Toronto, his wife's fare should be paid and she accompany him on part of the tour.

1943 became an eventful year. It opened with a visit to Washington at short notice and in answer to a telegram inviting Donald to be the main speaker at a College of Preachers' Course in place of a bishop who had been unable to come. A Quiet Morning for the clergy of the Niagara diocese on Shrove Tuesday was followed by preaching engagements in Montreal; all this in addition to his College teaching. It is salutary to recall that these activities of a fairly authoritative kind were carried on by one who was still only (Spring 1943) thirty-three years old. On 20 March, a few weeks before the

[20] 1877-1967 born London; educated Toronto; Missionary in China 1906-18; Wycliffe College from 1923-47.

start of the projected visit West, the blow fell: a letter[21] from
England suggesting that Donald should consider the post of Prin-
cipal of St John's Hall, Highbury; also known as the London
College of Divinity, a place of training for the ministry of the
Church of England.

The proposal, which came from the secretary to the Council of St
John's, Prebendary Hinde, head of Oak Hill Theological College,
was full of difficulties. The St John's buildings had been bombed
two years earlier and made uninhabitable. The former Principal,
T.W. Gilbert, had moved the students, who were greatly dimi-
nished in number (he had taken no new entries since 1939), to
Wadhurst in Sussex. At his death in the previous June only nine
students remained, and they had been transferred to Oak Hill.

In short, Donald was being asked to head a College which had no
buildings and next to no students. However, St John's had enjoyed a
sound reputation in Evangelical circles for eighty years; Prebendary
Gilbert had increased both numbers (up to one hundred during the
more recent years of peace) and academic standards. As soon as the
war was over, there would be serious need for the resumption of
training for the clergy to make up for the time lost.

> St John's must be ready . . . We are praying for the right man and have
> felt it right thus to approach you . . . If you are open to return, we believe
> we have a post worthy of anyone's consideration.

Here was a decision to disturb the most phlegmatic. Donald cabled
that he would consider the call but that he must have more time.
The proposition was hedged round with uncertainties. For one of
tender conscience, such as he, it was hard to determine the right
course. He and his family were happy in Canada and fresh opportunities were appearing all the time. On the other hand, he knew
himself committed to the cause of ordination training and to be
sufficiently young and energetic for the effort required for the
complete re-establishment of St John's Hall. His obligation to the
Evangelical tradition in the Church he saw as a serious duty. Donald
was conscious that this witness was both under threat and undergoing change; aware of a vocation to be part of this process, where
should he place his efforts – in England or Canada? A former
CICCU contemporary, then serving as a Chaplain-in-chief of the
Canadian Airforce[22], spent Christmas with the Coggan family; he

---

[21] It was a war-time photo-copied message (airgraph), greatly reduced in size for easy
transmission, dated 26 February 1943.
[22] Wing-Commander G.W.J. Gregson, RCAF Ottawa.

had given Donald a clear indication of his view of Canadian needs after the war, which he considered could be supplied by him through Wycliffe College:

> I do pray that Wycliffe men may be kept on fire for Christ with a real fundamental background, as I find more and more with my experience of men that this modern watery so-called theology never gets a man anywhere and I want my boys given truly sound training such as we knew in the CICCU. May men go out from Wycliffe on fire for Christ and for the souls of men.

Donald wrote a number of letters to those whom he trusted, asking for counsel. Meanwhile as soon as a second successful School of Preaching had been completed at Wycliffe, he set off on his tour of North and Western Canada. His first stop was Saskatoon, a journey of 1,756 miles and over forty-six hours on the train. A four-day School of Preaching there was followed by a similar Course and two sermons in the diocese of Saskatchewan at Prince Albert, a mere 98 miles away. In Winnipeg, 562 miles to the East, there was a heavy schedule of sermons and visiting Wycliffe graduates; then a week in Edmonton in Alberta, the beginning of the great Alaska highway (814 miles) and another School of Preaching. The journey to Vancouver in British Columbia (750 miles) across the Rocky Mountains brought Donald to his first sight of the Pacific Ocean. More sermons, including one in the Cathedral and a further School of Preaching, occupied Donald until 19 June when Jean arrived at the end of her rail journey of 2,695 miles which she had started in Toronto four days earlier. Together they set off for Victoria on Vancouver Island with its spectacular setting on the Juan de Fuca Strait, pleasant houses and rose gardens; two sermons in the Cathedral, a Quiet Day for clergy, and back to the mainland.

Long rail journeys took them to Calgary across the Rockies, to Edmonton once more, and on to Peace River 300 miles to the North in the enormous diocese of Athabasca, so called after the river which rises in the Rocky Mountains near Jasper and flows east into central Alberta. Four times larger than England and Wales, and thirty-seven times bigger than Donald's future diocese of York considered large by English standards, the Athabasca diocese presented difficulties of communication before the development of air travel. Nevertheless, the signatures of nineteen participants appear on an address of thanks presented to Donald after the Peace River Preaching School. In his recorded impressions, their dedication, with their meagre means, earned his praise and lasting admiration.

Singled out were the efforts of Women Workers who ran Sunday Schools, took services and preached, rode out on ponies to Indian reserves from morning till night. His memory of them doubtless contributed to his later enthusiasm for the ministry of women in the Church. A notable occasion during the School was an evening picnic at Sir Alexander Mackenzie Cairn, thirteen miles up the mighty Peace River, where the explorer had wintered in 1792-3, one hundred and fifty years before.

After three sermons in the Grande Prairie area, the Coggans took a week's holiday in the mountains near Banff and Lake Louise. However much they enjoyed the remarkable scenery, the thought of the decision that hung over them can never have been far from their minds. Two letters from Ramsay Armitage, Principal of Wycliffe, followed Donald out West.

> In regard to Highbury. I believe you are right in not giving immediate answer. It is not as simple as that.
>
> I hope that by the time we may discuss it on your return there will gather some further arguments for Canada and the Canadian Church. Naturally all in England who write to you will give emphasis and urgency for your acceptance. It will be no easy matter to see both Highbury and Wycliffe in one picture.
>
> It is not from any narrowly selfish College advantage that I urge your staying at Wycliffe. The Cause is something far greater than the College. We know what place you already have taken in the Canadian Church and it is of very great value and moment. I am sure that you are only at the beginning of what you will be able to undertake and accomplish for theological education in Canada and the common good of the whole Canadian Church . . . There are plans begun for a graduate School of Theological Studies in the University of Toronto. It will not be a happy circumstance if you will not be available for this new development.
>
> The more I think of your place in Wycliffe and your far-reaching influence across Canada through Wycliffe the more I am persuaded that your lot is with us[23].

The second letter[24] contained much the same argument as to the new ventures Donald would be initiating and developing if he remained in Canada. It ended: 'Not only do not give an answer to Highbury until you return but *do not give an answer to yourself.*'

Back in Toronto, answers to letters despatched to England in search of advice had arrived and were in a contrary vein. One upon

[23] 1 June 1943, both were addressed to 'Dear Professor Coggan'.
[24] 8 June 1943.

which Donald placed most weight came from his former Principal at Wycliffe Hall, Oxford, now Bishop of Sodor and Man, J.R.S. Taylor. Donald had enquired as to Evangelical Theological Colleges in England and especially of St John's Hall, Highbury:

> And not only in regard to the Colleges but the whole Evangelical position. What are the prospects of a strong forward move on the part of our forces? Is the time ripe for united advance? Is there a job to be done which would justify the giving up of a very full task here?

The bishop replied[25] in the affirmative. Highbury was important; the last Principal had greatly improved its status in London University. It would be a calamity if it went fundamentalist.

> In regard to the Evangelical position, I personally feel that the time is ripe for a forward movement, along the lines of what Wycliffe [Hall] has been standing for since 1925. Many recent appointments, e.g. in the CMS, show that people value a positive Evangelicalism, which has a real Gospel based on an inspired Bible, read with scholarly intelligence. I believe that the days of the Modernist AEGM[26] Evangelicalism are numbered. But our opportunity will be lost if Evangelicals harbour mutual suspicion and criticism. We must combine wholehearted devotion with a free generous spirit.

There were similar expressions of opinion from others, together with much pressure from the Council of St John's Hall which continued throughout the summer. Eventually on 18 August Donald felt that he could deny the call no longer: he would return to England and become Principal of the largely non-existent College; not for what the immediate present had to hold, but because he hoped in faith that St John's had a future.

He sent a cable with his decision, but asking that he be allowed to finish two more terms at Wycliffe in Canada and delay his return until the early summer of the following year; this was accepted. His most pressing need was to secure passages to England for Jean and the children; his own presented no problems; even in war-time his claim was recognized. In the event and after much delay, it became clear that exit permits were not to be granted for Donald's family to leave Canada until the war was over, or at any rate conditions had improved. Separation was inevitable.

The next nine months were again filled to capacity. The news of Donald's impending departure increased even further the number of invitations to preach and teach. There were many such in the

---

[25] 3 April 1943.
[26] Anglican Evangelical Group Movement.

neighbourhood of Toronto, some to churches where the outlook was not evangelical; short visits were made to Listowel; Huron College, London Ontario; Montreal; a third and last School of Preaching at Wycliffe; to farewell gatherings[27]. Somehow he managed to write another short work, once more on the Bible, *A People's Heritage*, as the Canadian Lent Book for 1944. Dedicated to Jean, with the inscription from Proverbs, 'The heart of her husband doth safely trust in her', the foreword was provided by the Primate of Canada, Archbishop Derwyn Owen. He commended the book as lending 'a helping hand to those who are in doubt how best to begin their study of the New Testament and more particularly of St Paul'.

Finally came the Wycliffe Convocation on 21 April 1944; Donald was presented with a Doctorate of Divinity *honoris causa* to mark his contribution to the College. A week-end with Jean to the fruit-growing area of Niagara on the south side of Lake Ontario with the trees in blossom, to the celebrated Falls and Goat Island, was the prelude to their parting. On 15 May he fetched the children from school and then left Toronto on the 4 pm train to Montreal en route for Halifax and a banana boat in convoy across the Atlantic. He counted it later as one of the worst days of his life. For Jean the experience was particularly devastating because she could not comprehend the need to accept the Highbury invitation: there seemed nothing to which to return. Here, of course, lay the crux of the matter; Donald had gone to rebuild. It was a long time before they were all as happy again as they had been in Canada; ahead were many homeless years and much adjustment.

Jean had parted with more than her husband: the possibility of a larger family, a settled base, shared expeditions to surroundings of great beauty, the outdoor life on summer holidays that is the heritage of Canadians, her own part in the Wycliffe community; entertaining students and their wives; all had been wrested from her. She moved from the Dean's residence and accepted the offer of the top floor of the Principal's house for herself and the girls, as she settled down to the life of a single parent in company with those whose men had gone to war.

Donald's years in the Church in Canada were at the end of an era that was passing. With peace and the progress in air travel, the development of the country with its vast resources and potential of its people, was no longer held back by problems of communication;

---

[27] Donald wrote to England on 29.11.43: 'The attitude here seems to be "As the man *is* going we'll kill him before he goes!" '.

the result was phenomenal. The Church advanced likewise and with good leadership assumed a significant place in the councils of the Anglican Communion.

On his arrival in Canada Donald already knew that he had the gifts that made a good teacher; they were to be greatly extended and to them was added the experience of administration. Above all, he developed an aspiration to help men to be more effective ministers of the Word and Sacraments. His initiative sharpened: the courses he devised, the extensive and intensive itineraries he undertook, were largely of his own making; testing grounds of value for the future. His views broadened. There were pastoral developments also; perceiving how to meet on equal terms with new acquaintances of every kind on an almost daily basis. He had learnt to come face to face and hold his own with the Canadian great: George Campbell Pidgeon[28], creator of the United Church; Archibald Fleming, first Bishop of the Arctic; Henry John Cody[29], almost alone among contemporary Canadian Evangelicals with his commitment towards society. One time Rector of St Paul's Bloor Street, the largest parish church in Canada, President of the University, Minister of Education, he declined several bishoprics and the Archbishopric of Melbourne in Australia in order to remain in the city of Toronto. When consulted by Donald as to whether he should do likewise, Dr Cody reluctantly agreed that Donald's place was in England; 'One day,' he said, 'you will be Archbishop of Canterbury.' It was a remarkable prophecy; the Canadian Church had helped to prepare him for its realization.

---

[28] 1872-1971; DD, Moderator General Assembly the Presbyterian Church of Canada 1925. Moderator for the General Council of the United Church of Canada 1925-6.
[29] 1868-1951; DD; CMG; Wycliffe College 1890-3.

CHAPTER FIVE

The London College of Divinity

It was not until 22 May that *SS Erin* left Halifax, Nova Scotia, with Donald Coggan on board. A circuitous route to confuse hostile shipping led them to see Iceland on the port bow on the 30th; by the early morning of 31 May the ship lay off the coast of Ulster. During the afternoon a small boat took the passengers to Belfast. A train journey to Larne, across the Irish Channel to Stranraer, and he boarded the night train to London where he arrived on 1 June 1944. Since this was the date upon which his appointment as Principal became effective, after lunch with his sister whom he had not seen for five years, he typically wasted no more time and went to Highbury to view his new territory.

What had been since 1866 St John's Hall was a forlorn sight. The buildings had not originated as an Anglican Theological College to prepare men for the ministry of the Church of England; from 1825 they were part of a Congregationalist College and later a Training Institute for schoolmasters. The original location at St John's Wood which had been occupied since 1863 had proved too crowded; the Highbury site with its seven acres of grounds in a then prestigious neighbourhood had seemed more than adequate, particularly since the founders of the College, the Reverend Alfred Peache and his sister, had been prepared to give funds for additions. In due course a new chapel and dining hall were built; an appeal to old students provided library, tutors' rooms and most curious of all, a new gateway was designed to resemble that of St John's College, Cambridge, as a compliment to the first Principal, Dr Thomas Parnall Boultbee, whose *alma mater* this had been.

The result represented a conglomerate of buildings not in the main purpose-built, and many of them dark, gloomy and unheated. But since a strong corporate feeling had grown up in the College, attachment to the site, as Donald Coggan was to find to his cost, was more enthusiastic than its quality deserved.

A landmine which descended by parachute on the College in November 1940 and exploded on impact, had damaged roofs, ceilings and windows and made the building unusable. Cox, the College gardener, was killed, but no students died; they were forced to move to Sussex. At first the basement was let as a stretcher-party depot; in 1942 the National Fire Service requisitioned the whole complex as a local headquarters and carried out a series of alterations to adapt St John's for its specialized use. The library provided the new Principal with the most melancholy spectacle: the roof leaked; furniture and bedding not required elsewhere was piled up to eight feet high; bookcases with glass doors could not be opened because of lack of space, but books inside were clearly damp and covered with mildew; open library shelves had been used for firewood and volumes, many old and valuable, were scattered everywhere. Samuel Fuzzard the porter for many years at the College and still in residence, gave Donald his only encouragement that afternoon with the words 'I'll stand by you, sir'.

As the first few months, even years, of the new responsibilities passed, it would seem that not by any stretch of imagination could Donald Coggan have been aware in advance of the magnitude of the difficulties with which he was to be faced. They came from many sources; some from quarters which might have been expected to offer him support. It was necessary for the Principal of a theological college to surround himself with good working relationships with a series of other bodies: the first was with the university to which the College was affiliated as a School of theological education; in the case of St John's Hall, the University of London. Donald's predecessor had enjoyed good standing. In 1930 Dr Gilbert had become Chairman of the Faculty of Theology and later Dean; had been an examiner for higher degrees; and he increased the number of men at St John's who were reading for the London BD, as opposed to the three-year course leading to the ALCD (Associate of the London College of Divinity) for non-graduates, a Diploma in theology finally approved by the Bishops in 1934.

Donald found no problems in his personal dealings with the University, given his good academic record and straightforward outlook. A year after his arrival he was appointed as a recognized teacher of London University and a member of the Board of Studies of Theology. The University provided an outside examiner to help in assessments in College examinations so that they might be kept in line with those in other Theological Schools. Visitations by Inspectors of the University were made of its constituent establishments; St John's Hall received its turn. No one could have been readier than Donald to take on the considerable labour of trying to achieve as high an academic standard as possible for his students. The tendency to underrate the value of study in relation to the need for personal holiness, such as put forward by a previous Vice-Principal who complained 'We are no longer a training college for Holy Orders, but are rather an establishment for preparing men to pass bishops' examinations', Donald did not share. The ordained ministry of the Church of God, in his opinion, called for the most exacting training that it was possible to provide. These were views that he had formulated in Canada and they did not change. He proceeded to put them into practice.

The second body to whom Donald was required to pay attention was the Central Advisory Council for the Training of the Ministry, known as CACTM, which had been reconstructed shortly before his appointment as Principal. Its new Chairman was the Bishop of Maidstone[1], its secretary Kenneth Moir Carey[2]; its composition representative of the Church of England: bishops, archdeacons, academics, religious, parish priests, and a few laymen. Periodical inspections of theological colleges were carried out by members of CACTM, who kept in regular touch with principals. Relations, in Donald's case, again appear to have been smooth: he impressed inspectors with his personal efforts and the only criticism of him in the Report of 1949 was that of probable overwork and carrying too great a share of the administration.

Donald was by nature sensitive to the need for authority and deferential to those placed in authority over him. This put him in a favourable position in regard to the episcopate, the third structure with whom he had to work. He succeeded in gaining the confidence of bishops who sent him men for training and accepted his students for ordination and as curates in their dioceses. He had written to the Bishop of London, Geoffrey Fisher[3], from Canada, preparing the way for their future relationship; the Bishop was Visitor[4] to St John's Hall. They met soon, at Geoffrey Fisher's invitation, and it was the beginning of a long acquaintance which was to be of much significance in the future. The bishops had at one time made difficulties for predominantly non-graduate theological colleges by demanding that candidates for Holy Orders should be proficient in

[1] Leslie Owen (1886-1947); Bishop of Jarrow 1939-44; of Maidstone 1944-6; of Lincoln 1946-7.

[2] 1908-79 Bishop of Edinburgh 1961-75.

[3] 1887-1972; Bishop of Chester 1932-9; of London 1939-45; Archbishop of Canterbury 1945-61.

[4] Final arbiter in any case of serious trouble or dispute.

Latin and Greek before proceeding to preliminary training. One of the effects of the war would be that no bishop could demand anything but a lower academic standard on entry than heretofore in cases where men offered themselves for the ministry after many years of service in the forces. From then onwards it was up to the colleges to provide as thorough a training as was possible.

The source from which most adversity sprang was the fourth area of concern, the Council of St John's Hall. Donald was in a position of considerable delicacy. His natural instinct, as has been mentioned, was to defer to his superiors. Where he saw that to do so was to jeopardize the future of the labour to which he was totally committed, his strategem was to carry on as before as unobtrusively as possible and circumvent obstruction; maintaining an attitude of outward calm and acquiescence. His loyalty to the Council was exemplary; his feelings and expressions of exasperation he kept largely to himself. His staff and students suspected at times that Donald was having a rough passage, but the full extent of his endurance did not reach others. When a period of struggle was over, he would sometimes allow himself a brief *post mortem*. After the eventual setting up of the new St John's at Northwood and years of travail, he remarked to a former student (now a bishop) that it had been achieved in spite of and not because of his governing body.

The Council was a phenomenon of a kind cogently described by Randle Manwaring in his *From Controversy to Co-existence*[5]. Strong in doctrine, determined to maintain the *status quo* and the Scriptural purity of the gospel message, its members could look only backwards when assailed by liberalism and modernism. Evangelicalism they represented in a defensive form, antagonistic to change and the search for new expression and identity; its methods were rigid and inquisitorial. Donald was at the end of a long line of principals for whom leadership had not been made easy: lack of trust was a particular feature. His predecessor, Dr Gilbert, though a distinguished scholar, was appointed after a long interregnum and much disagreement and a declaration by him not only as to his adherence to Evangelical principles, but also his views on Old Testament criticism. He was not permitted to join the governing body, nor appoint staff without approval. The same applied to Donald.

One of the contributory reasons for these reactionary views was

[5] Subtitled *Evangelicals in the Church of England 1914-1980*. Cambridge University Press 1980.

that of age. The average age of members of the Council was abnormally high: several had served for more than twenty years; their attitudes had become fossilized. As the new Principal moved on to the College scene, attempts were at once made to try and influence him. Within a fortnight a senior Council member had invited him to lunch at his Club. Though 74 years old, 'I desire to die in my armour,' he had written to Donald, 'I have ideas as to the future of the Evangelical ministry in general and Highbury in particular . . . I should like to talk over with you.' They were, Donald recalls, that the Principal should move in an extreme Protestant direction.

Prebendary Hinde had been Secretary to the Council for seventeen years and a member for twenty-one. He had paid two visits to Canada, on one of which in 1938 he had given talks to Wycliffe alumni. *Cap and Gown*[6], the student magazine, had published extracts from his stern message:

> The Gospel of today is a Gospel of social salvation rather than of personal salvation. The sovereignty of God needs to be revitalized in our preaching. Many clergymen are administering sedatives today instead of preaching the Gospel of man's need of Salvation. The world says it sees very little difference between the Church and itself. We need to get back to the severity of a sovereign God who hates sin and cannot tolerate it.

Donald was to restate the same truths with a different slant: the love of God for men and the grace available through Christ for man to start his life again. He recognized that it was possible to take too narrow a view of Christian doctrine; there were important revelations besides the Atonement. Moreover he became aware that the gospel had a bearing on the life of society as well as that of the individual. His part in the renewal of Evangelicalism with its accompanying recognition of and co-operation with other Christians, was not as visible nor dramatic as that for example of John Robert Walmsley Stott[7], its undoubted leader. There were two main reasons for this: first that Donald was never, to use a current popular phrase, a charismatic figure; secondly he was preoccupied during the next twelve years by the considerable pressures of his hard new world of post-war ordination training. Once he had become bishop and archbishop, as Randle Manwaring rightly points out[8], he was available to all traditions. He was not free to

[6] Number for 1939, p.29.
[7] 1921- ; Curate of All Saints, Langham Place 1945-50; Incumbent 1950-75.
[8] *From Controversy to Co-existence* p.103.

play an obvious role in the renewal process of one wing of the Church of England. But this does not mean that he was absent from the *dramatis personae*. What went on inside the London College of Divinity, to quote only one instance, makes this clear.

It would seem that the contribution of Donald Coggan, with his dislike of labels and partisan Christianity, towards a more positive and fearless Evangelical outlook, has been underrated. The attitudes which found their culmination at the National Anglican Evangelical Congresses of Keele (1967) and Nottingham (1977), he began to express earlier, when the going was hard. It was for this cause that he left Canada.

The morning following his arrival and visit to Highbury, Donald collected his identification card, gas mask and ration book. He visited Jean's parents and several members of his governing body during the next days; he discovered that a majority of them were averse to a move by the College from the depressing scene he had viewed on his first afternoon, in spite of the fact that it transpired St John's no longer owned most of the site and was paying rent. Shortage of funds in 1923 had persuaded the Council to sell a large proportion of the ground to the Arsenal Football Club.

On 5 June Donald took the train to Lincoln for a meeting of theological college principals. As the newest and youngest member (he was thirty-four years old) he found himself in august company; many of those present were to rise to prominence. It was an era when the Church of England tended to draw many of its leaders from this source: Michael Ramsey[9], later Archbishop of York and then Canterbury; William Greer[10], later Bishop of Manchester; Eric Abbott[11], future Dean of King's College London and of Westminster; Julian Thornton Duesbury[12], later Master of St Peter's College Oxford, formed part of this galaxy. During the Lincoln meeting came news of the D-day landings in France and the opening of the second front in Europe.

The chief matter under discussion was the final Report of the Archbishops' Commission on training for the ministry which had just been published. An Interim Report issued a few months earlier had contained some unpopular proposals and was withdrawn.

[9] 1904- ; representing St John's College, Durham; Bishop of Durham 1952; Archbishop of York 1956; of Canterbury 1961.
[10] 1902-72; Principal, Westcott House, Cambridge.
[11] 1906-84; Warden, Lincoln.
[12] 1902-84; Principal, Wycliffe Hall, Oxford.

Particularly disfavoured was the suggested substitution by theological colleges on a regional basis, of the current system of institutions of varying traditions spread over England, the existence of which was considered to protect the comprehensive nature of the Church of England and freedom of expression. This plan came to nothing, but the recommendation that Test School Conferences should be held, when groups of fifteen to twenty aspirants to ordination would attend lectures, interviews, and services over a week-end, was adopted. Donald accepted the Bishop of Maidstone's invitation to take part in the first of these.

The following months he spent in attempts to force a decision on the Council as to the future location of St John's. A sub-committee was appointed to examine the options; to remain at Highbury and, when the war was over and permission granted, to repair the damage; to find new premises; or to buy a site and erect a building when peace-time conditions allowed. Many localities were visited; some Council members still hankered not to move. Eventually, after a further visit to the devastated College, a majority vote reached a decision to leave Highbury and build on a new site at Brockley Park. Donald was still not satisfied and continued to search. By the beginning of 1945 he had found what appeared the most satisfactory solution so far; a piece of ground known as Broad Oak Field of seven acres at Northwood, still within the boundaries of the diocese of London. Adjoining the property stood a house by the name of Wetherby and a further three and a half acres; there was a chance that it might be also available.

The chance was fulfilled. But the formalities that were required in wartime and the fact that the Highbury buildings had already been sold for a low figure many years before and available funds were therefore insufficient, prolonged negotiations. Eventually on 15 March 1946 signatures were put to the purchase; the lease on St John's Highbury had already been terminated. The London College of Divinity now owned ten and a half acres at Northwood, empty space apart from a medium sized house suitable for the Principal. Permission to begin to build upon it was not granted until April 1954; an interval of another eight years.

Meanwhile back in the autumn of 1944, Donald was faced with reviving what was left of St John's in exile at Oak Hill: to build, if not with bricks and mortar, at least a community of staff and students. One of his concerns was with the future supply of men for training at the end of the war. He met and wrote to the authorities who were to regulate demobilization. From Kenneth Riches,[13] then vicar of Bredfield, Suffolk, who was responsible for service candidates on CACTM, he learnt that according to chaplains about 2,000 Anglicans would come forward for ordination when that time came. Donald wrote to all chaplains who were old students, some fifty in number, outlining his plans for the College. He spoke with a number of bishops: Ely, Rochester, Malmesbury, Liverpool, Oxford, Maidstone; he had lunch with Geoffrey Fisher, Bishop of London and met him again at his licensing. 'Friendly'; Donald wrote afterwards. 'Half (only half!) laughingly suggested formation of one strong college, King's and LCD.'[14] He saw a good deal of James Theodore Inskip,[15] Bishop of Barking, the chairman of his Council, who was 76 years old and had been a bishop for twenty-five years and chairman for nineteen.

Donald took a week off in September with his sisters at Barnstaple; it was the only break he had since leaving Canada. Then term began on 3 October. He lived in a bed-sitting room in a club in Queen Anne's Gate for the summer; now he moved into Oak Hill, at Southgate, London N1. The three St John's students of whom he had been apprised earlier grew to number eleven by November: a retired schoolmaster appeared from the Bishop of Truro for two terms and three candidates were sent by other bishops for a short course of a year. Donald's efforts to draw attention to the continued existence of the College had been rewarded. Teaching in the two establishments side by side was carried on by Donald himself, Prebendary Hinde and his vice-principal, and two part-time assistants, one of whom was Donald's former tutor for his own post-ordination training, Dr A.J. Macdonald.

London that summer was greatly disturbed by flying-bombs, so much so that it was at one time contemplated that Jean's parents should move away from the flight path and leave the capital for the country. With the new year of 1945, conditions improved as the allied armies progressed across Europe into Germany. Donald's mind turned to the possibility, as a consequence, of effecting his family's departure from Canada and joining him in England. After a good deal of letter-writing, he heard from the Ministry of War Transport that they were due to arrive in England at the end of May.

---

[13] 1908- ; Bishop of Dorchester 1952; of Lincoln 1956-74.
[14] Donald Coggan also conducted a School of Preaching on his Canadian pattern for clergy of the diocese of London.
[15] 1868-1949; Bishop of Barking 1919-48.

Since the war in Europe was by then over, Jean with Ann and Ruth left Canada on a troop ship in what was to be the last convoy across the Atlantic. The boat was crowded, the sea rough, the journey long, an unaccustomed seventeen days. Jean had agreed to bring two unaccompanied children who had spent the war in Canada, to join their parents; all the children were miserable with the cramped, turbulent conditions. It was expected that they would land at Southampton; the ship sailed up the Clyde to Greenock; Jean wondered how she could reach the parents of her charges or be in touch with Donald. As the tender which took them ashore grew near to the quay, the family recognized Donald's figure pacing up and down on the cobbles.

More difficulties lay ahead. Prebendary Hinde resigned from the Principalship of Oak Hill during 1945, but until he did so the Coggans and their children shared the Principal's flat with him and his wife (as also with his successor[16]), even to the point of using the same kitchen. Fuel and food were in short supply. A student of those days has left an account of trying to study in temperatures well below freezing indoors. Ann and Ruth Coggan reacted unhappily after their less restricted lives in Canada, grew thin and fretted to return. A relative commented that the tilt of their hats prevented them from looking English. The children replied that they were not English, but Canadian.

But if the family did not thrive under the new conditions, the College did, with numbers advancing steadily as ordinands left the forces; Donald laboured to make plain what it had to offer, in constant letters, interviews and meetings. 'Now we long to build *men* for the Master's use' he wrote to the Cambridge Fellowship, as the acquisition of the Northwood site became more of a certainty. During the Michaelmas term of 1945 the numbers of students for whom Donald was responsible grew to nineteen. As the war in all theatres was now over, it was clear that this figure would increase. Donald invited F.W. Dillistone, his former colleague in Canada, to join him as Vice-Principal; Ralph Dean[17], a former student and curate of St Luke's, Watford, also became a member of the staff.

Bishop Inskip of Barking decided in view of his age and long service to resign as Chairman, and made a warning announcement at a Council meeting in October. In a subsequent letter to Donald which revealed their warm relationship, he showed his disappoint-

---

[16] L.F.E. Wilkinson.
[17] BD, MTh., Bishop of Cariboo 1957-73; Anglican Executive Officer 1964-9.

ment that none of the members had felt constrained to mention his contribution to the College.

> I never like a lot of fuss or palaver, but I thought one at least might have made a brief reference to it. It suggests that my services are not much valued and that it is time I gave up. Anyhow I have done my best for the College amid very heavy work.
> Not a soul spoke to me going out, though I was almost the last to leave.

Donald did his best to redeem the hurt; he had considered, he said in his reply, that someone should have spoken officially after the resignation had been offered; he could not himself as he was not a member of the Council:

> Alas, I fear we Evangelicals are not noted for our graciousness, or indeed, our gratitude. How one longs to see a spirit of graciousness among us.

The sorry incident is worthy of the telling because of what it reveals about Donald. Always the most courteous of men, it was one of his most abiding characteristics; he hoped that graciousness would be the mark of those who themselves had received grace.

Worse was to come. The College was so full by the summer of 1946 that other accommodation than Oak Hill, and more staff, were essential. The Headmaster of Harrow offered as a temporary expedient a boarding house, 'West Acre', at Harrow-on-the-hill, that was not in immediate use. R.G.G. Hooper came as chaplain and Geoffrey Parke Taylor[18], a former student of considerable ability from Wycliffe College, Toronto, as part-time lecturer with a special brief to help in the teaching of Greek; also a housekeeper, Elizabeth Churchill.

Donald made some requests of his Council for equipment for the new premises with the greatly increased numbers. Letters have survived between members of the governing body which reveal the lack of trust that must have wounded so conscientious a man as he. Donald was forced to ask for even small sums of money by item, for example to have a cistern repaired. 'Now Coggan is asking for authority to buy an electric potato-peeler which will cost £40,' said one letter, 'I think you ought to know this so that we do not become too generous and easy-going in authorizing heavy expenditure'. The reply asked how potatoes were peeled at Oak Hill. The first writer agreed to find out; the matter should be discussed in the absence of the Principal. Donald was obviously not to be put off and returned to the charge. The correspondence continued:

---

[18] Bishop Suffragan of Huron 1976.

Sorry to trouble you again, but Coggan has been on to me again about a potato peeler. X seemed to think it was rather an extravagance and said so. I have enquired of Oak Hill and gather they have got one. They used to get every man in the College to peel two potatoes each day, but the result was so unsatisfactory in every way that they decided on this potato peeler . . . Perhaps we could persuade them to buy a cheaper one, not so expensive as the electric one'.

The Coggan family moved into 'Wetherby', the Principal's house at Northwood, during the summer of 1946; though commodious, it was to prove extremely cold. The adjoining site for the proposed college building remained empty for years to come. At last they had their own home, but the enjoyment was short-lived because Donald was to be there so little. A flat was created on the top floor of the house for Ralph Dean and his wife; provision of a cooker, sink and water heater (there was insufficient fuel that winter for central heating) was the subject of more lively correspondence; they were supplied with some unwillingness.

The Michaelmas term of 1946 was a milestone in Donald's life. Forty-three men crammed into West Acre at Harrow. He was for the first time on his own without the back-up of the Principal and staff of Oak Hill. His students were for the most part veterans of the war. Many were married, had formative knowledge of service life and responsibility. Donald's own experience was less varied and although it had increased in recent years, narrower than theirs. He had learnt to mix in Canada, but never at close quarters nor under battle conditions; most of all he had received no experience of command. To use an army metaphor, he was suddenly required to lead a regiment without having had charge of a section, a platoon, a company, as had many of his students.

Almost to a man, initially they found him unduly severe; some say harsh. There were members of staff who felt they themselves were treated as schoolboys. A little afraid of revealing weakness (and always to remain so), Donald chose this way of facing the challenge and staying on top. Particularly the married men who had been away from their families for several years, considered the restricted time permitted for home visits insensitive. There were children they hardly knew. The Principal did not ask of them anything he had not endured himself for the sake of the Faith, but the demands were indeed great. Considerably self-disciplined, he expected the same of others; Donald was incapable of compromise. He had always possessed a capacity for hard work; now his performance went into top gear and remained there for the rest of his active ministry. Former students describe the Principal's enormous energy and drive; always thrusting forwards on to the next undertaking, be it mission, books, lectures, new buildings; never content to stop. It produced if not a relaxed atmosphere, at least a purposeful one. Donald's dedication was total. 'Thy Kingdom come on earth' did not remain solely a prayer. He offered all that he had towards its fulfilment.

As students settled down at West Acre in the worst winter of the century, physical conditions were almost intolerable: men shared rooms; there was little or no heating; food was poor. Then came the realization that the standard of teaching they were receiving was very high. The Principal they found an exegete rather than an apologist; not an original or a philosophical thinker, but an outstanding exponent of the Scriptures which he taught often with brilliance, always cogently. His legacy to his pupils was that they emerged with a permanent love for the New Testament. Sloppy, inaccurate work and lack of regulation in their lives they realized were unacceptable.

F.W. Dillistone, known as Dilly, provided the balance; an able theologian of depth and ideas, his lectures provoked thought and interest, presenting a mind with which men wanted to engage. He took a concept and developed it from his own thinking without reliance on quotations, and showed men how to read and reflect. He was also understanding of students' problems. Latecomers from home visits on Saturdays could rely on Dilly to let them in through the fire-escape. R.G.G. Hooper who as tutor and chaplain carried most of the devotional aspects of the course, was a man of spiritual maturity.

The scope of the training surprised many men with its breadth and content. One former ex-service student of that period recalls that for those who, like himself, had come from a narrow ecclesiastical background, it was like emerging from prison. Although he remained somewhat rigid from a disciplinary point of view, the Principal's doctrinal position was undergoing a broadening process. Dilly was aware of new currents of theological thinking upon which he lectured and wrote in the College magazine. Lecturers of various traditions and viewpoints were invited to speak: Bishop Wand[19],

---

[19] 1885-1977; Archbishop of Brisbane 1934; Bishop of Bath and Wells 1943; of London 1945-55.

Sir Sidney Nicolson[20], Bishop Joost de Blank, Kenneth Sansbury[21], Dorothy Sayers[22] and so on.

For the Coggan family their occupation of the Principal's house at Northwood was hardly ideal, though it was a good deal better than what was to follow. Donald commuted each day during the West Acre period. Students used the unheated church at Roxeth, three hundred yards from the house, as their chapel; when they arrived for Morning Prayer each day shortly before 7.30 am in that terrible winter, Donald would have arrived already, having travelled from home in the dark. He was never known to have been absent. He stayed within the College until late evening. A student recalls

> I remember coming upon him lateish at night in his study struggling despite his tiredness and the coldness of the room, to complete his preparation for the next day.

'There will be no vacations' was a remark which former colleagues on the staff remember well. It was a figurative one, for all members of the College did in fact leave the premises three times a year; but plenty of work remained to be done.

Quite apart from continuing difficulties, there were some particular crises at this point. One was of a personal kind for Donald. Since he had returned from abroad, the Executive Committee of the Inter-Varsity Fellowship was anxious to secure his services once again as a speaker. He was invited to become a Vice-President to provide him with a position of authority. A prerequisite of acceptance was his signature on a declaration of doctrinal stand. It was required *inter alia* that he should declare his belief in the Bible as infallible, not merely to accept 'the divine inspiration and entire trustworthiness of Holy Scripture' as the International Fellowship Bible clause reads today. The connotation of the word 'infallible' in this context Donald could not accept. He pointed out that he had already, as part of his ordination vows, given his assent to Article 6[23] of the Thirty-nine Articles, would that not suffice. The IVF decided not; he and they parted company.

A problem felt by staff and students was the shortage of books. When Donald took up his appointment, he extracted from the wreck that was the library at Highbury as many volumes as space at Oak Hill would allow; these went on to West Acre. One May

---

[20] 1875-1947; Distinguished organist.

[21] 1905- ; Bishop of Singapore 1961-6; Gen.Sec. British Council of Churches 1966-73.

[22] 1893-1957; Writer of theology and detective fiction.

[23] Of the Sufficiency of the Holy Scriptures for Salvation.

evening in 1946 the old Highbury library became the centre of a conflagration. By the time the flames had been extinguished, what remained was covered in water, foam and ash. The damage to books was even more serious and extensive than that caused by the earlier bombing. From graphic accounts of the salvage operation, Donald worked as hard as the rest; though strict on discipline on account of his view of commitment, he was never princely. A former member of the teaching staff recalls that Donald cleaned his own shoes.

Relations between Council and Principal continued to involve him in walking a tightrope. On the resignation of the Bishop of Barking, the office of Chairman was offered to J.R.S. Taylor, Bishop of Sodor and Man, a happy outcome for Donald except that their former close association made it possible for others to accuse them of conspiring over College business. Building plans for the new St John's, appointment of an architect, costing and an appeal for funds, these were uppermost in the minds of all. Correspondence suggests that Donald took more initiative than was regarded as appropriate over the setting up of an appeal committee.

> I see the danger of the Principal and the President (Bishop Taylor) being too closely associated. They got their heads together at Oak Hill and fixed a date for the meeting of the Appeal Committee. Coggan has written me that he and the Bishop have discussed additional names for co-options and asked me to invite the co-opted members to come to our first meeting.

This did not please the governors; the composition of committees was required to remain entirely in their hands. Later correspondence shows the close attention paid to Donald's actions and motives.

> I have since realized that in as much as the Bishop himself would know nothing about old Johnians[24], the suggestion must have been made by Coggan.

Another *cause célèbre* of the time was the appointment of the new Visitor. Geoffrey Fisher had been translated to Canterbury in 1945; Donald had attended his enthronement in Canterbury Cathedral on 19 April. William Wand was appointed Bishop of London but several Council members were against his becoming Visitor on account of his unacceptable churchmanship. Archbishop Fisher was asked to continue, and declined as he had left the diocese of London. Donald, as Principal, pressed the candidature of Bishop

---

[24] Former members of the College.

Wand as most satisfactory from his point of view, since the College was already within his ecclesiastical jurisdiction. The matter dragged on until at the end of 1946, Bishop Wand was eventually appointed.

The weightiest matter was that of accommodation when Harrow School let it be known that West Acre would shortly be needed and must be handed back. An architect, R. Fielding Bond, had been appointed to design the new buildings at Northwood; plans were maturing. But there was no likelihood of government permission being given in the foreseeable future for either the release of materials or for the work to begin. A few members of the staff, detailed to make a search for alternative premises, found a home for the College in a country setting. Ford Manor at Lingfield, a sizeable house set in several acres of grounds on the edge of Surrey, Kent and Sussex, was found to be available, and a lease was drawn up for ten years at the cost of £750 per annum. It had been occupied by the Canadians as a base hospital, but was no longer needed. The owner[25] continued to live in a small area of the building.

Some men were still required to share rooms, but the over-crowding was less extreme than had earlier been the case. A dignified chapel was created in the drawing room; Fuzzard, still on the payroll, had brought some of the original chapel furniture from the old St John's. In course of time, and greatly daring, a cross was placed on the communion table.

Those who suffered most from the new arrangements were the Coggan family, who were separated once more. Jean, Ann and Ruth remained at Wetherby in Northwood where the girls were at school. Donald had a bed-sitting room at Ford Manor. F.W. Dillistone resigned and became Professor of Theology at the Episcopal Theological School, Cambridge, Massachusetts; his place as vice-principal was taken by Ralph Dean who with his wife moved into a cottage in the garden of the manor house.

Shortly before the move to Surrey, a Visitation of the College was made by London University. One of the Inspectors was Charles H. Dodd, the great biblical scholar. In their Report the Inspectors commented upon the courtesy of the Principal who had provided them in advance with a good deal of preliminary information; there had been a full and frank discussion of all aspects of the work of the School which had undoubtedly suffered a serious reverse through the damage to premises and equipment sustained during the war. In

[25] The Hon. Mrs Spender-Clay.

the opinion of the Inspectors, the scheme under which the School was governed had served its purpose. 'In some respects it is actually repugnant to the Statutes of the University . . . For example there are no arrangements for the direct representation of the Teachers on the Governing Body'. This had been raised after an earlier Inspection, but no action had been taken; the present Principal was not aware of the matter. The Report went on to comment:

> We are of the opinion that even when such considerations are taken into account as to the provision of free residence, the salaries paid to certain members of the Teaching Staff compare unfavourably with those in force in non-Theological Schools of the University. We are also of the opinion that the hours of lecturing of certain of the full-time Teachers are too heavy.

The small number of men taking the Bachelor of Divinity course, in relation to the Diploma candidates, was also the subject of criticism. The Principal had pointed out that the inclusion of Hebrew as a compulsory subject put too severe a strain on some students; now that it was optional, one would hope that numbers would increase. In conclusion, the recommendations were that the Scheme of Management be redrafted, attention given to salaries and the hours of Academic Staff and the Degree work developed.

The Council did not see its way towards implementing the suggestions concerning Principal or Staff. The presence of Free Churchmen as Inspectors, recommending the terms of deployment of the Anglican clergy, received adverse comment. Once more, Donald was placed in a position of difficulty; he was particularly anxious to maintain the connection between the London College of Divinity and the University; the struggle to keep the link continued for the next nine years.

Two years after the move to Lingfield, in 1949, CACTM made an Inspection. Once again, Inspectors recorded their admiration of the way the College was tackling the difficulties brought about by so many removals on account of enemy action: 'We are confident that it is doing very good work indeed in preparing men for the ministry.' Forty-five students were in residence; most of them ex-service men with government grants; many were married; about 85 per cent were non-graduates; not a few had no more than an elementary school education, and had passed a matriculation examination on spare-time study while working in an office, a shop or a factory. Two had been miners. The personal quality of many of the students impressed the Inspectors who conceded that the wide

difference in previous education perforce made it unusually difficult
to teach the group. Nearly half the men were working for the
London BD; a fair proportion obtained honours. The burden of
examinations lay heavy on the staff; there was little time to think or
talk about anything not directly related to examination questions.
Shortage of books, especially of a non-theological kind, was
obvious. The Inspectors were concerned lest the mens' general
cultural background should suffer. The staff they thought 'dis-
tinctly good'.

> The Principal, Dr F.D. Coggan, is a fine scholar and an experienced and
> stimulating lecturer . . . His forceful personality, liberal outlook and
> Christian understanding make him a power for good in the College.

A serious criticism was that both staff and students were over-
worked. Teachers should have more leisure to read and think. The
Principal, it was felt, bore too large a burden of administration.
'Although he carries this burden cheerfully and efficiently, he
should have more assistance'. Inspectors took note of the Principal's
seminars on Preaching, but recommended that the teaching of
Pastoralia should receive attention also. As a summing up the
Inspectors expressed themselves 'very pleased with what we saw of
the College and of the intellectual and spiritual quality of its work'.

The pattern of life at the London College of Divinity based on
Ford Manor did not change a great deal during the next six years.
Greater emphasis on evangelism and participation in parish
missions were the only major changes. Donald had laid down his
design. Discipline remained strong, but as the Principal became
older and the students younger, the tensions of the immediate post-
war years lessened, though the pace was still brisk. Some students
felt they were pushed too hard; some members of staff favoured
more consultation; many, looking back, express gratitude for the
high standards that had been expected and set.

Douglas Webster[26], who joined the teaching staff in 1947, has
left a vivid account of his five years at Ford Manor. Himself a
stimulating and evocative lecturer, he appreciated the hard-
working, dedicated atmosphere engendered by the Principal and
admired, though did not share, his austere and frugal outlook and
triumph over conditions. Douglas was a bachelor who liked his
creature comforts; the 'ghastly cold' and unattractive food he found

---

[26] 1920-86; Canon Residentiary of St Paul's Cathedral 1969-84.

difficult to bear. His day off in the parish at Crouch End where he had been a curate, spent in front of a warm fire with a hot meal, kept him going. When he was invited to go and talk with the Principal, Donald with his usual courtesy would recall that Douglas felt the cold and turn on a one-bar electric fire. The interview over, the fire had been switched off before Douglas reached the door.

Within the College Donald's pre-occupation concerned not only the provision of as thorough a training for the ministry as possible for each current student, but also looked ahead to the students of the future. The fact that stalemate seemed to have been reached in regard to the new premises at Northwood did not mean that he failed constantly to press the officials of successive governments to allow building to begin. In 1949, for instance, the Ministry of Works was not willing to meet a deputation asking for a licence; such could not then be granted. The Principal was advised to wait and try again. Meanwhile, changes had continually to be made to plans as prices rose. There was an on-going search for new sources of fund-raising; the spartan regime at Ford Manor helped to save money for future needs.

Donald's life beyond the College *did* change. It was a marvel that there was time and energy left for any other activity. It was, in fact, all part of the total commitment to the service of his institution and, through it, the whole Church. He needed to get around, meet people, be an ambassador for his College; to show that Evangelicals were on the move and had much to give, and were not the bigots they had often hitherto been held to be.

There were fairly frequent meetings with Max Warren, then General Secretary of the Church Missionary Society. They had two main consequences: one for the College, the other for Donald individually. Through this means, members of overseas Anglican dioceses would spend time at LCD. A Nigerian Churchman, now an academic in his own country, recalls his arrival in England as a young student and first meeting with the Principal at his club, the Athenaeum. Donald was waiting, escorted him to the dining room and insisted on his preceding him through the door. The courtesy with which he was treated made a lasting impression, as did Donald's gathering up of the plates and collecting firewood at the family home in Northwood when the young Nigerian spent some vacations with the Coggans.

Max Warren's influence led Donald to become a member of the Evangelical Fellowship for Theological Literature which Max had founded in 1942[27]. Max's was a profound contribution to the Evangelical renewal with his determination that Evangelicals should continue to have a vital role within the comprehensiveness of the Church of England. Not least valuable was his conception of the totality of human experience as the province of the Creator; Donald at that point still had a tendency to speak of 'higher things'. Max was concerned that Evangelicalism had been weak on the intellectual side and not least in the output of good theology. He gathered together a group of younger Evangelicals who were committed to serious reading and, if possible, publishing. Under this aegis Donald wrote his first book on returning to England, entitled *Ministry of the Word*;[28] Max wrote a further volume in the collection, *Strange Victory*; F.W. Dillistone's contribution was *The Holy Spirit in the Life of Today*; while D.E.W. Harrison wrote a commentary on the Book of Common Prayer. J.R.S. Taylor, Bishop of Sodor & Man, contributed a preface to the series. He said he felt that a revival of articulate Evangelicalism would be appropriate in the present phase of the development of Christian theology. Whilst welcoming the freedom of thought and discussion which Liberal Protestantism had encouraged, Anglican Churchmen had deplored its vague humanitarianism as a barren substitute for the full Christian gospel. It was important to maintain a right proportion between Traditionalism and Liberalism and to retain the advantages of both by combining single-hearted loyalty to the Apostolic faith with 'boldness to examine and faith to trust all truth'. This the current series set out to do. Donald Coggan's own book was the first of several that he was to write on the subject of preaching; it was based on material he had prepared for conferences in Canada and for the diocese of London.

As F.W. Dillistone makes clear in his biography[29] of Max Warren, 'the EFTL proved to be an admirable means of drawing together and holding together a community of research and writing which, by 1952, had a hundred and fifty members.' Max's own biography[30] explains an important by-product of the Fellowship in the form of an annual register which recorded names and addresses of members, their subject of research and publications. The register, as Donald was to find out, was used by Archbishop Fisher

[27] It wound up in 1972.
[28] Canterbury Press.
[29] *Into all the World*, p.59.
[30] *Crowded Canvas*, pp.223-4.

when he was looking for scholars of Evangelical outlook to serve on commissions or delegations.

In 1945 the Archbishop, concerned for the divisions in the Church of England caused by varying interpretations, called upon a group of clergy who held a 'Catholic' point of view to examine certain questions so that common ground might be established and differences resolved, if such were possible. The publication of *Catholicity*[31] was the result of their deliberations. Two years later, in 1947, he invited some Evangelical Anglicans to undertake the same exercise. All were members of the Evangelical Fellowship for Theological Literature; Donald and Max Warren were of the number. D.E.W. Harrison, currently Archdeacon of Sheffield, was chairman. The result, in their case after eighteen months of meetings, was the publication *The Fulness of Christ*[32].

Archbishop Fisher wrote a preface to each volume. In the case of the second he commented on the eirenic attempt to account for the contrasts of 'catholic' and 'protestant' theology.

> It is careful to uphold that the Church of England is in the proper sense Protestant as well as Catholic. To a large extent, it is an endorsement of words which occur at the end of *Catholicity* . . . Our Anglican unity in the past has rested on the assurance that certain things remain constant as part and parcel of the very structure of Anglicanism. Some of these belong specifically to our Reformation heritage, some of them belong to our Catholic continuity and it is vital to our unity that both are constant and unalterable.

After this promising start, there were no further developments. The Archbishop, for his part, became swallowed up in the demands of his onerous calling.

Donald wrote a further book in 1950 under the auspices of the Church Missionary Society, *The Glory of God*. Max Warren began the series with his *Together with God – a programme for Prayer*. (Hubert Higgs who later became Donald's Archdeacon at Bradford and later still, as Bishop of Hull, one of Donald's suffragans at York, was the Society's publications manager.) *The Glory of God* was short (61 pages) and, as was Donald's custom, written with a practical purpose, in order to help missionaries, clergy, lay-workers, Sunday-School teachers, to explore the subject. The term 'glory' was examined in the Old Testament, the Synoptic Gospels, St Paul and St John.

[31] SPCK 1947.
[32] SPCK 1950.

Donald preached at the service of thanksgiving for Max's life and ministry[33], but for all their long association, they were never so close that Donald became a member of Max's innermost circle. In spite of some shared interests and enthusiasms, they were very different. Donald's discipleship of Jesus Christ, his work and his family were his world; he had no need for intimate friends. Max was scared of over-simplification[34]; Donald has been accused of going to the opposite extreme; it is this fact that has led to his books being regarded as the least satisfactory product of this very able man. He was, in fact still is, above all a great teacher, so determined that the gospel message should be comprehended that he tended to clarify and simplify to the extent that in some opinions he ran the risk of trivializing. Moreover, the strictly biblical approach received some criticism and was viewed as a limitation, when such a large proportion of the population had no knowledge of the Bible. His gifts of exposition in talks overcame the difficulty, since he invariably made the Scriptures come alive, even to those who had no previous experience of them.

The year 1950 was significant for several reasons; it saw Donald a member of the Convocation of Canterbury as one of the Proctors for the clergy of the diocese of London. He decided to stand for election for the reason that he did everything else, to help his College. He topped the poll in the election; it was a personal triumph and showed that he enjoyed the confidence of the London clergy in general, and not only those who shared an Evangelical outlook. He did not speak much either in Convocation or the Church Assembly in these early days; it was not primarily to air his views that he had joined, but to listen and confer. His first attendance included a crucial moment. Pope Pius XII had just announced the promulgation of the Assumption as *de fide*. Archbishop Fisher included a reference to it in his presidential address:

> The Archbishop of York and I felt obliged to put out a brief statement in reply to the announcement that the Corporal Assumption of the Blessed Virgin Mary is to be made a necessary article of faith for Roman Catholics. We cannot understand their insistence on requiring acceptance within their own ranks of doctrines altogether outside the Bible and universal creeds.

Donald was at once placed on a Committee of both Houses on Baptism, Confirmation and the Holy Communion, under the Chair-

---

[33] 11 October 1977.
[34] F.W. Dillistone, *Into all the World*, p.158f.

manship of the Bishop of Leicester; other members included four other bishops and some giants: Dr T.G. Jalland, Dom Gregory Dix OSB, and Professor Geoffrey Lampe. If Donald had intended to broaden the base of his acquaintanceship, he had succeeded. He was re-elected during subsequent sessions. The Committee issued its Final Report in October 1954 under a new Chairman, the Bishop of Hereford. Donald was then invited to serve on the Committee appointed by the Archbishop at the request of the Convocation to consider relations with the Church of Sweden; its Chairman was Bishop George Bell of Chichester. Donald was already a member of CACTM, having been nominated by Archbishop Fisher in 1949.

The second major event of the year 1950 was the first return journey of many, to Canada. A request from Emmanuel Theological College, Saskatoon, to help in a crisis could not be denied. (He solved it with considerable self-sacrifice by suggesting that his Vice-Principal should fill a vacancy.) He left England by air on 12 September and returned on the 23rd. The journey to Western Canada was by this time able to be made by air also. There was a day and a half in Toronto spent seeing some old friends. The extent of Donald's programme by the early 1950s can be gauged by the fact that on his landing in England after a night flight across the Atlantic, he went straight to Gorlestone near Great Yarmouth to preach next day; then to Rochester to give two lectures and finally to Emmanuel Church, West Hampstead, to conduct a Quiet Week-end.

Most of the vacations from the College and many Sundays in term were spent on preaching engagements, lectures, talks, missions. Some were in London: the Islington Conference, a series of sermons in the Abbey, in St Paul's and many smaller churches. Some were as far afield as Bristol, Bath, Cambridge, Wolverhampton, Oxford, Plymouth, Norwich, Brighton, Liverpool, Lee Abbey and a host of schools. He preached twice in Bradford Cathedral, in 1948 and in 1953 when he led the Three Hours devotions on Good Friday. Shortly after, during the following month of May, he gave some biblical addresses in the diocese of Canterbury as part of a confer-ence called by Archbishop Fisher for the parochial clergy. (Anyone compelled to be excused was required to write to the Archbishop personally.) Donald gave three studies in St Paul. The first on the grace of Our Lord Jesus as seen in the Epistle to the Ephesians; the second one on the Love of God demonstrated in the first Epistle to the Corinthians; the third described the fellowship of the Holy Ghost as shown in the Epistle to the Philippians.

This kind of address Donald presented superbly well; here was no exception. It so impressed the clergy that those who were still serving in the Canterbury diocese when he came as their Archbishop in 1974, could recall the occasion. Geoffrey Fisher heard one address only, but his reception of it had a notable consequence. There were two important subsequent engagements in the Canterbury diocese during this period: Three Hours' devotions in the Cathedral on Good Friday 1955, and some addresses on preaching for clergy at Cliftonville in 1959.

That Donald was able to persist in the accomplishment of such a punishing programme was a source of amazement. His considerable physical and psychological stamina included much strength of purpose and inner reserves upon which he could draw. His previous experiences at Cambridge and in Canada had prepared him, for he had learnt to work fast and efficiently with economy of words, time and effort. Not a moment was wasted; Donald rose from bed every day at the same hour however late he had been the previous evening; it allowed him to know exactly how much time he had at his disposal and he disposed of it to the minute.

But there was a price that was paid for all this dedicated activity. It curtailed the time that could be spent with his family. Only a yearly holiday was really free. When the heavy burden of active ministry was over, the sacrifice made on all sides could be discussed openly. It was regarded to have been a combined commitment in which all shared and all suffered. The LCD period was the hardest. The continued separation between Donald and Jean during term became so painful on both sides that a decision was made that the girls should board at school in Northwood and Jean join her husband at Ford Manor and return with him to Wetherby in the vacations. As it turned out, it was not a solution to what was to become a further, deeper problem of Jean's health.

Many years later when the illness was long behind her, Jean back in Canada gave a talk to the wives of Wycliffe graduates as part of the centenary celebrations[35]. She emphasized the need that women have of disposable time and adequate space. She was obviously looking back to the pain of the days at Ford Manor when she had all the time in the world and nothing she could find to do with it; and no space whatever. The teaching staff and chaplain cared for the students; the running of the College and feeding arrangements were the concern of the housekeeper and caterers; the owner lived in a small private apartment. Jean had no kitchen, no personal sitting-

[35] 1977.

room until after the last student who had come to see Donald had left it at night, often filled with tobacco smoke; nowhere to sleep until a couch in that same room could be made each evening into a bed. In her case, absence of privacy may have been less important than absence of occupation. She was not primarily a woman of strong domestic inclinations; it would be difficult to imagine her surrounded by recipes or knitting patterns; she had wider interests than those, especially in the field of social service where she had received a professional training. She was essentially a person who had been brought up to be useful.

Her initial depression and spiritual desolation began to spread to distressing physical symptoms. Characteristically, she saw the affair as reprehensible on her part. She looked back to happy days in Canada, of rich shared experiences, visits, and a fulfilling role within the family and community. She accused herself of self-pity which she tried to attack with self-discipline. Understanding of such illness was still undeveloped thirty years ago; there was no professional help available to assure her that the physical body can take serious revenge if personality is under attack. Eventually she began to recover; she and Donald made outings by car into the country and talked out her feelings. Jobs were found for her; she helped to catalogue the library and became the College taxi-driver. She also began to work in a nearby epileptic colony. It was not thought prudent for students to be aware that Jean was unwell, probably for two reasons: first the Coggans' natural reticence and reserve; secondly because the condition of depression was still so little understood. A greater degree of openness might have been of pastoral benefit on all sides.

By 1954 Donald had been Principal of LCD for ten years. In a termly report he said that the College was again full; there were forty-nine students of whom two had to sleep in the village. He described its composition: men from universities, public schools, grammar schools, technical and secondary modern schools, with their varied experience; BD students formed over one third; the relationship with London University had been maintained; (when it had seemed threatened, the governing body had capitulated and in 1950 appointed the Principal to the Council). One hundred and thirteen men had been ordained since Donald's appointment. Whenever he was asked whether he had regrets over leaving the parochial ministry, he answered that this was so, but he had replaced himself with over a hundred others whom he had helped to train.

CACTM made another Inspection that year and lavished praise on Principal and staff. 'The extremely comprehensive range of subjects offered' was one of the compliments; there were others:

> The life of the College is inevitably – and rightly – dominated by the genius and personality of the Principal . . . a fine scholar, a really brilliant lecturer and a man of deep piety . . .
>
> The Principal himself lectures for eleven periods in the week – a full programme for a busy man. His lectures in Hebrew, both elementary and advanced, are a joy to listen to; he also is responsible for Homiletics, some Greek Testament, and a share in the Old Testament work. He is a born teacher, stimulating and satisfying . . . the College is indeed fortunate to have him.

Comment was made upon the quarters allocated to the Principal and his wife, 'almost unbelievably limited to one large bed-sitting room on the first floor . . . they cheerfully put up with totally inadequate accommodation in order to admit the maximum possible number of students for the College's benefit.' The Principal's large share in the administration, even to the point of paying bills, was also noticed.

'The final impression gained was that Ordinands have here a "reasonable, holy and lively" training for their vocation such as we have nowhere seen surpassed and by no means everywhere equalled'. The only omission which the Inspectors felt should be remedied was 'a more direct and definite attempt to keep the men acquainted with current secular thought and the changing structure of contemporary society in an industrial and mechanized age'.

As a reward, the Council granted Donald three months' leave of absence for a lecture tour in Africa in 1955, arranged through the Church Missionary Society, on which Jean was to join him in part. But the news in 1954 which would have pleased him most was that permission to start the building programme for the new St John's at Northwood was at last given. Work could begin on the site in 1955 with a view to completion in 1956. The original designs needed further modification. Space for fifty men rather than seventy-five was allowed for, and only one room each instead of the original bedroom and study. The buildings would be less ornate than planned and composed of two storeys rather than three. A new appeal was launched with a paid organizer.

Donald could look back to ten hard years, but they had borne much fruit; the only constant factor had been his salary, which had not changed since 1944. (During his last year at LCD his diary reveals that he gave over 10 per cent of it away to good causes.) Now he could look forward to easier days in the new premises, though it is doubtful whether if he had stayed to work there, he would have been able to relax his efforts. 'Gentlemen, pray for a tough assignment,' he would say to his students. He had certainly endured such himself. 'Not for ever in green pastures' was another of his aphorisms. Together with 'Always preach for a verdict', these characteristic phrases were embedded in the memories of the men Donald trained; not in any sense of mockery, although there was humour in it too, but with gratitude. As a former student, now an Archbishop in Canada, has said 'I owe him everything'.

That the Church would allow him to stay at LCD much longer was a doubt in many minds. In 1948 there was a moment when he considered becoming Secretary for Translations of the British and Foreign Bible Society. He was anxious to ease the housing situation for himself and his family, so that all could live together. 'Mine is a great job and I love it,' he wrote, but 'we are living fifty miles apart during term . . . we do not feel it is right to continue this indefinitely'. But the post itself was a minor one, the salary meagre and there was no house, so it did not provide a solution to the main problem. Later in 1952 came the offer of the post of General Secretary of the same Society, but the same conditions applied.

A good deal of pressure was placed upon Donald early in 1955 to accept appointment as Principal of Wycliffe Hall, Oxford. After much heart-searching he decided that it would not be proper to leave the LCD at that critical moment.

That summer he left London airport on 28 June for Nairobi for a long tour of dioceses in Kenya, the Sudan and Uganda supported by the Church Missionary Society. In Nairobi he preached by interpretation at St Stephen's Church and also in the Cathedral, which sermon was broadcast. During the next days he toured the villages declared emergency areas on account of the Mau Mau situation; he had meetings with local African clergy and a four day Clergy School for the Nyanza district. An Ordination Retreat at Limuru Theological College was followed by preaching at the Ordination in Nairobi Cathedral.

In Uganda, which he reached by July 25, he spent three weeks in the diocese of the Upper Nile, visiting stations and clergy, conducting Retreats and touring villages and Colleges including the Theological College of Bulawasi, and at Mbale. He then left for the Sudan. A mutiny in the South inhibited his progress, but he made a tour of parish districts, lectured for several days at the Bishop Gwynne Theological College at Mundri where he saw former student and Arabic speaker David Brown[36], and spoke in an important secondary school at Rumbeck. Jean should have met Donald at Juba, but was prevented by the uprising. She was diverted to Entebbe where after some days, Donald joined her in a military plane. A fortnight's programme back in Uganda, teaching three Clergy Retreats at Mukono, Mbarara and Fort Portal ended on 19 September. He had travelled over 10,000 miles. He wrote at the end of his copy of the itinerary, 'Holiday beyond the reach of man'. It was a reminder of the less care-ridden years in Canada. They returned to England on 30 September.

The foundation stone of the new St John's at Northwood was laid on 15 October 1955 by Bishop Llewellyn H. Gwynne,[37] aged 92, an old student of the College, 1883-6. The Chairman of the Council, Bishop J.R.S. Taylor, in his speech outlined the trials the College had endured; the damage to its fabric and constant moves. But now a new home was to rise and it was appropriate that the eldest and most honoured member of the College, with his outstanding missionary record, should perform this act. He did so, saying in a strong voice 'To the glory of God and in the faith of Jesus Christ, I lay this stone'. A short service with hymns followed in a marquee, with a large congregation; Donald read the lesson.

It was doubtless with some degree of anti-climax that the Coggans returned to Ford Manor. Three days later, on 18 October, a letter addressed to the Principal arrived from the Prime Minister (Sir Anthony Eden). It asked for Donald's agreement that a nomination be sent to Her Majesty for his appointment to the Bishopric of Bradford.

---

[36] 1922-82; Bishop of Guildford 1973-82; Chairman, Board for Mission and Unity 1977-82.
[37] 1863-1957; DD; LLD; CMG; CBE; Suffragan Bishop of Khartoum 1908; Bishop in Egypt and the Sudan 1920-46.

CHAPTER SIX *Bradford*

Archbishop Fisher and Cyril Forster Garbett[1], Archbishop of York, had been in correspondence with the Prime Minister since the summer on the subject of a new Bishop for Bradford. Bishop Alfred Walter Frank Blunt[2], who had held the see since 1931, was seventy-five years of age; he had narrowly survived a stroke in June which further impaired his already declining powers. In August he was persuaded to retire with effect from the 31 October. On 15 August 1955, Archbishop Fisher wrote to Sir Anthony Eden with a list of names as his suggestions for the Sees of Worcester (also vacant) and Bradford. Among them was that of Donald Coggan, 'an Evangelical' who was 'co-operative and understanding'. He combined more scholarship than the others mentioned with administrative skill; 'well respected for his judgement, leadership and spiritual power. I have heard him give first-class biblical addresses to the clergy of my diocese.' The Archbishop also gave the views of the Bishop of London (William Wand), who had been consulted: 'very sound, steady and industrious'.

The Archbishop of York wrote to the Prime Minister some days later with his list of names, on which Donald Coggan appeared once more. Himself a very sick man and shortly to resign, Archbishop Garbett emphasized that the Bradford Diocese was a difficult undertaking (in fact the 'tough assignment' for which Donald had urged his men to pray). The present Diocesan had been failing for some years and had lost grip; moreover, Bradford business men were not easy to handle. He described Donald as an Evangelical who worked well with men of different views; a first-class scholar with 'great spiritual gifts as well as administrative ability. He would greatly strengthen on the theological side, the Bishops of the Northern Province and would attract to Bradford a higher standard of Ordinand.'

The Prime Minister wrote to the Archbishop of Canterbury some weeks later to explain that he would have welcomed a talk, but if

---

[1] 1875-1955; Bishop of Southwark 1919; of Winchester 1932; Archbishop of York 1942-1955.
[2] 1879-1957; Scholar Exeter College Oxford; Fellow 1902-07.

they were to see each other, the public 'would be bound to think it was about Princess Margaret'. He thought it clear that the choice for Bradford was between two men: one was already a suffragan bishop; the other was Donald Coggan.

On the receipt of the Prime Minister's letter, Donald asked for time for prayer and consideration of the proposal that had been made. The following day at 5 pm he called, by appointment made at short notice, on Archbishop Fisher in his study which had been prepared as a dressing room for the Queen. She was to come at 6.30 pm for the dedication of the restored Lambeth Palace Chapel, followed by dinner with the Bishops. The Archbishop gave himself wholly to the decision in hand for twenty minutes. 'You must go,' he said, 'unless there is some overwhelming family or other consideration which forbids.' He and the Archbishop of York both wanted his acceptance. Clearly what concerned Donald most was whether he should abandon his College at a critical stage in its life, particularly when he was uncertain what might happen if his presence were removed. Geoffrey Fisher sympathized with the prospect of leaving, but thought it not altogether too unsuitable a time now the stone was laid. On his part trying to persuade Donald to accept, he spoke a little on the work of a bishop. Finally he gave as his opinion that no longer than a week should be taken in reaching a decision.

Next day at noon Donald called on Sir Anthony Bevir[3] at No 10 Downing Street and spent three quarters of an hour with him. Sir Anthony spoke as one who was not an Evangelical, but said quite frankly that Evangelical representation was wanted on the Bench in the North. What Bradford needed above all was a *Pastor*; that he stressed several times. Bishop Blunt had intimated in 1942, thirteen years before, that he perhaps ought to retire, but had not succeeded in getting round to it. No new churches had been built for twenty-five years. They spoke for a few moments on the matter of the Bishop's house, which was rented on a yearly lease. Bradford was the last diocese to have such a scheme. It would not be possible, Bevir said, for Donald to visit Bradford unless and until he accepted the Bishopric and the news had been made public.

Arrangements were made by telephone for Donald to see the Bishop of Liverpool, Clifford Martin[4] ('he is a saint and knows about this'), and at two-thirty in the afternoon their meeting took

[3] 1895-1977; KCVO; CBE; Private Secretary to various Prime Ministers. Secretary for Appointments to PM 1947-56.
[4] 1895-1977; Bishop of Liverpool 1944-65.

place at the St Ermin's Hotel in Westminster. The Bishop, who was an Evangelical also, was adamant: Donald had been chosen because the Northern Province needed a bishop of his outlook and gifts; it was important for the whole Church of England that he must shoulder the responsibility for the See of Bradford. Housing and the expenses of upkeep need cause no problems; the Church Commissioners had such matters in hand. If the Bradford house was not suitable, another would be found.

At six o'clock on the same day, Donald saw the Bishop of London at the Athaneum. He said that only Donald himself could finally decide whether to leave LCD at that moment, but in view of the united wish of the two Archbishops, he felt Donald should go to Bradford. He proceeded to give some fatherly advice to a prospective bishop; if funds were short, to ask one of the Missionary Societies if they had any second-hand episcopal robes; secondly, not to rush round a diocese at the start: 'get to know the clergy first', he himself in London had first met the clergy in Rural Deaneries; thirdly, only to preach once a Sunday at the beginning (without letting this become public knowledge) so that week-ends might provide time for thought, reading and prayer; fourthly, be prepared, if the Northern Convocation was like the Southern, to read the Latin Litany, and 'Mind your quantities'.

The next move was to ask the Archbishop of York whether there was anything he wished to say before a reply be sent to the Prime Minister. Archbishop Garbett at once wrote to express how gladly he would welcome Donald to the North:

> I feel certain that you will not only be able to do the work and give the leadership which is urgently needed in the diocese of Bradford, but you will also make a contribution to the Church life of the whole Province.

Lastly, Donald felt he should be in touch with Bishop Taylor, not only as his Chairman, but a valued counsellor (then staying in Cornwall). Bishop Taylor's reply revealed that Donald's fear for the College was not imaginary nor isolated, but shared. The news, the Bishop wrote, provoked a crisis that he had been hoping for yet dreading in the past few months.

> Yes, I want it for you and have been praying that it might be given to you, yet I fear its consequence for St John's and for the new building scheme. A diocesan Bishop's path is beset with perils – of position, of power, of popularity, and perhaps especially the peril of the Primates. I think you will understand – if not you will before long.

Be prepared for suffering and remember that even Christ entered into glory through suffering.

The Times of 22 October carried a news item that the Archbishop of Canterbury and Bishop of London had been to call on Sir Anthony Eden; the subject under discussion was thought to be episcopal appointments, the first of the Prime Minister's term of office.

On Sunday 23 October Donald replied to the Prime Minister; he agreed that his name might be sent to the Queen. Two days later he wrote to his elder sister, Norah, to warn her of what was about to appear in the press.

You can imagine what we feel like, approaching a task of this magnitude and leaving the beloved College. But the unanimity on the part of the two Archbishops and of such men as the Bishop of Liverpool (with whom I spoke last week at some length) has encouraged us to believe that this is the call of God. And, that being so, we can go forward without fear.

Both Donald and Jean considered that they should acquaint their children in person of the forthcoming major change in the lives of all of them. A telephone call to the Headmistress of St Helen's School, Northwood, resulted in an unprecedented step: Ruth was allowed to have tea in the town with her parents in term, to be apprised of the news. Ann was not present, as she was away in a school lacrosse match; the parental effort made to involve them both in the great matter was not forgotten by their daughters. The daily papers carried the news of the appointment to the Sees of Bradford and Worcester the following morning[5]. Donald had acted during the week with modesty, integrity, care in judgement and decision-making; there would be those in the future who would wish that he had continued to place such weight upon consultation. But it was his students who at that moment showed that they knew him best: a notice appeared on the Principal's door at LCD which bore the inscription 'BUSINESS AS USUAL'.

At last it was possible for them to see the new surroundings. On 12 November Donald and Jean made their first visit to Bradford since the appointment had been announced. In common with others who frequently made this mistake, their conception of the diocese did not agree with reality; Donald's previous experience had been limited to the built-up areas of the city.

The diocese had been created in 1919. Part, including the city of Bradford, had been within the diocese of Chester until 1836, when it

[5] 26 October 1955.

was transferred to the jurisdiction of the See of Ripon. In 1916 a scheme was drafted to form a new diocese by withdrawing six Rural Deaneries, including that of Bradford, from within the Ripon boundaries. The final Order in Council was dated 25 November 1919; Donald was to be only the third Bishop. By giving the diocese the name of Bradford, the illusion was created that here was a generally densely-populated, industrial area. Nothing was further from the case. The shape of it had been described by the previous Bishop as that of a banana, tilted slightly to the west. In the south, certainly, were the woollen towns of Bradford, Shipley, Bingley and Keighley, with their mills and dwelling houses in close proximity to each other; but going north the scene changed, and gave way to an area of moorland in the neighbourhood of Ilkley and Skipton; further north again lay the Yorkshire Dales, leading to wild, isolated mountainous country in the counties of Cumbria and North-West Lancashire, beyond Settle to Sedburgh. The one hundred and fifty-odd parishes were spread out in an environment of infinite variety, in a space sixty-five miles long and twenty-five miles wide at its broadest part.

Ironically, after all their former housing problems, Donald and Jean felt they could not occupy the former Bishop's residence, Horton Hall. The Bradford solicitors who negotiated the lease had offered to extend the tenancy for a rent of £150 a year. The house represented a hotch-potch of architectural styles; it was pretentious, rambling, cold, and difficult to maintain; the kitchen had equipment that called for the application of black-lead, and the garden was large and neglected. It did not in any way represent the Coggans' style, and wisely they said so. The Church Commissioners agreed to the purchase of an alternative, if such could be found. Meanwhile, Donald and Jean decided to start their lives in the Bradford diocese in a hotel: the Crescent at Ilkley was chosen as a central point. It marked the beginning of one of the strongest and most sensitive features of Donald's episcopate: the recognition that the various different cultural and vocational elements in the diocese needed to be welded together. For this, among other reasons, he is still remembered with affection in the Dales.

The next journey was to York on 19 December, to stay with Archbishop Garbett and his sister at Bishopthorpe. Cyril Garbett could not leave his room, but was still capable of shrewd judgement and wise advice. He had been a bishop for thirty-six years and was within twelve days of the end of his life. He said he was particularly glad to welcome Donald, as an Evangelical scholar, on the Northern

Bench and proceeded to outline the problems he would find at Bradford, and the areas where changes were required. Ordination needed tightening up: there had been some unwise proceedings as Dr Blunt had no use for CACTM. New housing estates needed assessing in regard to churches: little work had been done in this direction. There were some problems of extreme churchmanship: Archbishop Garbett was not in favour of extra-liturgical services. The appointment of examining chaplains automatically ceased with the resignation of a bishop: perhaps it might be wise to reinstate only those from within the diocese, not the others. If there were men who had scruples about stoles at ordination, the Archbishop had made it a practice to allow them to wear surplice only. He then outlined some priorities: there were certain essentials, such as Bishops' meetings, Convocation, Church Assembly and confirmations, although these should not be allowed to become too frequent, or could sometimes be combined. At the top of the list of priorities the Archbishop put a personal touch, particularly with the clergy. He described his methods: to ring round a day or few hours in advance to a group of incumbents; to visit them and let them talk, even when there was no special business to discuss. The Archbishop thought time set aside for reading each day essential: 'Always have a book on hand'.

A visit to the Dean of York[6] was made to discuss Donald's consecration, which had been fixed for 25 January 1956, in York Minster. To St Paul, the feast of whose conversion it was, Donald had a particular attachment. He made one or two requests for hymns and so on, especially for the anthem *Expectans expectavi*, to music by Charles Wood. This anthem was to reappear at his Enthronement as Archbishop of York in 1961 and Canterbury in 1975. Those who wish to draw close to an understanding of Donald Coggan can do no better than study his feeling for the second verse[7].

> With parted lips and outstretched hands
> And listening ears thy servant stands,
> Call thou early, call thou late,
> To thy great service dedicate.

Donald also asked whether it could be made possible for Jean to leave her place after the consecration and join him at the Commu-

---

[6] Eric Milner-White.
[7] Words by Charles Hamilton Sorley, killed at the battle of Loos 1915.

nion rail, so that they might receive the Sacrament together, rather than for her to wait for the general Communion of the congregation; the Dean agreed that this could and should be done.

Donald spent some days of Retreat at Lee Abbey in Devon and then left for York with his family on 24 January 1956. With the death of Archbishop Garbett in the early hours of the morning on 31 December 1955 (he was to have become a temporal peer in the New Year Honours' List of the following day), the duty of chief consecrator fell to Leslie Hunter of Sheffield, assisted by twenty-two other bishops. The Archbishop-designate of York, Michael Ramsay, Bishop of Durham, was gospeller, the Bishop of Newcastle, Noel Hudson, epistoler. The two bishops presenting Donald Coggan and invited so to do by him, were Clifford Martin of Liverpool and William Greer of Manchester. He had wanted to be supported by Spencer Leeson, his former headmaster and Bishop of Peterborough, who had been forced to decline on account of his health. Evered Lunt[8], Dean of Bristol, a friend of long standing and old student of LCD, preached on the pastoral duties of a bishop from the text 'Thy rod and thy staff, they comfort me'. The congregation included Donald's forty-six students from the London College of Divinity, whom he took out to tea in York after the ceremony. Two thousand clergy and laity from the diocese of Bradford thronged York Minster. The Diocesan Secretary had written

> In spite of the many problems that await you, I feel that the apparently unprecedented number who wish to attend your consecration, on top of the response to the cathedral appeal, is a very heartening portent for the future and will be a big encouragement to you.

Donald left York the same night in a sleeping compartment for London where he was received next day by the Queen and did Homage upon his appointment. The new Bishop of London, Henry Colville Montgomery Campbell[9], gave Donald at the Palace the best leaving present from the London diocese he could have imagined. The Bishop had found it possible to provide a grant of £760 per annum for an unspecified number of years towards the expenses of the new LCD.

The Enthronement or Inthronization of the new Bishop of Bradford took place in his Cathedral on the Feast of St Blaise, the patron saint of woolcombers, on 3 February 1956. Again a large congrega-

[8] 1900-82; Bishop of Stepney 1957-68.
[9] Bishop of London 1956-61.

tion greeted him as he was admitted through the West door, after beating upon it with his pastoral staff. He was placed upon the throne or *cathedra* by the Provost, John Tiarks[10] with a formula of words, before preaching from the text from Psalm 78.73, 'He fed them with a faithful and true heart, and ruled them prudently with all his power'. It was a thrilling time, he said, to have a part in the work of the Church of Christ. He could not align himself with those who dismally hankered for good days gone by. 'This is the day which the Lord hath made; we will rejoice and be glad in it.' The sermon was designed to usher in a new era and to warn that changes were on the way; Donald spoke of the need for 'swift action in many realms'.

If grip had been mentioned as a necessity to deal with the current situation in the diocese of Bradford, it had arrived. Their new Bishop was quick in his appraisal of what needed to be done most urgently. One of the worst features had not been mentioned by Archbishop Garbett: nineteen benefices were vacant and a further five would shortly have no incumbent. By the end of March Donald was writing for the April number of the *Bradford Diocesan Messenger* that he had sought to come to grips with some of the major problems of the diocese, at least in theory. An outline of some courses of action was beginning to emerge. By May he wrote 'A start is being made in filling the alarming number of vacancies in the diocese.'

Bishop Blunt, Donald's predecessor, was a man of considerable intellect and singular gifts. He had left Oxford, where he had been both scholar and don, with First Classes in Classical Moderations and *Litterae Humaniores* (Greats). His writings were exceptionally well expressed and had prophetic qualities. But he was cursed with a delicately balanced psyche and had endured at least four break-downs, some of them severe. His relationship with his wife, though deep and permanent, was not a steadying factor, and she played little part in the life of the diocese. His wells of sympathy were deep, and as a Christian Socialist his espousal of various political causes led him into some difficult situations. For instance, his attacks on the profit motive when directed against wool merchants had a deleterious effect on the Cathedral appeal. In 1936 he had ventured to criticize at a diocesan conference the apparent lack of enthusiasm shown for religious observances by the new King, Edward VIII, before his Coronation, a religious act. This was (quite mistakenly) regarded as an exposé of the King's matrimonial intentions, which it

---

[10] 1903-74; Provost of Bradford 1944-62; Bishop of Chelmsford 1962-71.

certainly was not. It has been pointed out[11] that Bishop Blunt never recovered the esteem of the nation, 'nor, quite, of his diocese'. Even when his words 'were powerful . . . the audience would hardly hear'. The gravest problem was that he clung to his responsibilities long after he could discharge them effectively.

Donald was accorded a rapturous welcome and carried diocesan opinion with him in almost all he tried to do. In June he addressed his first Diocesan Conference and outlined not only his plans for the future, but what he had been able to do so far. He had licensed a priest-in-charge to Wrose and instituted clergy to six further parishes: Menston-in-Wharfedale, Ingrow, Leathley-with-Farnley, Holy Trinity Bradford, St Augustine Bradford and Cross Roads-cum-Lees. He had made engagements to institute a further nine clergy to Rylestone, Marton-cum-Thornton, St Margaret Bentham, Riddlesden, Wyke, Oakworth, St Peter Shipley, Cowling and St Lawrence Pudsey. He spoke of the grave deficiency of curates; of the stipends of the clergy which he said he would try to have raised; and then devoted much time to his assessment of the need for new buildings, both churches and vicarages. There had been plans made as early as 1902 which had so far come to nothing.

The priorities included a mission church to serve Horton Bank Top and Clayton with a view to the formation of a new parish which would encompass the 'buildings which, like mushrooms, are rising full of young families all neglected by the Church of England'. The problem was aggravated by the fact that the Bradford Corporation, alone so far as it could be discovered, refused to sell land even for the erection of church buildings. (This was not a situation which Donald allowed to continue.) St James, Pudsey, had a good site and a Church Commissioners' grant for church buildings in new areas was available; plans should be drawn up. St Cuthbert, Wrose, a fast expanding area, had a totally inadequate church, an ancient hall into which the rain flowed, and a vicarage of which the diocese should be ashamed: no Church Commissioners' money was available so local effort would be required; the Bishop called for help from the business fraternity.

In order that these needs should be carefully co-ordinated, Donald announced that he had appointed two Committees. These words were to have a familiar ring about them in the next twenty years. One was a Survey Committee under the chairmanship of an

---

[11] By Owen Chadwick in his *Hensley Henson, A study in the friction between Church and State* (Oxford University Press 1983), p.227.

honorary canon who knew the diocese well, which would not only map out needs but enquire into and report on redundant churches (a nettle that had to be grasped), and would also estimate the manpower situation and assess the capital sum required. The second was a Ways and Means Committee to whom was given the task of thinking out the best way by which the money could be found. So that clergy could have a time of spiritual and intellectual refreshment, the Bishop had arranged a four-day clergy conference in Durham, subsidized by the diocese in the Autumn for prayer, study and conferring; 'Note the order', he added.

His own living problem, the new Bishop reported, had been solved by the purchase of a house at Heaton on the outskirts of Bradford to which he would shortly move. But he assured the members of the diocese who lived in the country areas in the north that he would not cease to be aware of their existence when he drew closer to the city. He had already seen much of the rural scene, and appreciated the problems there as keenly as he did those of new housing areas and towns: 'We are one family in Christ'. As an experiment, the diocesan conference would be held alternately in Bradford (in winter) and in Skipton in the north (in summer). The Dilapidations Board, which dealt with repair to clergy housing, would also meet alternately in those two centres. Instead of calling meetings three times a year, the Board would assemble monthly, so that there should be no unnecessary delays 'in matters which affect the happiness of clergy and their families'. Donald's concluding words showed the lines along which his thinking would develop: he spoke of the two primary functions of the Church as Worship and Evangelism. They would be hearing from him again on these themes; as also on the nature of the Church itself, as the people of God and not merely the clergy.

But the first six months at Bradford had contained activity beyond discovering the terrain, the parishes, the clergy, the people, the problems, and house-hunting. Before his preferment, Donald had received two requests from Archbishop and Mrs Fisher. The Archbishop had invited him to join a delegation that was to visit Russia in the summer of 1956: from this he begged permission to withdraw. Mrs Fisher asked that he should give some talks in Lent to a group of ladies, the wives of senior officials and Members of both Houses of Parliament and so on, who met under her guidance, but when the Bradford appointment was announced she offered to release him from the obligation; this however he refused, and kept to his agreement. He made a special journey by train to London on

three successive Wednesdays in February, 1956 and one in March.
The enthusiasm with which the lectures were received led to their
being printed under the overall title *Jesus Christ and the Experience of
Life* in four parts: Life in relation to God, Life in relation to others,
Life and the work we do, Life and its maintenance. Mrs Fisher
wrote at the conclusion:

> I cannot begin to tell you how much your four talks have meant to me and
> to the other ladies who have come this year in record numbers. We are all
> deeply grateful that you should have come so far each week, to let us
> share in your knowledge and experience of Christ. You have certainly by
> His grace opened a window in my spiritual house and made me long to
> know Him better and to love Him more.

Her secretary added her own testimony: 'In confidence I may add
Mrs Fisher suggested this morning we had all better move to
Bradford'.

In May, as the Bishop of London had predicted, the new Bishop
was required to say the Latin Litany in York Minster at the
beginning of his first meeting of the Northern Convocation. Archbishop Ramsey was in the Chair, also for the first time, having been
enthroned three weeks previously. In his address he referred to the
fact that three hundred years before, in 1556, Archbishop Cranmer
had gone to the stake. Two of those present were to become his
successors in office, though not in martyrdom.

The extent of Donald's diary did not prevent him from attending
the Speech Day at St Helen's School, Northwood in July. It was
Ann's last; she left school that term and proceeded in the autumn to
Edinburgh University. Ruth remained for another two years before
she began to read medicine. A letter, written about this time[12] to
the Cambridge Missionary Fellowship (still in existence after
twenty-three years) gave some of their father's views on the education of women.

> I do not number myself among those who think it is no use giving the best
> possible education to girls because they get engaged (or married) the day
> after graduating from their university. Even if they do, it seems to me
> worth-while, for their whole life is enriched and their capacity for
> enjoying the cultural side of life enlarged. Further, in these days when
> *money* values are very uncertain, cultural and educational advantages are
> well worth parental sacrifice.

There had been little or no free time since going north; a day off on

[12] 9.10.56.

21 May had been specially noted. A month of holiday at the end of August was spent partly in Edinburgh and partly near Keswick in the Lake District. Donald's daughters speak with enthusiasm about his capacity for enjoyment at times such as these, so that they enjoyed family holidays also. When they were younger their father invented stories, some strange and ghoulish, about the places they would visit, showing gifts of the imagination not generally revealed. The move into a new home (renamed Bishopscroft) of reasonable size and accessibility in Ashwell Road, Heaton, provided a welcome background to family life, and that of the diocese.

Jean began to develop pursuits of her own. Among them, she identified herself particularly with activities that concerned the wives of clergy. The 1950s were a time when clerical stipends had not risen in relation to the cost of living, and there was some hardship and isolation. Jean's friendship and empathy proved particularly acceptable.

In the autumn, Donald's interest in the dissemination of the Scriptures was recognized on a world scale. At the meeting of the Standing Committee of the United Bible Societies[13] held at Bandung, Indonesia from 25 September to 1 October 1956, it was announced that the Bishop of Bradford had been appointed a Vice-President. That same month of October, at the York Convocation, he was appointed by the Upper House of Bishops to represent them on the Joint Committee on the translation of the Bible under the chairmanship of Dr A.T.P. Williams[14], Bishop of Winchester.

By December 1956, the Bishop could tell his Diocesan Conference that he had instituted or licensed twenty-six incumbents, and before his first year was out the figure would have reached thirty. A few critics voiced the opinion that their new Bishop was filling the diocese with Evangelicals, but this was unfair. In the main he chose men he knew and trusted, since he was concerned with the quality of the clergy; some were his own former pupils. A remark of his that has survived gives another slant: when interviewing a prospective vicar for a parish he said: 'I have a different outlook and emphasis from yours, but I haven't come to be a party Bishop'. He warned that during the second year of his episcopate he hoped to have outlets for any energy that he might have for spheres other than providing so large a harvest for new cures. They were prophetic words. One of the problems which had hindered him, as he went

[13] The Federation of all the national Bible Societies.
[14] 1888-1968; Bishop of Durham 1939; of Winchester 1952-61.

about his diocesan business, was the lack of help from his principal officers, the two Archdeacons, *oculi episcopi*[15], one of whom was ill, the other old. A new appointment was made at the end of the year by reason of the death of the latter. Another move to increase communications came with the embellishment of the diocesan magazine, renamed *Bradford Diocesan News*, steered by a small committee, to which all were urged to subscribe in its new guise and format.

A number of evangelistic efforts in the diocese were announced for 1957: a campaign in Keighley, a big woollen town; seventy Church Army Evangelists would work with local churches; the Bradford Churches Campaign would begin in March, after careful preparation and the visiting of homes; and the Village Evangelists had planned a Mission in the Craven Archdeaconry in the north. Under the Bishop's guidance a School of Evangelism was planned to take place in Bradford once a month from November to April. Donald provided the lectures under the title 'the New Testament basis of Evangelism', and so many attended the first session that the second was held in a larger hall. The School, which was designed to be practical, included a monthly visit to the Thorpe Edge Estate in Bradford.

Donald's main thrust in his second year of office was the Bishop's Appeal for funds for new buildings. It began with a Press Conference, a day of Prayer throughout the diocese on 5 June 1957, and luncheons for captains of industry and other leaders of the community in Bradford, Yeadon, Keighley, Skipton and Settle, addressed by the Bishop. Meetings of Donald and the clergy in four groups had by that time already taken place during the Spring, to examine needs and explore the best way of meeting them. Six working parties followed, composed of lay men and women who drew up lists of those to whom the Bishop should write. A group of businessmen with the Provost of the Cathedral gave advice; with the result that Donald's twenty-five thousand letters asking for funds were despatched by voluntary workers helped by the facilities of a dozen business firms. The keynote throughout the enterprise was a personal approach by the Bishop; no money for the new churches was to come through the diocesan quota[16]. The manner in which the operation was carried out with speed and efficiency demonstrated that local help was willingly given in response to Donald's personal involvement.

---

[15] 'The eyes of the bishop'.
[16] Money required annually from parishes for diocesan expenses.

Bishop Coggan was again responsible for the Litany, but no longer in Latin, at the Convocation of York in May of 1957. Archbishop Ramsey's presidential address was concerned primarily with the question, 'How can we bring home the gospel of Christ to the millions who are indifferent to the Christian faith'; whether the gospel must be presented as an ideology, because the age demands a gospel which speaks to the condition of communal man; whether the gospel, thought-out and re-stated, should be the subject of a concerted national mission. These were matters of the deepest consequence to Donald and uppermost in his mind for the whole of his ministry. His response to the second question was always that the presentation to the indifferent millions must be Jesus Christ: 'Apart from him, the Church has nothing to proclaim'[17]. Consideration of the third question became a crucial issue during his last years at Canterbury. At Bradford he gave himself over to some discussion on the matter of popular lack of interest in human *finitude*[18]. Awareness of human finitude should be stimulated, he felt; his own thought had been inspired by reading Harry Blamires' *The Faith and Modern Error*[19] by which he had been much impressed. He did not consider that it was the primary task of the Christian apologist to answer questions, but rather to ask them. It may well be that his *Call to the Nation* of 1975 may have had some of its origins here, amidst his thinking in the 1950s.

The part taken by the laity in the worship of the Church was a theme explored and expanded by Donald at Bradford, partly triggered off by his first long intervention in the Upper House of the York Convocation on the subject of the need for a new translation of the Psalter. The matter had been discussed earlier, in 1945 and again in 1949 when the then President had promised to confer with the Archbishop of Canterbury. In his summary, Bishop Coggan said that a new revision of the Psalter was needed

> first because of the advance in Old Testament studies since Coverdale's day; secondly because of the great changes in the English language; thirdly because of the unintelligibility of very much of what was now in Coverdale, and which they were forced to sing and say in the course of the year; and fourthly because it was the duty of the Church to take out of the way of clergy and laity all that prevented their offering to God worship that was at once intelligible and beautiful.

[17] F.D. Coggan *The Ministry of the Word*, pp.64-5.
[18] Bradford Diocesan Conference, 6 June 1957.
[19] SPCK 1956; republished as *The Secularist Heresy*, SPCK 1981.

These were sentiments which Donald had expressed before in articles written as Principal of LCD. He saw no virtue in retaining forms of words in worship which were no longer understood, whether in Prayer Book or Bible. Donald was a life-long believer in linguistic revision of sacred texts and rites, and in every effort that might make them more comprehensible. Whether Archbishop Fisher became aware of the speech is not known, but when the appointment of the Commission to revise the Psalter was announced in 1958, the Bishop of Bradford was invited to be Chairman.

The laity's part in the Word was not the sole area of the Bishop's concern; he emphasized also their proper participation in sacramental acts when he said[20]: 'If one thing has become clear about early Eucharistic worship it is this – it was *the corporate act of the whole Church*. As a priestly society the Church acted corporately whenever the Eucharist was celebrated'. He went on to quote Dom Gregory Dix, with whom he had served on the Southern Convocation's Committee on Baptism, Confirmation and the Holy Communion from 1950-4:

> the whole Church prayed in the person of Christ; the whole Church was charged with the office of proclaiming the revelation of Christ; the whole Church offered the Eucharist as the re-calling before God and man of the offering of Christ . . . Christ and His Church are one, with one mission, one life, one prayer, one Gospel, one offering, one Being, one Father.

'Dix is undeniably right,' Donald went on, 'to this we must give expression in every way'.

The resignation of a second Archdeacon gave the Bishop the opportunity to appoint Hubert Higgs, with whom he had collaborated in the production of *The Glory of God* for the CMS Press, as Archdeacon of Bradford. With his impressive academic record, he proved an apt choice as the bearer of the burdens which Donald placed upon him. Mindful of Archbishop Garbett's words on the necessity to ensure a succession of ordinands of good standing, and his own observations, he decided to place the care of the studies of the younger clergy with the new Archdeacon, besides his usual duties. Higgs would also look after all those who were preparing for or contemplating the possibility of Ordination, the Bishop announced: he would formulate a well thought-out policy in regard to education, both clerical and lay, and would become Chairman of the Diocesan Missionary Council. Co-ordination and vision were

[20] Diocesan Conference, 12 December 1957.

needed if the diocese was to play its part in the great world-wide task of the Anglican Communion.

It was to this subject that Bishop Coggan addressed himself in the summer of 1957. Starting in Canada, his own horizons were broadening all the time. He warned his diocese of the danger of self-centred parochialism. It must not be forgotten that it was part of the great Anglican Communion which stretched over the world's surface and which itself was but a part of the great Catholic Church of God[21]. In a characteristic and often-used phrase, he urged that men should lift up their eyes from the comparatively narrow sphere of their own surroundings and 'look on the fields'. In this interest, he invited Bishop Frank Johnson to speak on the Church in the Middle East to that same diocesan assembly. The following year saw the advent of his first Lambeth Conference; both this experience, and his meetings with the Anglican Bishops who had been invited to the Bradford area as part of the run-up to the Conference, were formative in furthering his appreciation of the nature of the Anglican Communion of Churches. The future was to bring acceleration and development; nevertheless, Donald's early predisposition to be receptive to the concept of a world-wide community was important, especially as his own Evangelical background was often held to denote exclusiveness.

Every bishop attending the Lambeth Conference was invited to make his choice as to the Committee on which he would most like to serve. Donald chose the one which was to consider 'Progress in the Anglican Communion'. It was divided into three sub-sections: Missionary appeal and strategy; the Book of Common Prayer: Ministries and manpower. For the first of the sub-sections he became half of a drafting Committee of the Report. A list of subjects of special urgency was compiled which it was considered should engage the attention of the Advisory Council; Donald felt personally drawn towards two of them: African Townships and, as a result of a recent visit, South America. Here was the beginning of a particular interest and influence in missionary work in the 'neglected continent' that was to stretch into the future. Most importantly, the Committee brought him into touch with Stephen Bayne[22], Bishop of Olympia, Secretary of the Advisory Council on Missionary Strategy, whose clear mind and forceful personality Donald much admired, and they became good friends during Bishop Bayne's term

[21] Diocesan Conference, 6 June 1957.
[22] 1908-74; Bishop of Olympia 1947-69; Anglican Executive Officer 1960-64.

of office in England as Anglican Executive Officer. The Bishop of
Bradford anticipated his arrival and booked him to speak at the
diocesan conference of December 1960, while he was still on the
American West coast.

After a bare year as vice-president of the United Bible Societies,
Donald had been invited to be President as successor to Bishop
Eivind Berggrav of Norway, an office to which he gave himself
wholeheartedly, with much expenditure of time and energy and a
great deal of travel, for the next nineteen years. Thereafter he was
made Honorary President; a position specially created for him. On 9
July 1957 he set off for the Council Meeting at San Paulo and Rio de
Janeiro, Brazil, where his appointment was ratified; a tour on Bible
Societies' business in Santiago, Valparaiso, Lima, Colombia,
Panama, Jamaica and New York followed.

The next year he attended the International Missionary Council
Conference in Ghana in his capacity as President of UBS. On his
way home he visited the work of the Bible Society in Nigeria and
saw not only the headquarters, Bible House in Lagos, but flew to
Kano, a morning's journey by plane to the North. At this centre of
paganism on the edge of the Sahara, with Islam, Buddhism and
Hinduism making converts in a revival of ancient faiths, he met
Christians in the old walled city who were making translations of the
Bible into Hausa, the main local language, and also an old
missionary scholar, author of a Hausa dictionary.

As soon as he returned to England Donald was swept back into
the world which he had left: the consecration of the chapel of his old
College. Building operations had been proceeding ever since his
departure and troubles too, some of which he could have foreseen.
The affiliation to London University hung in the balance, and was
eventually withdrawn. The matter of Donald's replacement had
proved difficult and protracted. The post was offered to various men
who, no doubt realizing the problems that would ensue, declined to
accept. Eventually a candidate was persuaded to become the new
Principal. Douglas Webster wrote to Donald, 'I can scarcely bring
myself to write about the LCD appointment, I feel so distressed,
and I try to imagine your feelings'. The new Principal was a 'nice
man and a good' but very rigid and no scholar.

> The Council being what it is I was not very hopeful from the start, having
> neither a theologian nor a moderate evangelical among them . . . they
> don't seem to have looked very far and presumably they are unaware
> even of the existence of the EFTL, not to mention a very good set of dons
> at Oxford and Cambridge in the theological faculties. If all one can live

1 Donald Coggan's grandparents, William and Elizabeth, with five of their sons and the presentation silver from the members of the National Federation of Meat Traders, circa 1901. From left to right, *back row:* Leslie and his wife Murray, Herbert, Cyril Edgar; *front row:* Frederick, Elizabeth, William, Fanny (Donald's mother), Cornish Arthur (Donald's father).

2 Cornish Arthur Coggan, as National President of the Federation of Meat Traders, 1937–8.

3

3 Fanny Coggan with Norah, circa 1903.

4 Donald Coggan circa 1912.

5 Donald Coggan circa 1920.

4

5

6 Hebrew class, Merchant Taylors' School, 1927. From left to right, *back row:* D. A. Parker, W. S. C. Moon, I. E. S. Edwards, P. H. Biddlecombe, A. C. Beevor, J. M. Plumley, F. D. Coggan, B. F. Dupré; *front row:* P. S. Taylor, The Revd F. J. Padfield, S. H. Clark.

7, 8 Donald Coggan and Jean Strain at the time of their engagement, Autumn 1934.

9 Donald and Jean's wedding, 17 October 1935. From left to right, *back row:* Bertram Masterman (best man), Cornish Arthur Coggan, Donald Coggan, Jean Coggan, William Loudon Strain; *front row:* John Vellacott, Fanny Coggan, Jean Foster, David Vellacott, Dorothy Strain, Elizabeth Vellacott.

10 On honeymoon, Bournemouth, October 1935.

11

2

11 Confirmation of the election of Donald Coggan to the Archbishopric of York in Lambeth Palace Chapel, 5 July 1961. Archbishop Ramsey of Canterbury on the right.

12 Archbishop Ramsey of Canterbury and Archbishop Coggan of York leaving Lambeth Palace, July 1961.

13 Family Christmas at Bishopthorpe, 1961. From left to right: Ann, Ruth, Donald, Jean.

14 In the garden of Bishopthorpe with Chad, October 1974.

14

15 Archbishop Coggan entering Canterbury Cathedral for his enthronement, 24 January 1975.

16 Archbishop Donald and Jean Coggan at Lambeth Palace with a group of Protestant and Roman Catholic children from Northern Ireland, July 1975.

for is the preservation of north end and 1662 and a battle against stoles, then I see no future for Evangelical Anglicans save unhappiness, division and complete irrelevance. 'Oh that my head were waters and mine eyes a fountain of tears'.

Donald also received a letter from the appeals organizer for the LCD Building Fund, disappointed that his services were to be dispensed with, although the full amount needed had not been raised. From his distant point of vantage, Donald made some suggestions about the ceremony that was to mark the opening of the new buildings. At the time of the laying of the foundation stone, one of the Governors had attempted to exclude the Bishop of London from the proceedings on account of his churchmanship, and quoted Romans 16.17[23]. Donald had already tried to press for some new Governors: 'It is of very great importance that we should appoint men of vision and men who will carry some weight with the University.'

At 7 pm on the night before the Opening day, news came that the Bishop of London had been involved in a motor accident, and would be unable to dedicate the chapel, as had been arranged. After a series of telephone calls it emerged that the Archbishop of Canterbury, who was to declare the buildings open, was willing to dedicate the chapel also, and that the Bishop of Bradford had agreed to preach. Geoffrey Fisher was in particularly jovial mood and full of compliments; he was astonished at the quality of the food (one of the students who had been chef of the Adelphi Hotel in Liverpool, took over the catering for the day). The Archbishop's speech was long and rambling, but most friendly and warm-hearted; it ranged over a wide variety of subjects, from the College plumbing (for he had heard that at one point all taps had produced hot water) to ministry, trust, wisdom and the Church of South India.

After the Archbishop had unveiled the commemorative plaque and inspected the College, the bell tolled for chapel, packed for the dedication service which was in the form of Evensong. Donald Coggan preached from a text from Psalm 44.3, 4. It was surely a great moment as he looked back to past struggles. He spoke of his own vision:

> I see this College as a place supplying fit persons to serve God in the ministry of His Church . . . may God send from its portals men who care very little for cushy jobs . . . but who pioneer where Christ is not known.

[23] 'I implore you my friends, keep an eye on those who set up quarrels and lead others astray, contrary to the teaching you received'.

He prayed also that it might be a place of sound learning, increasingly as the years went by. 'For this the Church of England has stood down many centuries and for this it still stands' where the 'beauty of holiness is seen.'

The new Principal proved himself better able than had been expected to keep the College on a steady course, maintaining many of the traditions that had been the hall mark of the Coggan era: scholarship and an openness towards the existence of other Christians beyond the College boundaries. His rough passages illustrate the kind of tensions with which Donald Coggan had struggled, largely in silence. During the months following the opening of the new buildings it became known to the Council that the westward position had been adopted for the mid-week Holy Communion services in the chapel. It was ruled that the practice be discontinued. The senior student sent a letter of protest in the name of his colleagues, as they felt that what they had been trying to do did not in any way militate against true Evangelicalism, but would promote the unity of the Church. The matter of doctrinal tests for new members of staff was raised again, and of whether students should be made aware of alternative points of view. Over this issue, a tutor resigned, and R.V.G. Tasker, Professor of New Testament Exegesis at King's College, London declared that he as an Evangelical had never previously been subjected to these pressures, and withdrew from the LCD governing body[24].

With the closing of one chapter of his life in relation to the building up of an institution, Donald Coggan proceeded to give support and encouragement to another: one of the main achievements of his episcopate at Bradford was the creation of Scargill.

It had long been in the minds of some churchmen in the north of England that there was a need for a centre in their region similar to that which had flourished so successfully since 1946 at Lee Abbey in Devon. A group of men and women had established a Christian Community where guests could go for rest and refreshment of body and spirit. The visit of the team of Village Evangelists led by Bernard Jacob[25], then vicar of Ulverston, to four little Dales parishes north of Skipton in the spring of 1957, led them to discover a house for sale near the village of Kettlewell. For several miles

[24] In 1970 the College left Northwood and was reconstituted under a completely new governing body and system of management at Nottingham, where it began a flourishing new existence as St John's College, near Bramcote.
[25] 1921- ; Archdeacon of Kingston 1976.

beyond the small Dales town of Grassington two roads run parallel on either side of the River Wharf. About a mile short of Kettlewell, on the lowest slopes of the Great Whernside mountain which rises 1,600 feet above the valley, a turning off the easternmost road leads to a modest estate. Originally it consisted of a main house, four lodges, two farms, some land and local shooting and fishing rights. A natural wall of grey limestone immediately above the house on the side of the hill gave the house the name of Scargill. The Bishop of Bradford together with Harold Frankham[26], Bernard Jacob, and the Warden of Lee Abbey and one or two others viewed the prospect and later met in Harold Frankham's rectory in Manchester. Donald was at once enthusiastic over the possibilities the acquisition of the house would provide, but the diocese was very stretched financially. The call for money for extensions to the Cathedral shortly before his arrival, had been joined by his own appeal for new church building. Almost at once, three landowners approached him with the suggestion that they should form a consortium with him and combine to buy the whole estate and then divide it; the farms and sporting rights would go to the landowners; the house, four lodges, two cottages and seventy acres, which included a vegetable garden, to the Bishop. One of the three offered to advance the Bishop's share of the cost.

With loans, gifts and a scheme known as 'Scargill Partners' whereby a group of interested lay people gave regular contributions and publicity to the venture, Scargill was launched at the beginning of 1958. Despite, or perhaps because of, its isolation, it proved an immediate success, and the initiative was amply justified. The scenery was dramatic and provided adventurous activity for young people, while others could feel remote from the stresses of urban living. A Community of about seventeen Christians made their home there, under the guidance of a warden, sub-warden and chaplain; and courses, conferences, and houseparties were run most of the year for guests of all ages, walks of life and states of mind. Use of the house was not confined to members of the Bradford diocese; it was open to all, but those who came were predominantly from the north of England.

After a new dining room and other extensions had been built, the group who had planned Scargill asked their architect, George Pace, to design and build a chapel. He provided a brilliant structure of

[26] 1911- ; Rector of Middleton, Lancs. 1952-61; Provost of Southwark 1970-82; now retired.

glass and wood in the Scandinavian style which was not only exceptionally pleasing inside, but blended well with the rugged country setting. Jean Coggan put the foundation stone in its place on 23 May 1960 while her husband laid his hands upon it to bless it. Though the opening of Scargill was the culmination of the work and inspiration of a number of interested people, they are the first to say that the scheme would never have come to fruition without the continuous active participation of Donald and Jean Coggan. It would seem that they put a great deal of themselves into the enterprise because it was a place after their own hearts. They had come to admire the countryside of the north of the diocese, with its direct people, awesome beauty and lack of sophisticated diversions; Donald's rural origins were awakened and allied him to the surroundings. The conception they shared of the guiding and healing properties inherent in Christian home life made them feel that Scargill had a part to play in a torn world. The presence of Frank Lake, originator of Clinical Theology, among the planners was clearly important here, as also were Donald's happy memories of his days at Keswick.

Donald was full of ideas as to how Scargill could be used. A meeting at Old Jordans, Beaconsfield, in March 1959 when he was in the forefront of the discussions, decided that a College of Preachers be set up in England. It was to be designed on similar lines to that established in Washington, so well known to Donald in his Canadian days. The English version was to have no permanent base but be peripatetic. At once he decided that courses of preaching should be held at Scargill, and in November 1960 they became a reality. Donald remained Chairman of the Scargill Council long after the Bradford days were over, and Jean endowed the library in memory of her mother.

By the middle of 1958 Donald had completed the first half of his ministry at Bradford. More than a third of the sum which he was trying to raise in his Bishop's appeal had come in; the building of new churches and vicarages had begun; and the earlier spate of institutions had turned to one of laying foundation-stones. He described it on 5 June: a stone for a new church for Wrose had been laid on 15 February; at Barnoldswick on 10 May. At St James, Pudsey, the foundation-stone was to be laid two days later on 10 June. Work would begin on the new church at St Aidan, Horton Bank Top shortly; the foundation-stone-laying ceremony was planned for 20 September. The church of St John, Great Horton, destroyed by fire in 1956, was to reopen on 27 September. Plans for

Thorpe Edge new church and vicarage were before the Pastoral Committee and would soon go out to tender; a site for a new church on Tong housing estate was under scrutiny. The new vicarage at Thornbury, he announced, would be ready for occupation in the autumn; that at Ingleton even sooner; and a new vicarage at Gargrave was planned to take the place of one that was too big for modern conditions. The parish of Esholt had built a new hall to house the Sunday School, largely from its own funds, but augmented, which the Bishop was to dedicate the following week; the children would no longer need to meet in a garage.

Donald's drive and energy were behind this considerable list of achievements. But the most remarkable feature of his ministry at Bradford, in the opinion of countless clergy and laity, was his role as pastor, wherein he showed a good deal of development. He had an exceptional gift for names and faces, of care for the well-being of the men under his jurisdiction, their families and flocks. His approach was humble, unassuming, friendly, personal and direct, giving the impression that his only concern at a given moment was with the lot of the individual with whom he spoke. Donald preached often in parish churches, where he would meet incumbents and their families, play the piano in their homes (extremely well), and for ever thereafter remember them in detail. Loose ends would be followed up by personal letters; the examples offered are legion, and give credibility to the legends. A vicar's son, for instance, was shortly to sing in a voice trial to be a chorister at Ripon Cathedral; Bishop Coggan asked to be told of the result, and when the boy was unsuccessful he received a letter in the Bishop's own hand to tell him that he was not to regard his life as permanently blighted, there would be compensations in the future. This despatch of short personal notes was to continue even during the busiest of the Canterbury days, an indication of the pastoral basis of his ministry.

Only those who failed to work hard, who lacked order and application, or whose Services were sloppy, noisy or had particularly bad music, had anything to fear. 'He could be judgemental with those who did not come up to scratch.' Some of these may indeed have needed his help most; and here Donald may have been uncomprehending, but he had a high standard in everything done in the Lord's name. There were some complaints that he expected too much from his clergy, and that one reason was that he himself lacked parish experience, had never been an incumbent and therefore did not appreciate some of the pressures. The problems that difficult lay people could create was one of those areas; some felt that he lacked general exposure to the world of work: 'he had never experienced the hurly-burly'. They were criticisms which were to follow him to York and Canterbury, though it is difficult to imagine how he was expected to make up for the short-comings of his younger days in this respect. Unfortunately, as time went on, he had less and less time available for local, individual encounters; for instance, he hardly ever went out to private meals with lay people, or to social gatherings or entertainment. His engagements took him increasingly outside the diocese, to events on a national scale and of a kind remote from the more mundane experiences of ordinary human beings.

In the earlier days at Bradford, Donald as Bishop could not resist exercising his capacity as a teacher: he gave several courses of talks in centres in the diocese which varied throughout the years. These were among the engagements that became crowded out, but his diary shows that he continued to accept a number of formal invitations of a civic and commercial sort, which he thought important in order to indentify the Church with public affairs. He became well-known as an accomplished after-dinner speaker, addressing Rotary Clubs, the Bradford Textile Society, Building Societies, Chambers of Commerce and organs of Local Government, and was admired for his humour and openness. It is said that he found the enthusiasm for money-making as a way of life difficult to accept; however, he did not withdraw from association with the creators of wealth, but found opportunities, such as an article he wrote in the *Yorkshire Post*[27] on 'Dangers of Luxury', to express his own views. Donald was particularly adept at making a success of an occasion by producing a note of identification. His words of Hebrew at a dinner given by the large Jewish community in Bradford to honour their Lord Mayor (who was a Jew), and his drawing attention to a mistake in written Hebrew, caused his speech on the danger of anti-semitism to be received with especial enthusiasm.

After mid-1958 there were only three new areas where Donald introduced ideas of his own, as well as keeping up work he had already started; there was no time for more. One was Christian Stewardship, the second, relations between the indigenous population and immigrant minorities and the third a book, which was his only publication of the Bradford period.

Christian Stewardship, as a matter of giving back to God as

[27] 9 February 1961.

creator the fruits of his creation enjoyed by men, was an issue which came into the open in the late 1950s. Bishop Coggan introduced the subject to the Diocesan Conference of 4 June 1959:

> I think a new era is beginning to dawn in the Church of England in regard to the churchman's attitude to his money, or rather the money that has been entrusted to him by God. We are his stewards; nothing is ours; all is His.

Donald appointed a small Commission under the Chairmanship of the Archdeacon of Bradford to advise him on the application in the diocese of principles outlined in a book of Christian Stewardship produced by the Central Board of Finance. The Diocesan Conference of 10 December 1959 was devoted to talks by two experts and discussion. This remained very much Donald's method of introducing new ideas. It led to planned giving campaigns in those parishes who were interested in this course.

By the mid 1950s Bradford had received a considerable addition to its population in the way of immigrants from Asia. They were mainly from Pakistan, and were drawn by the opportunities of employment in the woollen industry. Certain problems of relationship with the local people occurred. Church and State made efforts to defuse the potentially inflammable situation, particularly where economic issues, such as means of livelihood and housing, were raised, and social issues such as education and varieties of culture. Earlier, Bishop Coggan had presided over a rally of two thousand people packed into a hall in Bradford, addressed by Bishop Trevor Huddleston of the Community of the Resurrection at Mirfield and then Bishop of Masasi, on the subject of Race Relations. 'Prayer and care for the dark folk living in these islands are two practical things to be done', he subsequently wrote to the Cambridge Missionary Fellowship[28]. When the York Convocation met in January 1959, the Bishop put a motion to full synod on the subject of Multi-Racial Communities. It commended 'the problems inherent in the current situation to the study of the Church and the welfare of these people to her especial care'. The five lines of approach he advocated, study of the problem, reconciliation, hospitality, clubs, centres, and employment of former missionaries as interpreters, were taken up by the media and received much notice. They were matters to which he returned many times and on which account he received rough treatment.

[28] 29.3.57.

Stewards of Grace[29] was a small book of just over a hundred pages which was concerned once more with the theme of preaching. There was general amazement when it appeared, as to how the Bishop could conceivably have had time to write anything more than his letters. He worked fast at his desk; his former secretary comments on the speed and flow of his mind: no wasted time, no coffee breaks. The book was designed as a work of practical help to parochial clergy, theological students, lay readers and fourthly 'the thoughtful listener who Sunday by Sunday "sits under the Word" '. It was dedicated to the clergy and lay-readers of the Diocese of Bradford 'my fellow-labourers in the Gospel of Jesus Christ'.

There were more foreign journeys: to Holland in September 1958 for the United Bible Societies and in May 1960 to Grenoble for a UBS conference for Latin American Countries; nearer at home, to Edinburgh in 1959, again in Bible Society interests; to Geneva in 1960 in preparation for the World Council of Churches meeting in New Delhi in 1961. Mercifully, there were some holidays abroad also; to France, Switzerland and Portugal. Engagements throughout England became greatly accelerated: sermons and addresses to schools, groups of clergy, diocesan conferences and so on, were much in demand. But it was due to the Archbishop of Canterbury that the heaviest and most continuous burdens fell upon the Bishop of Bradford.

Geoffrey Fisher's admiration for Donald Coggan was transparently obvious. They had much in common: one had been a Headmaster, the other Principal of a theological college; they were both authoritative, friendly, jocund, optimistic family men with a strong sense of purpose and concept of the part the Church should play in the life of the nation; neither ever spared himself. Ever since their paths had first crossed, everything Donald had done had received the Archbishop's approval and more. Archbishop Fisher, with approbation, likened the Bishop of Bradford to a man with a wheelbarrow: 'however much you pile on him, he goes on pushing'. He had asked Donald to lead the Commission to revise the Catechism; to this he added the Chairmanship of the Commission to revise the Psalter later in 1958; in 1960 came the request to head the Liturgical Commission. It seems that he mentioned to a wide circle that, on his retirement, he would like to be succeeded in the Chair of St Augustine by Bishop Coggan.

In the Autumn of 1960, Donald was summoned to an interview

[29] Hodder and Stoughton 1958.

by Harold Macmillan, then Prime Minister (temporarily at Admiralty House, as No 10 Downing Street was under renovation). The conversation, which lasted seventy minutes, was general in content; Donald gained no indication of a particular appointment in view. Early in January 1961, he was commanded by the Queen to preach at Sandringham. On the 17th he went with Jean to stay the night at Bishopthorpe with the Archbishop of York and Mrs Ramsey for the Northern Convocation, the invitation preventing their having to return to Bradford in winter for the night between the two days of the session. Early on the morning of 18 January Bishop Coggan was called to the telephone. He emerged, so it was noticed by those present, as white as a sheet. Not a word was said as he was driven to the Convocation to deliver a long, major speech on the revision of the Catechism. The call had been from Mr Macmillan. Archbishop Fisher had announced his intention to resign; Archbishop Ramsey was to go to Canterbury. The Prime Minister had asked Bishop Coggan to be the next Archbishop of York.

CHAPTER SEVEN *York*

'Bradford is proud'! *The Telegraph and Argus*[1] (the Bradford edition of the *Yorkshire Observer*) issued a fulsome leader once the news was made public that their Bishop was to be moved to a higher sphere. On all sides, inevitable sadness at his departure was tempered by pleasure that Bishop Coggan's remarkable achievements in his short period in the diocese had been recognized by his translation to primatial status.

It was not, except to him, an unexpected outcome. Various national newspapers had described him as a likely candidate for the Archbishopric of York, or possibly, even at his early age of 51, of Canterbury[2]. Bishop Stephen Bayne, who was consulted by the Prime Minister's Secretary for Patronage, considered that Donald could fulfil either role, but was perhaps somewhat young and relatively inexperienced for the last named. During only five years in the North, Donald had made a profound impression. It was agreed that he had 'achieved more than many would have done in twice or thrice the time'. His courage in launching his appeal, his building programme of new churches, his extensive visiting all over the diocese, not only in the southernmost parts, were all emphasized. 'I would like to thank him very sincerely for the wonderful work he has done for Bradford,' wrote the Lord Mayor. Churchmen followed with appreciation of their Bishop's unremitting labours, sense of purpose and optimism, friendly spirit and administrative gifts.

There has been a tendency, particularly noticeable during the Canterbury period, but also earlier, to assume that Donald Coggan began each new sphere of ministry with, if not some kind of master plan, at least a firm list of specific objectives. This would seem to be out of character; such assumptions have been made as a result of pure conjecture, and ignored the fact that no man was ever less concerned with personal achievement. Donald Coggan's aims on a new appointment were always expressed in very general terms

[1] 20 January 1961.
[2] The Bishops of London, Winchester, and Sheffield were all over 70: Hereford 69; Salisbury 68.

(which more than once led to such specific ones as were mentioned being exaggerated or taken out of context in the interest of dramatic impact). The Provost of Bradford (John Tiarks) recognized this in his personal appreciation of his Bishop.

> It was his expressed hope when he came among us that together we should get through the pressing financial and material problems facing the diocese as quickly as possible, so that under his leadership we could get on with the more vital work of deepening the spiritual life of the Church and of reaching the outsider.

In short, Donald's method would seem to have been to try to meet current problems and needs on an immediate basis, rather than as part of a long-term strategy. This emanated from his understanding of response to the promptings of the Holy Spirit, clearing the way for the Church's primary function of mission to the world. However, it did not mean that all his initiatives were invariably conceived *ad hoc*. Like his ideas for sermons and addresses, some of his schemes were of long gestation and had lain in a mental filing cabinet, to be released when he saw a need and opportunity. The pace of his labours in Bradford was dictated not by what Donald Coggan wanted personally to achieve there, nor by expectations of a short tenure, but by a determination quickly to solve problems that impeded the progress of the Kingdom. It was in this light that he regarded both the shortcomings in the diocese pointed out to him by Archbishop Garbett, and those he discovered himself.

Donald was greatly assisted by two factors: first that the depleted and dispirited nature of the diocese was visible and plain for all to see, so that he had a clear, unhindered run towards its reform and advance (his next assignment was in this respect of quite a different sort). Even his passion for order and decency in the conduct of Services[3], in regard to the speed of hymns, psalms and readings; congregational participation in responses and Amen; and correct treatment of collects and following of lessons, was accepted because a relationship had already been created. Secondly, Donald's own nature and capacities responded to the challenge, and it was well within his compass. His record both inside and outside the diocese of Bradford during the five years 1956-61 was indeed remarkable for initiative, thoroughness and involvement on a personal level.

It is not, therefore, surprising that the elevation to the Archbishopric of York was not the first attempt to give him wider responsibili-

---

[3] Set out with great clarity in *Bradford Diocesan Notes, December 1960*.

ties. In the autumn of 1958 he had been nominated for election to the Archbishopric of Sydney in Australia. If the newspaper reporting of the event can be relied upon, doubts were expressed as to Donald's suitability to lead this ultra-conservative evangelical diocese, since it had been rumoured that he had embraced some liberal tendencies; it was Hugh Gough, Bishop of Barking[4], who was elected. In 1960, Christopher Chavasse of Rochester pressed for Donald to succeed him there, but Archbishop Fisher, who clearly had other plans, no doubt prevented the request from going further.

During the months before the move to York, Donald's activities did not abate. A significant occasion was the visit of the former Archbishop of Canterbury to Bradford[5] following his retirement, in order to lay the cornerstone of the new East end at the Cathedral. It rested on two stones, one from the Cathedral of the mother diocese of Ripon and the other from the Metropolitical Cathedral of York. As we have already seen, the building programme alone during Donald's episcopate at Bradford had been formidable: first, new western transepts in the Cathedral, then plans for five new churches, the Centre at Scargill, new diocesan offices in 1959 and now a new chancel.

Outside the diocese, honours and engagements proliferated: they included an Honorary Fellowship at St John's College, Cambridge, (a considerable pleasure), becoming an Honorary Freeman of the Merchant Taylors' Company, and celebrations relating to the commemoration of the 350th anniversary of the Authorized Version and the completion of the New Testament of the New English Bible, with which Donald had been so closely associated as a member[6] of the Joint Committee. Culmination came with a service of thanksgiving in Westminster Abbey on 15 March 1961 at which Charles Dodd, as General Director and chief architect of the new translation, was the preacher. Donald was called upon a good deal to justify and interpret the need for a new version, which he did with fervour and conviction in sermons and writings.

As the days at Bradford came to a close, the Coggans were overwhelmed with expressions of gratitude and goodwill. Jean received her share of thanks, for it had been recognized that she had not spared herself in her efforts to identify with the lives of clergy families, and that her discipleship was as committed as was his.

---

[4] 1905- ; Bishop of Barking 1948. Primate of Australia 1959.
[5] 29 June 1961.
[6] Eventually Chairman.

Their silver wedding during the previous Autumn had brought them countless local wishes of affection and esteem; these were renewed, and letters flowed in from all over the world. Kenneth Sansbury, recently become Bishop of Singapore, provided one of the most telling in its grasp of current requirements[7].

> The more I think of the particular solution the P.M. has found to the problems of the two Archbishoprics, the more wise and right it seems. You and Michael will make a splendid pair – both devoted, both with gifts of scholarship and yet also with so much individuality that will complement the gifts of the other. Your easy manner and friendliness, your directness of approach to the problems and needs of the ordinary parish priest, your concern for Scargill and all it stands for, these things will supplement admirably the more 'magisterial' gifts of Michael. And you will be wonderfully placed to gain the confidence and give a lead to the Evangelicals . . . I want to see a strengthening of the *central* group – those who were responsible for the report *The Fulness of Christ* a decade ago, who have no journal and no organization to back them. I am sure you will give that group new confidence and will be the means of drawing towards it others of the Evangelical School whose main concern is a positive proclamation of the Gospel rather than a negative resistance to more 'Catholic' ways.

Kenneth Sansbury ended by supposing that Donald would need to give up the chairmanship of the Liturgical Commission on account of pressure from his new duties. It would be important, he wrote, to find someone wise to succeed him in that not very easy body (of which Sansbury himself had been a member). Donald replied with thanks for the insight that had been shown. Characteristically he indicated that it was his intention to retain the chairmanship, urged on by a 'kind of parting shot of great solemnity' by Geoffrey Fisher. It was typical of his incapacity to say no to extra burdens.

Donald's election by the Dean and Chapter of York took place on 26 June. On 5 July came its Confirmation by the Archbishop of Canterbury (now Michael Ramsey), and he paid Homage to the Queen on 7 July. It was therefore as Archbishop of York that he and Jean and their two daughters set off on a much needed and prolonged holiday at the beginning of the following week. They took sleepers to Innsbruck and travelled by train slowly through Austria to Salzburg. Retracing their steps a fortnight later, they went through the Brenner Pass and Dolomites to Venice. Visits to Padua, Ferrara, Ravenna, Florence, Arezzio, Perugia and Assisi followed. Eventually they reached Rome, where on Sunday 30 July

[7] 23.1.61; Archives Borthwick Institute, York.

they worshipped in the Anglican Church at 8 am and 10.30, and next day saw Codex B[8] in the Vatican Library. On 1 August they flew to Athens and made excursions to Eleusis, Corinth, Nauplia, Epidaurus, Mycenae and the Island of Poros. A flight to Tel Aviv took them to Israel, where Donald preached in Jerusalem on two successive Sundays, but otherwise he continued his holiday with visits to biblical sites in the Holy Land. The Coggan family returned to England on 15 August and reached their new home next day. For Donald and Jean, the long break on the outset of the new life must have provided refreshment and renewed vigour. Ann, 23 years old and Ruth, 21, had enjoyed a Grand Tour of almost 18th century proportions.

The enthronement of Donald Coggan as Archbishop of York took place in the Minster on Wednesday 13 September before a large congregation, with music, surroundings and ceremonial of considerable splendour. There were also some highly characteristic touches for those who were sufficiently tuned in to Donald's wavelength to be able to recognize them. The text of his sermon was, as he explained, deliberately down to earth, taken from 1 Corinthians 9.16: 'Necessity is laid upon me; yea woe is unto me if I preach not the gospel'. It was for him a significant and familiar theme, evocative of his days in Canada, as the motto of Wycliffe College, Toronto; moreover these were words engraved on his pectoral cross given to him on his consecration by his students at the London College of Divinity. If such a gospel were to be proclaimed by the clergy, two needs, the Archbishop said, must be supplied: a fresh awareness of God the Holy Spirit, and secondly a fresh understanding of the Bible. He urged on every Christian soul in the building and each one listening beyond, with phrases of a kind to which members of the York diocese would soon grow accustomed: 'Back to the love of Jesus our Lord; *forward* to a new obedience to the Holy Spirit; *out* to a needy world in pity and compassion.' He moved to the great west door at the close to bless the people gathered outside. To the amazement of many he was seen to be wearing a cope and mitre[9]. Where was the Evangelical Archbishop?

To ask that question was a failure of understanding that betrayed ignorance of Donald's outlook. His concern was not with trifles such as clothing, but with what he saw as the essentials of the faith and the authority to proclaim them. The office of Primate, not his own

---

[8] 4th-century MS of the Greek Bible, known as *Codex Vaticanus.*
[9] He had worn a cope on ceremonial occasions in Bradford, but never before a mitre.

person or whims, was always the criterion. (His insistence on being preceded by the primatial cross had a like significance.) It has often been commented that as he moved among congregations on ceremonial occasions in such apparel he seemed surprised in his humble way to find himself in those circumstances, as if he thought himself in a dream from which he would wake. High office changed Donald Coggan hardly at all; 'to keep himself unspotted from the world'[10] was an injunction he continued to obey.

But the sphere Donald entered as he emerged from the Minster at York, and his function in it, had changed, and was of a different kind from any in his previous experience. There was in addition a major contrast to the early days at Bradford, in that he was now following a predecessor much revered and of very great stature. True to form, he sought neither to emulate Michael Ramsey, nor to pursue deliberately different policies. Donald Coggan continued to be himself. He described[11] the nature of his demanding new roles in terms of a series of widening circles: the diocese, the Province, the Anglican Communion and the world-wide Church. In each he now had a responsibility. Spectators viewing his work-load in each marvelled; few saw the whole picture or there would have been even greater astonishment.

The image of concentric circles provides a useful framework within which to see Donald Coggan's ministry as Archbishop of York: and the largest circle provides the best starting point. It is ironical that one who spent his youth in secluded and rather static circumstances should become, after he was fifty years of age, the world's most widely-travelled Church leader. Only two months after his enthronement, and shortly after his first meeting as a Privy Councillor on 25 September and introduction to the House of Lords on 8 November, he was off to New Delhi for the Third Assembly[12] of the World Council of Churches. It was his first experience of a meeting of the World Council and first visit of a great many to India. The impact that this land of contrasts made upon him he described in a later sermon[13]: a culture that went back two thousand years, and the beauty of sunshine and deep blue sky, of flower and bird, of local art and architecture, impressed themselves deeply upon him. He was also mindful of the high rate of illiteracy, which problem

---

[10] General Epistle of James 1.26.
[11] *Convictions*, p.23.
[12] The two previous sessions had been at Amsterdam 1948 and Evanston (USA) 1954.
[13] ibid., pp. 83-8.

was especially close to his heart. He addressed the Assembly on December 1 in order to make known one of his main enthusiasms: not only the provision of copies of the Scriptures, their translation and distribution, but the whole matter of developments in reading ability. 'When the infant Church of Jesus Christ went out into the world, it went with a book in its hand. That book was what we now call the Old Testament . . . The book in the early days of the Church became a book of two Testaments.' In whole or in part it had been translated into 1,150 languages; but another 1,000 languages, mutually unintelligible, remained without the Scriptures, a matter of urgency. He spoke of the fact that each year saw vast numbers of new readers, and those not only children. Here was a challenge that should be met by the provision of Christian literature[14].

Donald never became a World Council figure in the manner of some English Bishops, notably George Bell, William Temple, Oliver Tomkins[15]. They bore the heat and burden of the early years when the going was hard; their international outlook was of long standing, while he was a relative newcomer to this scene. But it would be unfair to suggest that Donald simply used the Assembly as a platform on which to air his own views, or his stay in India to further his other interests. He certainly made the most of his visit with a host of engagements; for Bible Society work and meetings of various kinds. But this disinclination to waste time was his standard practice. He was genuinely impressed by the Assembly, its variety of Christians of diverse traditions from all parts of the globe: 625 official delegates and as many again in other capacities. The Orthodox Churches of Russia, Bulgaria, Romania and Poland sent delegates for the first time; it was also the first Assembly to which the Roman Catholic Church sent official observers. Donald warmed to the theme, 'Christ, the Light of the World', sub-divided into three emphases: unity – that the Churches should strive for visible as well as theological unity, witness, and service. He was in the last named section and commented:

> Again and again we found ourselves confronted by the fact that Jesus did not pursue the way of power – indeed He constantly refused it – but He went the way of the humble Servant of God. As preacher, as teacher, as leader, *He ministered* to the crying heads of those around Him.

[14] Donald Coggan's lively interest in this area led to his establishment of the Archbishop of York's Fund, and participation in the *Feed the Minds* campaign, see p.139.

[15] 1908- ; Bishop of Bristol 1959-75.

This to Donald was the message of New Delhi as he comprehended it.

The following year, the World Council's Division of Mission and Evangelism held a week's conference in August in Paris which Donald attended, preceded by a short holiday with Jean at Chenonceaux on the Loire. Few of his visits abroad were so leisurely. By flying from Manchester airport it was possible to reach most destinations in western Europe the same day. This he did in September, when he made his first visit to Germany. He delivered two lectures, one in each half of Berlin on behalf of the Bible Society, and met its leaders in both East and West of the city. True to form, he added other engagements during the four-day visit: a service of Confirmation at St George's Anglican Church in West Berlin, dinner with the Lutheran Bishop Otto Dibelius, whom he had met in Delhi, and a meal with members of the British Army stationed in Germany.

The final overseas engagement of 1962 was a return visit in October to Uganda, where several of the clergy had been his pupils. The occasion was an invitation by the government of Uganda to the celebrations attending Independence. Sunday 7 October was the heaviest of his programme: he celebrated the Holy Communion in Namirembe Cathedral at 8 am and later in the day preached at three other churches; the last time at Makerere University.

1963 was a decisive year for the Anglican Communion: there were developments, redeployment and reorganization in which Donald Coggan played a significant part, and which was to give him a wider experience of the constituent Churches than any previous Archbishop. Since his first visit to Latin America in 1957, Donald had become particularly interested in the matter of Anglican presence in that continent with its huge unchurched millions. A contributory reason might at one time have been that Anglican missionary activity there had tended to be on Evangelical lines, but his increasing response to wider Christian traditions reduces the weight of this argument. Acquaintance with Sir Kenneth Grubb[16] will have been important, and Donald's meetings and conversations with Bishop Stephen Bayne, with whom he was clearly on very good terms, and who also viewed the South American situation sympathetically, certainly reinforced his concern. A resolution they helped to secure at the Lambeth Conference of 1958, calling for Anglican advance in South America, gave it substance. When, therefore,

[16] 1900-80; Chairman, House of Laity.

plans were made to hold a pan-Anglican Consultation on this development at Cuernavaca in Mexico from 20-24 January 1963, Archbishop Coggan was a not unexpected choice as Chairman. Other members were Arthur Lichtenberger, then Presiding Bishop of the American Episcopal Church, Archbishop H.H. Clarke of Rupertsland (Canada), Bishop Eric Trapp, Secretary of the Society for the Propagation of the Gospel, Gilbert Baker, General Secretary of the Overseas Council of the Church Assembly[17]. It was not Donald Coggan's last visit to Latin America. Moreover he gave expression to his continuing commitment in a letter[18] to Cyril Tucker[19] who asked Donald to preach at his consecration as Bishop in the Argentine in the Autumn of 1963:

> How I wish I could accept your invitation
> (a) for Auld Lang Syne's sake,
> (b) to say, in the very act, how deeply concerned I am about Latin America . . . the diary says a plain 'No' . . . I've got you and Howell[20] entered up in it, however, so that at 7.45 in Bishopthorpe Chapel that morning we shall be praying for you. The pre-Toronto meetings are good (London, Ontario). Out of them emerged a document which we shall be presenting here on Saturday. If followed up it might alter the whole 'missionary' picture . . . Latin America is well in the picture. I think a new day is dawning, God prepare and guide you as you take your central part in these affairs. Pray much; think big; plan boldly!

But before his participation in the Toronto Congress, Donald had some further assignments out of England. At the beginning of May he made a four-day visit to Northern Ireland and preached at the Cathedrals in Belfast, Down (twice) and Downpatrick. This was closely followed by a major tour in the Far East for the United Bible Societies (though he was able to squeeze in other engagements also). He attended an All Asia Regional Conference in Bangkok, then left for a full programme in the Philippines and Singapore (as guest of the Sansburys), en route for Japan. The UBS, like the Anglican Communion, was experiencing change and development, and this was a crucial period of growth. A report written thirteen years later[21] described the process: the years up to 1957 had seen the need for consultation between the national Bible Societies; between 1957

---

[17] Later Bishop of Hong Kong 1966-80.
[18] Written from the Anglican Congress at Toronto 14.8.63.
[19] 1911- ; Vicar of Holy Trinity Cambridge 1957-63.
[20] Kenneth Walter Howell, who was being consecrated Bishop in Chile, Bolivia and Peru.
[21] 6 September 1976; Dr Ulrich Fick, General Secretary, to Archbishop Coggan.

and 1963 the emphasis turned to co-ordination: the implementation of programmes developed by consultation. It came to a head at a Council meeting at Rikko University in Tokyo, where Donald took the chair and in an unusually impassioned speech which spoke of the 'hunger of the mind, a hunger for ideas, for ideologies, for a way of life to live by, for truth', launched a campaign called *God's Word for a New Age*. Its object was to increase the world circulation of the Scriptures from roughly 50 million copies a year to 150 million by the end of 1966, in order to keep pace with the rise of population and the increase of literacy. For the next three years Donald worked to achieve the target with a number of personal initiatives.

He reached home at the beginning of June, the Japanese visit having been concluded by engagements in Osaka and Kobe and an honorary Doctorate of Divinity from St Paul's University, Tokyo. Within two days he was back in Belfast to preach at Clogher Cathedral in order to celebrate the 1400th anniversary of the arrival in Ireland of St Columba; he preached at Derry Cathedral the next day. Six weeks later another Canadian tour claimed him, and he left London for Winnipeg, Vancouver, Kamloops, Jasper, Banff, Calgary, Regina, Saskatoon; an intensive three weeks of sermons, lectures, TV interviews and addresses to clergy and lay people. On arrival at Toronto he made straight for Huron College, London Ontario, where the Advisory Council on Missionary Strategy (Primates and others) was about to meet before the Anglican Congress. Certain papers were before the Council which had their origin in a Missionary Executives' Conference of the preceding week, when Bishop Trapp, Gilbert Baker, David Paton[22], J.V. Taylor[23] and Max Warren were among the most prominent and experienced of the group. Bishop Stephen Bayne, who had been chairman, gave the Advisory Council a brief review of the proceedings of the week before. The chief gain had been a draft paper on mutual responsibility for Mission which envisaged a move towards responsible partnership between the Anglican Churches. It underwent much discussion and several revisions: the term 'mission' came out, and what was finally proposed amounted to a new form of Anglican Communion.

The paper was then submitted to the Consultative Body of the

[22] 1913- ; Former missionary in China; Secretary Church Assembly Council for Ecumenical Co-operation.
[23] 1914- ; CMS Africa Secretary 1959-63; General Secretary 1963-74; Bishop of Winchester 1975-85.

Lambeth Conference, the Primates, who decided that under their names, after final editing, it should be reported to the Congress shortly to begin at Toronto. Thereafter it should be transmitted to member Churches for appropriate action. The aspect of mutuality contained in the document was further strengthened by a decision by the Primates to meet every two years.

The Archbishop of York was chosen to join the final drafting committee, headed by Leonard Beecher, Archbishop of East Africa; in addition he was asked to read the document to the Congress. On Saturday 17 August, to great effect, Donald introduced *Mutual Responsibility and Interdependence in the Body of Christ*[24]. The Church, he said, was not primarily a debating society,

> it is the Body of Christ at work in God's world and at war against God's enemies. The Anglican Communion has its part in that war. It is vital that we hear what God has to say to us in Toronto in 1963.

He then read the final version of the document. It called for new forms of unity and obedience: for a comprehensive study of needs, commitment of funds on a strong, sustained and expanding pattern of giving in order to support the vast development that was called for in training, buildings, needs of new provinces, manpower. The nature of the Anglican Communion should be faced squarely, and

> the implications for all of us of the one Lord whose single mission holds us together in one Body. To use the words 'older' or 'younger', or 'sending' or 'receiving' with respect to the Churches is unreal and untrue in the world and in our Communion. Mission is not the kindness of the lucky to the unlucky, it is mutual, united obedience to the one God whose mission it is.

It was a historic moment, and for Donald in particular. In a Church Assembly debate[25] in the Autumn he disclosed an episode in the final drafting process. The MRI document was designed to end 'the peace of the Lord be always with you'. He suggested, somewhat typically, that a more adequate version would be 'the disturbance of the Holy Ghost be with you'. An Anglican compromise was reached: 'the power of the Lord Jesus be with you'.

Canada made some further claims upon him: several preaching engagements and three lectures to Wycliffe Alumni[26], before he and Jean escaped to a short holiday in isolated countryside near

[24] Edited by Stephen F. Bayne, Jr., SPCK 1965.
[25] 6 November 1963; Report of Proceedings Vol. XLIII no 3, p.609-12.
[26] On the use of the Psalms as prayer; St Paul on prayer; St Paul at prayer.

Montreal. There were meetings in London the morning he returned after a night flight.

In April 1964, Donald attended the gathering in Canterbury of the 'Wider Episcopal Fellowship': bishops of Churches in Communion with, but not part of the Anglican family. This was followed by a meeting of Anglican Primates. In May he preached at the University of Aberdeen and in the Episcopal Cathedral.

The commitment which Donald had made in Japan, as to the provision of copies of the Scriptures, he took steps to implement in June 1964. He called a conference of younger leaders of the Churches to him at Driebergen in Holland: 100 came from 48 countries, half of these from Asia, Africa and Latin America. A few weeks previously, the Archbishop had summoned the General Secretary of the UBS and Laton Holmgren, then Chairman of the Executive Committee, to Bishopthorpe to discuss the agenda. One of the most important outcomes of the Driebergen meeting was the impetus it gave to the beginning of talks on the provision of the Scriptures with Roman Catholics, notably with Cardinal Bea whom Laton Holmgren met at the Vatican Secretariat for Promoting Christian Unity. Later he saw Cardinal Willebrands also. Fr Walter Abbott, SJ, became Cardinal Bea's representative for the continuation of combined Bible work; the production of a Common Bible was mooted. Eventually two hundred and forty-two common Bibles in various languages were published.

Donald Coggan's second initiative was to launch a campaign in the Autumn of 1964 which he called 'The Archbishop of York's Fund to Feed the Minds of Millions'. The intention was to find a million pounds to finance publishing and book distribution projects in co-operation with other denominations and Societies, for the provision of Christian and other literature mainly to developing countries. It was to grow and develop as a continuing movement under the title *Feed the Minds*. Donald remained closely associated with it and he secured the patronage of Queen Elizabeth the Queen Mother for the cause, to give it support and status.

On a five-day visit to Germany in October 1965, when he visited Herr Willy Brandt and British Army Units, Archbishop Coggan had a further opportunity to speak of Bible distribution at a rally of ten thousand people in the Deutschlands Halle in West Berlin in the presence of two Lutheran Bishops[27]. Speaking on the rally's theme 'Millions throughout the world need Bibles', he said that it

[27] Bishop Otto Dibelius of Berlin and Bishop Hanns Lilje of Hannover.

depended on the Churches what the masses in developing countries learning to read and write would be given as reading matter. It was a theme to which he returned repeatedly; and immediately on this occasion, to a group of clergy in East Berlin.

Donald Coggan spent the 10th anniversary of his Consecration back in South America in January 1966 in San Paulo, Brazil, presiding over a Conference of leaders in the Anglican Communion who made plans for the future. He wrote in the York Diocesan Leaflet[28]:

> Real advance has been made during these three years . . . further growth will take place . . . it is coming to be realized that we cannot leave this vast area simply in the care of the Church in the United States . . . The Roman Catholic Church cannot compass so huge a task and it realizes this to the full. As we enter more significantly into this field of opportunity, we do so with no desire to proselytize, but with a great passion to make Christ known to millions of people hitherto unchurched. It was the expressed desire of the San Paulo Conference that . . . work in Latin America should be planned on an ecumenical basis of co-operation.

The decrees of the Second Vatican Council (recently ended) made this a possibility.

On 22 April he went by plane to Cairo, where the main event was the anniversary of the Consecration of the Anglican Cathedral. He then flew to Amman in Jordan and drove via Jericho to Jerusalem where the Lambeth Consultative Body met for a few days. There were some interviews with local dignitaries: the Armenian Patriarch, the Governor of Jerusalem, Archbishop A. Campbell MacInnes[29], Bishop Najib Atallah Cuba'in[30].

1966 marked the 150th anniversary of the founding of the American Bible Society and the 50th of the UBS, and there was a considerable programme in New York to mark these occasions. Donald arrived straight from the airport to a large gathering and mounted the stage at the Philharmonia Hall. He then led a crowd of three thousand people down Broadway to the new Bible House, which he blessed standing on the spiral staircase leading from the lobby to the second floor library. In his major speech at the Waldorf Astoria hotel on 13 May, under the title 'Obstacles and Opportunities', he spoke first of achievements (the American Bible Society had just presented to President Johnson the 750-millionth copy of

---

[28] No.453, for March 1966.
[29] Anglican Archbishop in Jerusalem 1952-69.
[30] Anglican Bishop in Jordan, Lebanon and Syria 1958-75.

Scripture), and then turned to the torn world of walls, referring to the one in Berlin which he had re-visited so recently. He spoke of opportunities presented to Christians by obstacles.

> And when the Word goes out then the Church is born, and when the Church is born then healing begins in a broken society, and the walls get broken down, and then God's plan for His world begins to take shape.

There followed a sermon in New York Cathedral, a journey to Detroit, more sermons, press interviews, TV and radio, three McMath lectures[31], dinner at the Roman Catholic University, then a flight to Buckhill Falls, Pennsylvania to take the chair at a three day United Bible Societies Council meeting. Donald was planning for more than the Province of York. Considerable organizational reconstruction of the Bible Societies had been carried out; the world sphere was divided under four regional offices which 'replaced the mother-daughter or headquarters-branch office system of communication'. In order that the Bible Societies should not work on their own, 'but closely connected with Christian communities', co-operation became the keynote of the next phase.

Immediately, there was more to come: meetings in Boston, supper with Dr Eugene Carson Blake, General Secretary of the World Council of Churches, and attendance at the General Assembly of the United Presbyterian Church; a breakfast address; on to Cambridge, Massachusetts, to speak to the students of the Episcopal Theology Seminary; thence to Princeton, Newark; a sermon in Hartford Cathedral, a Quiet Hour for clergy, and at last the overnight flight to Manchester.

There was no holiday until the end of July, when respite came in the shape of nearly a month in Ireland: Killala, Kenmare, Co. Kerry, Galway and Armagh. But the year's travelling was not over: visits to the Churches of Denmark, Sweden and Finland took place during a fortnight in September. Preaching the University sermon at Cambridge in October, Archbishop Coggan drew on his experiences during the year and spoke of the challenge of the world-wide increase in literacy.

In 1967 came a long journey of combined purpose and heavy programme: some Bible Society work, an intention to be in touch with the Church of each country visited, calls upon British forces overseas. The itinerary covered a good deal of the Far East, Australia and New Zealand. Donald and Jean, with Michael Turn-

---

[31] Later published as *The Prayers of the New Testament*, Hodder and Stoughton, 1967.

bull the domestic chaplain, left England on 16 February, and they did not return until 5 April. It is clear from what Donald wrote that it was the meetings with unsophisticated congregations in India that were most enjoyed: New Delhi, Bombay, Cochin, Kottayam and Ernakulam in Kerala, Vellore, Madras, Calcutta.

> There are many places where the Church is a tiny minority, and the opposing forces of Hinduism, Islam, or sheer stark materialism are almost overwhelmingly strong. Nevertheless, we 'found the Church there' in South India where I dedicated a tiny thatched church structure erected overnight for the people of the local village . . . in Borneo where I celebrated in the chapel of the Bishop of Kuching whose jungle terrain was such that it took him twenty-four hours to reach an outpost church forty miles away; in RAF stations on lonely islands in the China Sea. One could go on. Suffice it to say: thank God for the Anglican Communion in which the worship of word and sacrament goes on quietly, steadily, persistently[32].

From Bangkok the Coggans flew to Singapore and on to Auckland, New Zealand for a tour which covered both North and South Island: Napier, Rotorua, Ohinemutu, Ngongotaha, Hamilton, Nelson, Wellington, Dunedin, Christchurch; these were no mere courtesy calls; addresses and sermons, retreats, conferences were required. At the beginning of March they arrived in Australia. Here the programme changed, for it was the 150th anniversary of the Australian Bible Society, and it was as President of the UBS that Donald spoke for the most part. Four days in Sydney and Paramatta were followed by a flight and quick visit to Hobart, Tasmania; then to Launceston, Melbourne, Adelaide, and to Perth, 1,500 miles away, where he delivered a paper on *The Relevance of the Bible for Today* at the University of Western Australia[33]; then two thousand miles back to Brisbane in the East, Canberra, and Sydney again en route for Singapore. A Royal Air Force Andover aircraft flew Donald to Kuching in Sarawak and to Labuan. In Malaya, small five-seater Beaver planes took him into the interior, to Kluang, Seremban and other small locations; then back to Singapore by helicopter for two days at the Cathedral and with the Royal Navy. On his return he told his diocese of the disparities of wealth and opportunities that he had seen.

By May, Donald, with Jean, was back in the United States. The atmosphere and pace of American life seemed to give him increased

[32] York Diocesan Leaflet No 467.
[33] *Convictions* pp.221-233.

energy; his programme was once again intensely demanding and included an address at the General Theological Seminary, sermons in the Cathedral of the Incarnation on Long Island, a Quiet Day for clergy and Bible Society activities. The occasion of Canada's Centennial year took the Coggans North to the Bible Society of Canada and meetings of the General board. Other engagements naturally followed, even a flight over nearly two thousand miles of terrain from Toronto to Edmonton, in order to return once more to Peace River in the diocese of Athabasca, scene of his activities as a young man more than twenty years before. The demands laid upon him were even greater than they had been earlier and it is a cause of astonishment that he was able to maintain the pressure, but the loyalty that continued to be offered to him was a powerful stimulus. Visits to Ottawa and Expo '67 in Montreal rounded off the Canadian tour.

Consultations in preparation for the Lambeth Conference of 1968 took the Archbishop of York several times to London in the preceding Autumn, but before it took place Donald was required to attend another Assembly, that of the World Council, meeting on this occasion at Uppsala in Sweden. Beginning on 4 July 1968, it was on a larger scale than ever before, with two thousand members and visitors. The biblical theme was 'Behold I make all things new'. There was a large gathering of Orthodox which caused the Uppsala Assembly to be the most ecumenical so far. Another salient factor in this direction was the considerable size of the party of official observers from the Roman Catholic Church, fourteen in number. Fr. Roberto Tucci, SJ, who gave an address, said that Roman Catholics 'no longer regard themselves as outside spectators who are indifferent or merely curious' but as engaged on a similar quest for unity.

Donald Coggan played no major role in the Assembly as part of the delegation from the Church of England and Archbishop of York, except in his recommendation that at least some of the youth participants (135) who were there for the first time, should be accorded increased status. They were critical of the conservatism of the proceedings, but their views had few accepted channels of communication. As World President of the UBS, however, Donald spoke as part of the Bible Society presentation, following a film shown on many screens entitled 'This Book-This World'. 'The Church must always go on her mission to the world with the Bible in her hand,', he said, and called for a plentiful supply in all languages. He drew attention to the encouragement which the Roman Catholic bishops were giving to Bible-reading and to those sections in the Constitution on Divine Revelation promulgated during the Second Vatican Council, which stressed the need for a Common Bible. From the WCC meeting Donald hurried back to England for the Lambeth Conference, which, with 467 Archbishops and Bishops, seventy-five official observers and twenty-five Consultants, opened a few days later, on 25 July, but he did not forget the lessons of Uppsala. The speeches of Lady Jackson (Barbara Ward) who pointed out that eighty per cent of the world's wealth was in the hands of twenty per cent of the world's population, and of the American Negro writer James Baldwin on 'White Racism and World Community' made a profound impression. He spoke later[34] in the Northern Convocation:

> We who are *Christians* should take action in regard to racism *not* because we want to avoid a blood-bath in America or Africa or Birmingham or Bradford, but precisely because we are Christians who believe that the black man has rights to certain standards of living by reason of the fact that the same God made him as made us and our children, and the same Christ died for him. This . . . is the *theology*, the religion, lying behind the politics and the action.

Donald was to have a major part in the proceedings of the Lambeth Conference. The theme, the Renewal of the Church, reflected that of the World Council Assembly just ended, and was treated under three main headings: Faith, Ministry and Unity. As Archbishop of York he provided the main presentation of the section on Ministry on the opening day; he chaired the discussions that followed on this topic, and bore a good deal of responsibility in detail for the drafting of the resolutions that emerged. It was for him a happy choice, for the concept had been for many years close to his heart and he viewed his whole life entirely within its terms.

He began in a characteristic and Pauline way:

> Ministry – the work of the servant, the slave (doulos) of Christ, the man or woman who has been laid hold of by Christ . . . the man who, to a greater or lesser extent is finding that slavery to be in fact his freedom . . . this is our theme.

These were self-revelatory words, important because they make clear a good deal about the speaker, and go a long way towards explaining his motivation and style of living.

St Paul described his ministry in terms of proclamation 'we proclaim

Messiah Jesus as Lord' – that is the *first* thing, the assertion of the crown rights of the Redeemer, the Lordship over all life of Him who was the archetype of all ministry; and *secondly*, we proclaim 'ourselves as your servants, because of Jesus'. Here is a strange combination of ideas; who would proclaim himself a slave of man? But this is precisely what the Christian does; here is his only pride. He does it 'because of Jesus', that is to say, because of what he is (the Servant of the Lord, who washed men's feet), and because of what He has done in calling and commissioning others to follow in his steps.

Much had been written, he went on, since the last Lambeth Conference, on the subject of the Servant Church and of the Christian as 'the man for others'. But he must be more than a humanitarian, he must be 'the man with God's Word for others'. One who ministers finds himself in a position of tension which by its very nature can be creative.

As he engages in the two functions for which in Christ he is being recreated, namely worship and mission, he finds himself very much one of the men to whom he ministers. He cannot stand apart from them. If he is *justus*, he is still *peccator*. Though redeemed, he is still part of this groaning creation. He is bound up in the bundle of life with all the rest. He, like them, is an inquirer, a learner, a listener . . . But . . . he is also a man of deep and profound convictions. He has been 'apprehended by Christ Jesus my Lord' and that apprehension . . . is the very essence of his ministry. 'Give me a place where I can stand, and I will move the world.' He has such a place. It is the Cross of Christ.

He spoke of three areas with which the subcommittees on Ministry would be confronted in particular: the office of Deacon in relation to its primitive place as a distinctive order in the Church; the order of deaconesses; and thirdly the whole matter of the ministry of women. He called for advance in attitude in this sphere, and gave a clear sign of his own thinking and the initiatives that he would be taking in the next decade.

In relation to the Conference as a whole, Donald Coggan pressed for the needs of Latin America to be made more specific so that they could be more adequately met; for increased recognition of the problem of illiteracy. His diary during these Lambeth days was a full one, for he took the opportunity to meet and speak with many overseas bishops; the flat in Westminster placed at the disposal of the Archbishop of York by the Church Commissioners proved a useful base. He made good use of the presence of his former vice-principal from LCD times, Ralph Dean, who acted as Episcopal Secretary of the Conference.

A short visit to South Africa and Kenya from 18 November to 2 December rounded off the year. It began in Durban and Johannesburg and ended in Nairobi. At a press conference in Durban, Archbishop Coggan declared that Christianity could not be separated from politics. He proceeded to attend a packed multi-racial rally on the subject of 'Christianity's challenge today' where there was singing in the Zulu tongue; he attended a Provincial Synod, and in Johannesburg visited Soweto township and met the Reverend Beyers Naude[35] and Mrs Helen Suzman, MP[36].

In Kenya, there were meetings with the Church Army and the Bible Society, three addresses to clergy and a diocesan synod, lectures to Church workers and sixth formers in a school of twenty-six different races, two Cathedral sermons and a talk to a thousand African Sunday School pupils. Jean Coggan carried out her own programme for part of the tour, and visited hospitals, housing projects and local industry.

An important event that concerned Donald Coggan in the Church beyond his own Province came with the visit to York in April 1969 of Leon-Joseph, Cardinal Suenens, Archbishop of Malines/Brussels, Primate of Belgium, which had lasting consequences. In the years 1922-1926, unofficial conversations on the subject of Christian reunion took place at Malines between Cardinal Mercier, then Archbishop, with some Roman Catholic theologians, and a group of Anglicans headed by Charles Lindley Wood, 2nd Viscount Halifax[37], whose family home, Garrowby, was in Yorkshire. On the death of the Belgian Cardinal, the English peer received, by legacy, his episcopal ring. In order to keep alive the link between Malines and York, Lord Halifax's heir had the ring set in the stem of a 16th-century silver-gilt Flemish chalice which he gave to the Minster. It was this connection which Cardinal Suenens came to renew by presenting a plaque from his archdiocese to commemorate the conversations, and to dedicate it with the Archbishop of York. A plaque from the English side had already been placed in Malines Cathedral in 1966.

The visit was a considerable success in that the two Archbishops liked each other and a warm personal relationship was the result. Cardinal Suenens and some of his suite stayed at Bishopthorpe; he preached in the Minster at a service of Mattins, then both Archbis-

[35] Director of the Christian Institute.
[36] Member of the Progressive Party.
[37] 1839-1934.

hops changed into cope and mitre and stood side by side for the dedication of the plaque. The dinner party at Garrowby was a happy occasion, for the Earl[38] and Countess of Halifax were particular admirers of the Coggans.

It was therefore no surprise that a return visit to Belgium was planned in 1971, when Archbishop Coggan, accompanied by his wife, the Earl and Countess of Halifax and a small suite, went to Malines on 14 May. An atmosphere of friendly informality again prevailed: there were some prepared speeches, but also a good deal of unofficial talk on common diocesan problems. A mass in the Mercier Chapel was celebrated by Cardinal Suenens in English and he spoke simply of the ways to unity: holiness and closeness to Christ. Nothing could have endeared him more to Donald Coggan. A visit was included to the monastery of the Eastern rite at Chevêtogne, where the Litany was sung in Slavonic and French. All this was outside Donald's previous experience, but he seemed to enjoy himself and adapt to what was expected of him

On Sunday 16 May Archbishop Coggan preached at the Eucharist in the Anglican Church in Brussels on 'The Grace of our Lord Jesus Christ, the love of God and the fellowship of the Holy Spirit'. The Cardinal and the Orthodox Archbishop in Belgium were both present, and a visit for lunch to the Convent School at Tildonk followed. Donald spoke briefly to the few Anglican girls, and then a large concourse filled the chapel, prominent among them the five hundred pupils in sailor suits and white gloves. The Cardinal, Archbishop Coggan and Orthodox Archbishop sat with other clergy including Reformed pastors, for the Ecumenical Liturgy of the Word: good singing, readings, litany, prayers and sermon by the Cardinal. Many in Belgium had waited a long time for such a moment.

The last day's events began at the Catholic University of Louvain, where Donald addressed a large gathering of academics and students of the American College on 'Unity and the Scriptures'. He spoke of the need for the prayerful joint study of Scripture, joint biblical research and translation, work together with the College of Preachers, and co-operation within the Bible Societies. In the questions that followed he was asked what he saw as the next stage in Anglican/Roman Catholic relations, since there was already common worship, friendship and work. He replied, 'Is the Holy Spirit leading us to make a breakthrough with Intercommunion? Is

[38] 1912-1980; 2nd Earl and 4th Viscount.

it the case that we are held up on other points because we have not taken this step, without which they will remain insoluble?' In answer to another questioner Archbishop Coggan replied that fear was what kept most men apart. Lunch with the King and Queen of the Belgians completed a visit which was memorable on several counts. Mutual confidence had been increased; Archbishop Coggan was relaxed with his Roman Catholic hosts (who were to pay many further visits to York) with a possible caveat of the car journeys: the Belgian clergy drive at an average of seventy miles an hour on their long straight country roads.

There were to be eight more official journeys out of England in the York days, and even on holidays opportunities to meet local leaders were not missed. Thus it was that a family holiday to Cyprus, Israel, the Greek Islands, Turkey and Istanbul in the Summer of 1969 yielded meetings with Archbishop Makarios, the Mayor of Jerusalem, the Greek Patriarch, members of the Israeli government including Abba Eban, the Foreign Minister, the head of the Hebrew University, and in Istanbul the Oecumenical Patriarch. In December, Donald made a rapid week-end visit to Paris for two sermons, dinners, and a meeting with leaders of the Église Reformée.

By the beginning of 1970, Donald had been Archbishop of York for nine years. An invitation from the Trustees of the Missionary Lectureship founded in memory of Alexander Duff, the pioneer of missionary education, gave him the chance of a certain respite. In order to write the lectures (which later became the substance of the book *Word and World*)[39], he needed to have greater leisure and circumstances of quiet than his own surroundings gave him. He decided to make an extended visit to South Africa and accept the offer of hospitality that had been offered there in which to begin to write his book, and also (there was always also) to make visits to provincial capitals for Bible Society work and other addresses. He and Jean were away from the York diocese from early January until the middle of March. How he was able to achieve much writing is a mystery, for the tour was arduous and he did a great deal of speaking at a host of towns, cathedrals and churches and the Universities of Witwatersrand, Cape Town, Pretoria and Stellenbosch. He called on the Prime Minister and members of the Black Sash movement, and descended the deep Goto mine outside Johannesburg.

Unexpected occasions took the Archbishop half way across the

---

[39] Hodder and Stoughton 1971.

world; later in 1970 to Australia for little more than a week, in connection with the celebrations commemorating the voyage of Captain Cook, a man of Yorkshire, two hundred years before. A hectic programme ('I was worked hard', he wrote to Ruth) varied from a call on the Governor General to tea from a billy-can on a sheep station. He gave distinction to his travels by making a journey of circumnavigation, returning to England by way of Fiji, Honolulu, San Francisco and New York.

His last Canadian visit as Archbishop of York was a visit primarily to Ottawa in 1970 to lead a Canadian Congress on Evangelism with an attendance of 700. After preaching in the Cathedral he gave the opening address on 'the Evangelist as the man for others, the man for God, the man of God'; the second represented a familiar Coggan theme, 'the Evangelist as Servant of God'; the third, 'the Renewal of the Church'. A short visit to West Germany for Church, civic and British Army engagements, took in Kaiserworth Deaconess Institute, where Florence Nightingale received her medical training, and Münster, York's twin city. His last American visit from the Northern Province occupied eight days of 'much kindness and hospitality and too much food' at the end of October 1971, the main reason for it being the centenary of the Episcopalian diocese of Bethlehem, Pennsylvania, an old Moravian stronghold. Donald preached there and also in Norfolk, Virginia.

It had been the Coggans' intention to include a visit to their daughter Ruth at her hospital at Bannu in Pakistan, in the Far Eastern tour at the beginning of 1972. The war in Pakistan intervened, and Donald set off on his own, restricting his visit to the Church of South India which was celebrating its silver jubilee. However, the longer tour was only postponed, and took place over Easter after a visit to British troops in Belfast and Londonderry. Jean remained at Bannu for a month while Donald went on to Kenya for a Provincial Conference of Church workers.

In September 1972 the World Assembly of the United Bible Societies took place at Addis Ababa in Ethiopia with Archbishop Coggan in the chair. The Emperor was present at the opening of the Assembly; Donald responded to the speech of Haile Selassie; he also visited the Coptic Patriarch. Oliver Béguin, the much admired General Secretary, had died and there were decisions to be made. One concerned whether simplified versions of the Scriptures should be contemplated; it was resolved that an attempt be made at five levels under the title *Good News for New Readers*. Donald pressed at this meeting for recognition of the work which women had done. It was largely women who formed the greater number of Bible Volunteers and who carried copies of the Scriptures over long distances. He emphasized the need for prayer in the life of the Bible movement.

This was Donald's last overseas journey as Archbishop of York. He had travelled far and widely; had extended his knowledge and acquaintance, especially within the Anglican Communion, but beyond it also, and had gained in particular insight into the lives of simple as well as sophisticated people. These factors were to be of benefit when he became Archbishop of Canterbury, as opposed to other experiences which were to be construed as less helpful.

The second sphere of Donald Coggan's influence and activity from 1961 was the Province of York: fourteen dioceses from the Scottish border to the river Trent. Chairmanship of the Northern Convocation (in two Houses: Bishops, and representatives of the clergy drawn from the dioceses) occupied him twice a year. He became chief consecrator of bishops within the Province and he was called upon to give advice as to their appointment; they could call on him for support and counsel, and he made visits to dioceses as invited.

As one of the Primates of England, much of his work had its focus in London: he was a chairman of the Church Assembly and member of many of its committees, a Church Commissioner, a member of the House of Lords. He had already been appointed to several Commissions, on the Revision of the Catechism, the Psalter and the Liturgy. His ministry was called upon by the Royal Family, by Lord Mayors, the City of London, civic and academic bodies, schools and some private individuals, though this number was nowhere near as great as it was to become after the move to Canterbury.

Even before his appointment to York became legal, Donald spoke in the Church Assembly in July 1961 as Archbishop designate, to welcome his predecessor, Michael Ramsey, as Archbishop of Canterbury. His own introduction to the presidency of the Northern Convocation came on 3 October, when he addressed the full synod for the first time in characteristically optimistic terms. People had reminded him constantly of the darkness of the world situation, and the need for the church to act, asking 'Cannot the Church give a lead?' He suggested it should do so along these lines:

First, prayer. God is on the throne . . . We mortal men are in touch with that God through prayer. Prayer is not a means by which we persuade a reluctant God to do what we will. It is a means by which we align our wills with the will of God; by which we see His design for His world, and we receive power to share in the realizing of that design. Secondly, support for the United Nations Organization . . . Thirdly, sacrificial effort to improve the conditions of the underprivileged.

His future initiatives were to show how deeply these words reflected his own outlook.

The new Archbishop was greeted by enthusiastic speeches, particularly from the Prolocutor (the Archdeacon of Manchester)[40], underlining the esteem with which he was regarded for his past record and invariable clear exposition in the synod. Special mention was made of Donald's part in a clergy conference in Blackpool some years before; a Bible study which won golden opinions. The high expectations were justified by his performance as chairman throughout his years as Archbishop in the North. He kept a firm grip on the proceedings as to time and subject matter: he was fair minded and shared round opportunity to speak, but did not allow debates to drag on.

Donald himself launched directly into discussion of the Report of Archbishop's Commission on the Catechism, apologizing as he did so for monopolizing so much of the agenda, but as usual presenting the issues with clarity. He had conducted the business of the Commission as chairman likewise, in the brisk yet courteous manner that was intrinsic to his style. The terms of reference were to 'consider the revision of the Prayer Book Catechism in order to enlarge its scope and cause its language to be more suitable for modern conditions'. The Commission met eleven times in the initial two-and-a-half years, twice on a residential basis. Three other diocesan bishops and two suffragans served as members, also C.F.D. Moule, Professor of Divinity at Cambridge, some clergy, no lay people. But there were unmistakeable signs of Donald's influence in the Report which made its first appearance before the two Convocations of Canterbury and York in January 1961. In no section was this clearer than in that on Christian Hope which, with mention of the Bible, was entirely new; also in the general attitude thoroughly to modernize the language and to change the attitude of Catechist to Cathechized. It reflected the chairman's overall outlook which was constant: to clarify was to effect understanding. Amendments were invited; several became incorporated in the revised Report reintroduced before the Convocations for acceptance, which

---

[40] The Venerable Arthur Selwyn Bean.

it eventually received. After frequent reissue, it continues to survive.

Their President reminded the members of the Northern Convocation of the breadth of his activities, for at the same meeting he proceeded to propose a second motion, this time on the New English Bible, as a member of the Joint Committee responsible for its overall supervision. After twelve years work by a group of scholars, an entirely new translation of the New Testament, not merely a revision, had been produced; he commended it for use in the public worship of the Church. 'I believe' as he wrote in the *Church of England Newspaper*,[41] 'there will be a sharpness to the cutting edge to this book which has been blunted by the "venerability" and familiarity of the Authorized Version'. He continued to serve on the Joint Committee for the new translations of the Old Testament and Apocrypha[42] (becoming chairman in 1968 on the death of Alwyn T.P. Williams, formerly Bishop of Winchester). He spoke at length on the use of the New English Bible at the service of Holy Communion in the Church Assembly later that Autumn[43].

To follow the debates of the Church Assembly over the following nine years (until the creation of the General Synod in 1970), is to discover a clear and consistent representation of the thinking of the Archbishop of York, and of his particular spheres of interest: ministry, including that of women and of the laity; theological education; liturgical revision; mission and the reunion of Christians. During the first four years of the life of the General Synod, before Donald was appointed to Canterbury at the end of 1974, he expressed some strong views in that place on the ordination of women, crown appointments, evangelism, and the treatment of immigrants. The period 1961-74 was one of extraordinary activity in the councils of the Church of England in the face of the threats of change and (in some cases) of decay; of almost incessant schemes and Commissions to plan for new situations and growth. In this process Donald took up identifiable positions.

As President of the Northern Convocation, his attitudes emerge in his Addresses, although the subject matters to which he directed his Province were regulated not so much by personal choice as by the fact that certain items were on the agenda. Nevertheless his comments reveal much.

---

[41] 17 February 1961, p.9.
[42] Published 1970.
[43] 9 November 1961, *Report of Proceedings*, Vol.XLI, No. 3; pp.536-8.

Donald's attitude towards renewal in the Church's life must be a first consideration. His enthusiasm for revision of the written word has already been touched upon in relation to the Catechism and the New Testament. In May 1962, on the eve of a Joint session of the Convocations of Canterbury and York, he spoke of the revised Services for Morning and Evening Prayer, some Litanies, Intercessions and Thanksgivings, which were to be presented the following day. He had been Chairman of the Liturgical Commission since 1960, placed there by Archbishop Fisher, not (as all were agreed) on account of his expertise in matters liturgical, but because he had established a reputation for being a firm and even-tempered chairman. His predecessor had become increasingly deaf, the Commission unruly and the Secretary independent. Moreover his position as Bishop of Bradford gave the Commission a much needed spokesman in the Church Assembly and Convocations.

Donald's influence was soon apparent: he began to broaden the composition of the Commission, which had been exclusively clerical, by introducing laymen and eventually laywomen. He sent the draft Services of Mattins and Evensong to C.S. Lewis to seek his opinion on the new material from the literary point of view, and he invited Helen Gardner (later Dame and Professor), daughter of his former teacher, to speak to the Commission in the same interest. He asked (and obtained) the permission of the Archbishop of Canterbury to seek the opinion of other Churches. He set up a small committee for specialized areas, such as the form of Thanksgiving after Childbirth, on which he invited a mother of three children who also had good academic qualifications[44] to serve as a member.

Archbishop Coggan's Address which referred to the revised Services[45] provided the basis of this activity: Liturgy, he said, must not be allowed to lapse into antiquarianism. It was a living thing, 'ministering to the present needs of the People of God as they do the work of worship'. Liturgical revision, he went on, was not the concern of the Anglican Church alone.

> The winds of Liturgical reform are sweeping through most of the great Christian Churches, including the Roman, and we shall be indeed foolish if we do not make full use of their insights, if not by incorporating any representatives on our Commission, then by close personal and postal co-operation with them outside the Commission.

In 1964 Donald Coggan resigned from the Liturgical Commission.

[44] Elizabeth Montefiore, who later joined the Commission itself.
[45] 16 May 1962, *York Journal of Convocation*, pp. 14-17.

His preferment to the Primacy of York had presented certain difficulties, in that he was required to report not only to the Archbishop of Canterbury, but also to himself. This was an unusual step, for he seldom withdrew from an assignment to which he was committed. It is unlikely that the frequency of the meetings – at least six a year and several of them residential – played a major part in the decision, but it may well be that realization of his lack of specialized knowledge was a crucial factor, as also the consideration that the Commission would be well served by the appointment as chairman of Ronald Jasper[46], who had been a member since the beginning.

A third field where Donald was engaged in amending the Church's language was in the revision of the Psalter. During four-and-a-half years, from 1958-63, a Commission with Donald at its head laboured 'not to concern ourselves with questions relating to the manner of using the Psalter in public worship. Our sole duty was to revise the text.' The members of the Commission were G.A. Chase, who resigned as Bishop of Ripon during the course of the revision; two musicians, J. Dykes-Bower and Gerald Knight; T.S. Eliot, the poet; C.S. Lewis and D. Winton-Thomas, Regius Professor of Hebrew at Cambridge.

To read Donald's comments is to learn something, though never a great deal, about the man. It was work clearly enjoyed: he was able to harness his knowledge of Hebrew, his passion for accuracy, his love of music and his desire to make Holy Writ more comprehensible. It affected, as his other biblical work had done, his attitude towards what some considered the flawless transmission of Scripture from earliest times, and this, in turn, qualified the opinion of certain elements in the Church of England towards him. Unlike the New English Bible, it was not intended that the Revised Psalter should be a new translation, but an emendation of an old one in which there were shortcomings. A first Report containing a revision of the text of Psalms 1-41 was presented to the Convocations in May 1961; agreement was given to proceed on those lines. Archbishop Coggan introduced the Revised Psalter before the Convocation of York in May 1963[47]. The work, he declared,

> has been necessarily of a somewhat specialist and detailed character. Calling for skill in Hebrew and its cognate languages, in English and in music . . . it is our belief that we have so revised the text as to eliminate

[46] 1917- ; Canon of Westminster 1968-75; Dean of York 1975-84.
[47] 7 May 1963, *York Journal of Convocation*, pp. 47-50.

those passages in Coverdale which either made no sense at all – and there are such – or else give a translation which was unfaithful to the original.

He ended by submitting that the Commission had enriched and not impoverished the meaning of the Psalms by being accurate in the translation; and when the musicians had completed the pointing of the new Psalter, a major contribution to worship would be provided[48].

In parish churches, the Archbishop was known to bring congregational singing of the psalms to a sudden halt if he thought them badly rendered; if sung too slow or too fast, or if participation was patchy. If the organist was at fault, he would suggest that it were better to finish a psalm by saying alternate verses with him. He was driven to such a course partly by his insistence that worship be of the highest standard it was possible to reach, and on account of his own feelings for the psalms as a means of personal devotion. His work on the revision of the Psalter had clearly been done with these ends in mind. It was true of everything he touched: all was for God.

Apart from exhortation to prayer, Donald Coggan urged his Province to bring in the Kingdom by increased personal dedication, effort and application. He called for radical change within the hearts of men rather than in the structure of Church and government. During the period of office as Archbishop of Canterbury, this outlook was considered as having produced a stabilizing rather than wakening effect on the nation. 'Think big', he told the Northern Convocation in the Minster, in relation to the debate on Anglican-Methodist relations. It was a favourite phrase, but it was not as a thinker on the grand scale, as strategist, that men saw him; but more in terms of think boldly and think beyond the immediate to the ultimate goal of men.

No one initiated more schemes, commissions, councils to carry out specific short-term objectives than Donald during the Bradford-York period, but there was a sense also in which he was impatient of them. In 1965[49], referring to the increasing number of committees and Commissions of the Church Assembly that had been created, he

---

[48] It is only fair to say that the Revised Psalter was criticized by Professor D.R. Jones of Durham University in the General Synod on 8 July 1978. (Report of Proceedings Vol. Nine No 2 pp. 451-2) as having provided some clarifications based on arbitrary decisions. Since it seems that many Hebrew words are liable to diverse interpretation, the debate is likely to continue.

[49] 18 May 1965, *York Journal of Convocation*, pp.18-21.

said that however necessary these might be, the Church should give much more attention to the proclamation of Father, Son and Holy Ghost.

> When the Church concerns itself first and foremost with God, Creator, Redeemer, Sanctifier, its griefs will not be cured overnight. Its frustrations will still be there. The creaking of its machinery will still go on. But we shall address ourselves to those griefs, those frustrations, those creakings with a good heart as we renew our grasp on the fact that God reigns, the God of love and grace revealed in Christ. Thus the glory will return to the pastoral and evangelistic task on which we are engaged at the command of our Lord.

Donald's conception of 'thinking big' would seem to have been cast in these terms. In answer to the question as to how this was to be translated into action, in view of the gap between the Church and a large proportion of society, he provided few new guidelines; the *Call to the North* was one. Meanwhile he had some piece-meal changes to suggest, but no radical, structural ones, for the creaking machinery.

In the field of ministry, Archbishop Coggan looked for renewal in two areas: the Ministry of women and that of the laity, which he regarded as different in essence. Although he saw the whole matter of women's ministry as wider than the question of ordination, he accepted this possibility; it formed the separation.

> A Christian theology of the secular must not mean a secularized theology . . . the more we stress the secular job of the layman, the more strongly do we need to guard the sacred ministry of the clergy[50].

Ordination remained for Donald a calling of great significance. Changes that were proposed in the 1960s in regard to the clergy[51] did not find him springing to his feet in debate, although he was invariably sensitive to the need for adequate means of livelihood for the clergy and fair working conditions. The creation of a completely new set of structures was not his forte; he pressed on in the hope that it was possible to operate within the status quo, with what he saw, but others did not, as minor sub-structural adaptions. One of these concerned the Ministry of Women; it was not for him a matter of either expediency or justice. He was led to believe that in this sphere

---

[50] 27 July 1968; Lambeth Conference 1968; quoting Bishop F.R. Barry.
[51] The Paul Report *The Deployment and Payment of the Clergy*, 1964; the Morley Report *Partners in Ministry* and the Pastoral Measure, before the Church Assembly 1964-8.

development would bring good to the Church's work in the world, that no doctrinal *changes* were involved.

During the Spring session of the Church Assembly of 1962 he spoke[52] on a Report under the title *The Men He wants*. There should have been a section, he said, on the Women that God wants; the approach to the problem of Women's Ministry he thought out of step and out of date; CACTM as a Council for the Ministry should give careful and quick attention to it. Mrs M.B. Ridley[53] expressed gratitude for the Archbishop's speech, which she said would bring hope to countless women who had despaired of the question ever being taken seriously. The Archbishop continued to press for better theological training for women and where possible joint training with men; for women to be permitted to say Morning and Evening Prayer in churches, to become Lay Readers, and eventually to be accepted for ordination to the diaconate and priesthood. He did not find it easy to recognize the validity of the case for the opposition; and quoted St Paul: 'There is no such thing as Jew and Greek, slave and freeman, male and female; for you are all one person in Christ Jesus.' It was not a new idea, but an old one. He acknowledged that 'the path of those who engage in discussion of this subject is bestrewn with perils. We are all prejudiced, one way or the other. Is there such a thing as a totally unbiased man or woman?' He recognized that relations with the Roman Catholic Church might be jeopardized, and the issue was a serious one, but

> the thinking of the Roman Catholic Church is far more open today than it was in pre-Vatican II days . . . it is possible that in the near future we shall see a change in this area of thought such as in recent years we have seen in many others.[54]

He showed, and this was not an isolated instance, that he was more in touch, through his travels, with grass-roots Roman Catholicism than with attitudes in Rome itself. The contention that:

> the voice of the laity should be heard *as of right* and not merely of courtesy in the central counsels of the Church . . . An over-clericalized Church is not a healthy Church

was part of the Archbishop of York's introduction[55] to the debate on Synodical Government in October 1962. He was faced by a

[52] 14 February 1962; *Report of Proceedings*, Vol XLII, No 1, pp.104-5.
[53] 1909- ; Later Dame Betty, and Third Estates Commissioner.
[54] 6 July 1973, *General Synod July Group of Sessions* 1973, Vol. 4, No. 2 pp.534-7.
[55] (Read by the Bishop of Durham since the Archbishop was in Uganda) 9 October 1962, *York Journal of Convocation*, pp.11-13.

difficult piece of chairmanship when the Lower House (clergy) of the Northern Convocation voted against the adoption of the majority scheme because it considered it removed from the clergy the final power of veto on matters of worship and doctrine. (The scheme had been adopted by the Upper House of Bishops and both Houses of Canterbury.) A new scheme had to be worked out by the two Archbishops in consultation with representative members of all Houses and the House of Laity. This failed to gain the support of the Upper House of York. Ultimately a compromise was reached, for a General Synod was the concerted wish; as also the retention of the Convocations. What was demonstrated, above all, was the often quite fierce attitude of the Northern Convocation in defence of its independence as a Province. Loyalty towards their Archbishop can be seen as a concomitant; any Archbishop of York translated to Canterbury would be bound to feel the sudden exposure.

Closer relations with other Christians was an issue where Donald Coggan expressed himself often during his ministry in the North. He was deeply committed to Anglican/Methodist reunion, and the eventual failure of the Church of England to achieve the required majority for the scheme for unity wounded him. As always, his commitment was to the cause beyond the cause: not so much to the Schemes themselves than to what would be possible as the result of them.

> It cannot be denied that our debates sometimes show us as experts in elaborating *ad nauseam* the lesser matters, the comparative trivialities while the *great* issues of unity 'that the world may believe' get pushed into the background . . . The Church must be always on her guard against the temptation to fasten on and become engrossed in, small matters while the great ones go by default.[56]

He cited the deceased Wife's Sister's Marriage Act as a *cause célèbre* which had exercised the Church in the 19th century; the passage of time altered perspectives. What were to him 'comparative trivialities', however, represented matters of principle in other quarters. He was once more accused of over-simplification.

He returned to his theme after the Anglican/Methodist débâcle of 1969, and spoke of the effect that he thought it would have on the mission of the Church.

> Many of us had deeply hoped that we might be able to turn our attention *outwards* from matters of Church Relations to matters more clearly and

[56] ibid., 14 May 1968, pp.29-30.

more obviously connected with a world in chaos – to the needs of men and women 'without God and without hope in the world'.[57]

He urged how hard a blow it was to some younger Churches (of which he had recent personal experience), especially those engaged in working out schemes of union. Divisions had been exported. Archbishop Coggan expressed dismay at the effect on the Church's image of the failure to unite:

> This is a cause of great stumbling. The sin of disunion remains and it is worst at the point where most clearly our unity should be manifested, namely at the Eucharist. United in Baptism, we are divided here.

Intercommunion was to become a subject of discussion after Donald's visit to Pope Paul VI in 1977. It had long been in his mind. The Report *Intercommunion Today* of 1968 had declared that it was the one loaf which had the power to create unity out of disunity. He believed that to be true, confounding those who held that intercommunion was the fruit rather than the means of unity.

The Archbishop of York's relationship with Rome had been affected by the seeming lack of concern by Roman Catholics for the Bible. How could they hear the gospel? But this situation was seen to be changing. In addition, he began to meet Roman Catholics in person on his travels all over the world. His encounters with Basil Hume[58], then Abbot of Ampleforth, and visits to the Abbey; with George Beck[59], Archbishop of Liverpool, during the Call to the North; and with Cardinal Suenens, all bore fruit. After the Malines visit Donald said to the Northern Convocation[60]:

> The outstanding impression left on my mind was that made by contact with the Cardinal himself. Here was a man of courage, a man of hope, a man prepared to take risks in the interest of Christ's Church and of the progress of the gospel.

As a former theological Principal, Archbishop Coggan remained preoccupied with the training of candidates for the ministry; he did not shrink from expressing his views, and continued to press for a high proportion of graduates. An extract from his speech in the debate on the Annual Report of CACTM for 1965 reads:[61]

[57] 7 October 1969, ibid., p.15.
[58] 1923- ; Archbishop of Westminster and Cardinal 1976.
[59] 1904-78.
[60] 12 October 1971, ibid., p.18.
[61] 6 July 1965, *Church Assembly Report of Proceedings Spring Session*, Vol. XLV, No. 1, p.337.

He wanted parish priests who were experts in biblical theology; and if not experts, to know what the issues were, so that when the great ethical and theological questions came, they were not led astray by shaky doctrine, and their preaching was strong in didactic element and in relation to life.

Others in the Assembly did not agree; years on a factory bench or in a shop were worth more than an Honours degree. The Paul Report pressed for more Secondary Modern schoolboys who would reach a wider segment of British society. But Donald proved remarkably consistent, as well as persistent: in a debate on the Reorganization of the Theological colleges in 1968[62] he spoke at length in the same vein:

> . . . if we let through the ministry a large proportion of men intellectually ill-equipped, we shall be doing something dangerous for the future of Christianity in this country.

The problems that attended upon the drop in the number of vocations to the ministry, closure and amalgamation of theological colleges amongst them, followed him to Canterbury. The size of committees was a bugbear: he criticized the number of members of the committees of CACTM in 1965: it took men away from work for which they were ordained and spent too much money on railway fares and subsistence; the bigger the committee the less effective the work done, he maintained. On the matter of Crown appointments, he believed that discussion on too broad a front led to difficulties. In 1963 he congratulated the Christian Stewardship Central Staff for cutting their numbers from five to two. Similar compliments followed the fusion of the Overseas and Ecumenical Co-operation Councils in the same year.

There would invariably be speeches from the Archbishop when questions of mission and evangelism were under discussion:

> It is my hope that when Government by Synod becomes a reality . . . we shall determine to move out of the sphere of internal reconstruction and reorganization and the consideration of our own affairs . . . to that mission which is the very essence of the Church[63].

In 1974 he made a major contribution to the debate on Evangelism Today[64] when he spoke on the relationship of evangelism to the search for unity. When the Church is obedient to Christ in the

---

[62] 7 November 1968, ibid., *Autumn Session*, Vol. XLVIII, No. 3, p.801.

[63] 14 February 1968, ibid., *Spring Session*, Vol. XLVIII, No. 1, p.148.

[64] 6 November 1974, *General Synod November Group of Sessions 1974 Report of Proceedings*, Vol. 5, No. 3, pp.724-6.

matter of evangelism, he said, He of the greatness of His heart throws in as a kind of bonus a growth in unity. Evangelism after all, is simply obedience to the Lord of the Church. 'Not to evangelize is to engage in disobedience to the Lord of the Church. It is as straightforward as that'.

Donald at York seldom missed an opportunity to speak in a debate that touched on help for the third world and questions of world development. He had gathered wide practical experience of the problems. On the matter of solutions he was considered less skilled. People criticized his lack of economic expertise and his small interest in politics. He had a firmer touch always on questions of 'Why', and less sure on 'How'. That the Western nations should have a lesser share of the world's wealth was a favourite theme; he wrote and spoke often on a topic which he named 'the creed of greed'. He could always be relied upon to bring up the subject of reading-material for the newly literate; sympathy for immigrants since the Bradford days was a further characteristic. All these interests were to endure into the Canterbury period; Donald's attitudes remained remarkably stable.

Donald Coggan's relations with Evangelicals as such as Archbishop of York were not close during the 1960s. This was not entirely on account of his efforts to be in touch with all Churchmen, but also partly because he had begun to be regarded with something near suspicion by the Evangelical wing of the Church of England, as having embraced some liberal tendencies. But changes were on the way. In 1967 a radical upheaval took place in Evangelical circles, and although the doctrinal stand remained firm, some new positions were adopted which amounted in several instances to those which had been Donald's for many years.

The movement had started in the North, where Evangelicals had felt isolated. Groups of thirty to forty clergy began to come together for annual conferences under the leadership of Raymond Turvey, vicar of St George's Leeds (1958-72). By the early 1960s, an attendance of 200 from the whole of the Northern Province could be relied upon. A wish to join with Evangelicals elsewhere, and particularly in London, led to a meeting in May between Raymond Turvey, John Stott of All Souls', Langham Place, and Peter Johnston, Vicar of Islington and chairman of the Islington Conference. Plans were laid for the first National Evangelical Anglican Congress, to take place at the University of Keele in April 1967. In anticipation of the Congress, Peter Johnston outlined some of his hopes for it,

and described the current state of ferment in the Church of England
and the changes that were affecting Evangelicals.

> Not in doctrinal conviction (for the truth of the gospel cannot change)
> but (like any healthy child) in stature and in posture. It is a tragic thing,
> however, that Evangelicals have a very poor image in the Church as a
> whole. We have acquired a reputation for narrow partisanship and
> obstructionism. We have to acknowledge this, and for the most part we
> have no one but ourselves to blame. We need to repent and to change. As
> for partisanship, I for one desire to be rid of all sinful 'party spirit'.
> *Evangelical* is not a party word, because the gospel as set forth in the New
> Testament is not, and never can be, a party matter. We who love the
> adjective *evangelical*, because it declares us to be gospel-men, must take
> great care, therefore, that what we are seeking to defend and champion is
> the gospel in its biblical fulness and not some party shibboleth or
> tradition of doubtful biblical pedigree[65].

Many of these sentiments could equally have been expressed by
Donald Coggan.

The Archbishop of Canterbury, Michael Ramsey, opened the
Congress with an address that concentrated on its theme 'Christ
over all'. Archbishop Coggan was unable to accept the invitation
because of a long tour abroad, but sent his assurance of prayers and
good wishes and voiced his thankfulness for the theme chosen.

> I believe that the weakness of the Church in certain quarters is due to the
> fact that it has allowed itself to be side-tracked from the centrality of
> Christ. May your Congress help to bring us back to that.

The long and careful planning of the Keele Congress bore remarkable fruit. 1,000 participants, 519 clergy and 481 lay people who had
been prepared for the agenda by previously circulated study
material, were steered into discussion groups whose findings were
conflated into the Congress statement which received general acceptance by the Church at large. It was noted that without deviating
from what were regarded as theological fundamentals, a new willingness had been shown:

> to face without fear the winds of change, to welcome truth from any
> quarter, to encourage free discussion, to trust the rank and file rather
> than to impose the party line, and to move . . . into fields such as the
> social application of Christianity, that Evangelicals have for some genera-
> tions neglected[66].

David Paton remarked that the change that he saw as the result of

---

[65] Philip Crowe, ed., *Keele '67* (Falcon Books 1967), p.8.
[66] ibid., p.15.

Keele was not in the body of evangelical doctrine, but in the way the doctrines were held, and in the readiness to tackle new questions. In this respect Keele seemed not unlike Vatican II. Kenneth Sansbury, then General Secretary of the British Council of Churches welcomed

> the stress on theology, the desire to take a responsible part in the corporate and central life of the Church of England, and the recognition that Christians must show the implications of the Gospel for the social, moral and international problems of our time.

New possibilities were opened up by the outcome of the Keele Congress in relationships between Evangelicals and Christians who cherished other emphases; also between various Evangelical wings. What did not change to any discernible extent was the degree of joint activity undertaken by the two Archbishops of Canterbury and York, as it was hoped might be the case. There would seem to have been two reasons for this: the first was that such was not the tradition. Successive Primates tended to plough their own furrows, and did not look towards that of the other. Secondly, the occupants of the two sees were separated by such a gulf of difference in personality, methods and outlook, that combined action would have been particularly difficult. But a closer relationship between the Archbishop of York and his Evangelical brothers was now possible as a consequence of the increased convergence of views. There is evidence that it took place; an immediate example came a year later. At a time of considerable pressure, just before the Uppsala World Council of Churches and the 1968 Lambeth Conference, Donald accepted an invitation to take part in a Conference on Evangelism, again at Keele, where he preached and gave three Bible Studies.

The problems that were besetting the Anglican-Methodist Scheme in 1972 led a group of churchmen to make contingency plans to further the cause of unity if the scheme folded up. 1972 had seen the Church Leaders' Conference at Birmingham and the inauguration of the United Reformed Church. It was considered that leadership of fresh initiatives towards reunion by this newly created body would have credibility. A conference of a hundred men and women at Christ Church Oxford was set up in January 1973 to launch this proposal, and Donald Coggan was invited to take the chair. It was a representative gathering of the Church of England, the Baptist Union, the Churches of Christ, the Methodist Church, the Roman Catholic and United Reformed Churches. The outcome was a resolve to hold 'Talks about Talks'. The URC agreed to take the initiative and issue the invitations.

Donald Coggan outlined the plan to begin official conversations between all the English Churches, with a view to their union, at a press conference on January 18, 1973, the first day of the annual Week of Prayer for Unity. As a result, the Churches' Unity Commission came into being in 1974, and its report containing 'Ten propositions' as an acceptable basis for continuing the search for unity, to which constituent churches were asked to give a reply, was issued in 1976. A covenant to seek visible union was thereby put up for acceptance. Many of the debates on these issues took place during Donald Coggan's tenure as Archbishop of Canterbury.

The suggestion that he should chair the Oxford Conference may well have been consequent upon the initiatives which he had recently taken in the ecumenical field in his own Province under the title *Call to the North*. It is a subject that requires attention, particularly in relation to Donald's later, more publicized, national call of 1975.

The seeds of the movement that was to become the *Call to the North* originated in the mind of Stuart Blanch[67], Bishop of Liverpool (1966-75), who, on return from the Lambeth Conference of 1968, drew together some church leaders on Merseyside for private conversations about mission. George Beck, Roman Catholic Archbishop, and Rex Kissack, the Chairman of the Methodist District were among those present. The intention was to make evangelism a leadership exercise, not to try and sell to church leaders a plan developed by a group of enthusiastic Evangelicals.

After six or eight months Bishop Blanch approached the Northern Primate. He chose an opportunity when Donald Coggan came to speak in Liverpool parish church during Lent 1969 and arrangements were made for him to meet Archbishop Beck who had taken particularly to heart the ecumenical message of the Second Vatican Council. The two men began to explore and think together, and Donald conceived the idea of designing a venture with the whole of the North of England in mind. It would not be primarily an essay in Christian unity; that would be a by-product. It was to be an essay in evangelism, 'in outreach to those on the fringe of Christian life and activity and those virtually untouched by the Christian faith'. But if evangelistic activity could be achieved together by the churches, 'God in His goodness will show them something new in the sphere of Christian unity'.

A meeting of Church leaders in the North was called at Bishop-

---

[67] 1918- ; Archbishop of York 1975-84.

thorpe in May 1969. The response was remarkably representative. Donald sat at the end of his long table in the dining room facing the terrace on the bank of the river Ouse, with Archbishop Beck beside him. Round them, and stuffed into every corner, were the Anglican Bishops of the Northern Province and most of the Roman Catholic Diocesans. Rex Kissack had secured the presence of fourteen Methodist Chairmen, three Baptist Superintendents, representatives of Congregational and Presbyterian churches, and some Pentecostals.

The meeting took shape only slowly. There was some initial murmuring which was silenced by a withering glance from the Archbishop who showed himself an able chairman of the remarkable gathering. He had been under suspicion by Evangelicals for liberal traits; now he faced opposition from other quarters who felt he was likely to want to mount an old-style evangelistic campaign on Billy Graham lines. It was eventually made clear that what was envisaged was a combined exercise to work out the implications of saying, 'Can we together speak the Word of God to the North?' A more positive response followed.

Some years of meetings and careful planning on an ecumenical basis followed. John Hunter, Diocesan Missioner for Liverpool, became the co-ordinator. At the suggestion of Archbishop Beck, for every two days of business there was a day of prayer. The area of operation was fixed as coterminous with an Anglican diocese. (Anglicans were anxious lest this should not be thought proper, but it seemed wise to use existing structures.) In each area the Churches were free to plan what was thought appropriate, provided it was done together and simultaneously. Annual gatherings of church leaders continued to take place at Scargill. Archbishop Coggan continued to guide, plan and lead in prayer. Finally, it was decided that the *Call to the North* should be launched in Holy Week 1973. A joint letter, signed by Donald Coggan, George Beck and the Chairman of the Northern Free Church Conference, was read on Palm Sunday in every church and chapel. Donald was active throughout the Province. He stressed that at last it was possible to say in unison 'Christ Crucified is risen. We commend Him to you.' Fears were expressed that the Archbishop would wear himself out.

Considerable activity followed, which varied from diocese to diocese: ecumenical house-to-house visiting, concerts in cathedrals, Cardinal Heenan[68] in Sheffield football stadium, study groups,

[68] Born 1905. Died 1975.

joint efforts in factories. Although the results were uneven, a new sense of unity had been brought into being.

One further effort of Donald's on a provincial scale during his ministry at York must receive notice. In 1967 it was discovered that the failure to keep pace with the backlog of repairs to the Minster, due to insufficient funds, had resulted in a dangerous situation where expensive treatment could no longer be postponed. The sum of £2 million, which exceeded any previous Cathedral appeal was the initial calculation of needs. (Later it was found that not all the damage had been identified.) Archbishop Coggan applied himself to the promotion of the appeal with determination and expenditure of time, and allowed his home to be used for the money-raising activities.

Nor should his membership of the House of Lords be omitted. He did not speak a great deal, perhaps twelve or thirteen times in as many years at York and usually on topics which could have been predicted: refugees, the rehabilitation of offenders, education, alternative Services, homosexual offences, and the abolition of the death penalty, where he was deeply in favour of the proposed legislation.

> Men, weak fallible men like ourselves – have often to be the means of executing judgment . . . But there comes a point – I believe it is the point whence there is no return, the point of the death sentence – where weak and fallible humans must say 'Hands off. This is the sphere where *we* give place to the divine wrath. Vengeance belongs to God. *He* will repay'.

National public functions and invitations claimed the Coggans a great deal. The hospitality of the Queen at Windsor Castle (April 1973) and the Queen Mother at Royal Lodge gave much pleasure, as also Royal visits to York. Donald was the ideal courtier, as he remained himself in whatever company he found himself, and Jean likewise. She enjoyed the unexpected in her experiences. Once she happened to mention William Temple to her neighbour at a formal dinner in the City. 'I live in the country and therefore do not know him,' was the reply.

The third circle of Donald Coggan's activity was his diocese, an area of some 2,660 square miles running from Cleveland in the north to parts of Humberside in the south, and from Northallerton to the East coast; with the Archdeaconries of York, Cleveland and the East Riding comprising 470 parishes, twenty-seven rural deaneries. He had the assistance of the three Suffragan Bishops of Selby, Hull and

Whitby (at the start, Carey Frederick Knyvett, George Frederick Townley and George D'Oyly Snow), together with three Archdeacons (Charles Forder – known as 'the wisest man in the diocese' – William Palin and Frank Ford). A domestic chaplain, a private secretary and some clerical assistance completed his initial staff. Later he added a lay chaplain in the person of David Blunt, a former schoolmaster, son of his predecessor at Bradford, who did a great deal to ease the administrative burdens in the Bishopthorpe office.

The domestic chaplains, James Scott[69], Michael Turnbull[70], Michael Escritt[71], and Colin Still[72] saw the Archbishop most, as they went with him to Institutions, Confirmations and many of his other engagements. He liked to be accompanied. In spite of persistent in-built reserve, he would relax on the journey home, treated his chaplains as the sons he had not had, and they were welcomed into the family circle with warmth and humour. There was, however, always something of the teacher in the relationship. No opportunity was missed to give a biblical exposition, with a hint to look up a point in the Greek. Chaplains were aware that everything Donald did contained a thread of evangelism and proclamation; all else was subservient to this, 'so that the world may know'. Disunion, they recognized, he thought a scandal. They regarded the Archbishop with admiration and affection, but the pace was unremitting and there was little spare time. Thoughts of watching Yorkshire play cricket, or evenings spent with friends, had to be set aside.

Donald Coggan has acknowledged that he found the York period heavy going, but he did not help himself by the extra burdens which he undertook in addition to his daily diocesan routine and programme already outlined in the Church overseas and the Province. The teacher in him, as indicated, came readily to the surface, and he did not seem able to resist invitations to give series of lectures[73] and write books, reviews, and forewords to the works of others, nor to visit schools and educational establishments of all kinds. He helped in the foundation of the University of York, was Chairman of Governors of St John's College, and gave time and thought to City projects, such as the Civic Trust and the Cambridge Society where he never missed Annual General meetings. John

[69] 1961-5.
[70] 1965-9.
[71] 1969-72.
[72] 1972-5.
[73] See Donald Coggan, *Convictions*, for some of the texts.

Shannon, former Lord Mayor and close co-operator in these fields, testifies to the respect with which the Coggans were held in York, he for his good chairmanship and ability to mix with all conditions of citizens, his impatience with minutiae and sense of proportion, and she for her modesty and desire to put all at their ease. Her disarming tendency to disclose situations which were to her own disadvantage comes through in John Shannon's memories. Once more the scene is Jean Coggan at a dinner, this time in York, where a visiting speaker was her neighbour at table. When she asked him where he was staying he replied, 'With you!'

York was probably the happiest period of Donald Coggan's ministry. He enjoyed being stretched, and although the programme was always heavy there was not quite the degree of strain that was to accompany the Canterbury assignment. Nor, although he received a large enough post-bag of a critical sort, did it contain the constant attacks which are levelled at the head of any institution, and which he was to receive in the future. The Coggans had developed a love for the Yorkshire countryside; they enjoyed their cold, rambling three-storey home on the banks of the Ouse with its 18th-century strawberry Gothic facade, 13th-century chapel and formal reception rooms. Donald and Jean played table tennis together on some cold winter evenings in order to restore their circulation. Gradually some modifications were made, and more convenient offices, kitchen and small family sitting room were created. They entertained more at York than at any other time, although never to any great extent. Prospective ordinands came at least once a year, and candidates for ordination stayed at Bishopthorpe for their days of Retreat before the ceremony in the Minster; Bishops came before their Consecrations with their families, when the Coggans were at their best, supportive and concerned. Otherwise occasional small lunch parties were the chief means of providing hospitality. Large-scale entertainment did not rate high in their scale of priorities; their respective family *mores* will have been partly responsible, together with the view that where there was starvation in the world, expenditure of food and time in preparing it were inappropriate. It was certainly not through lack of generosity. Donald Coggan continued to give away what was surplus to his own personal needs. In view of his frugal habits and modest tastes (he would in person visit rooms temporarily unused and turn off radiators), it was a high proportion of his salary.

To the parishes of Yorkshire, the clergy, their families, lay people and the problems of the diocese, Donald Coggan brought the same close attention, concern and interest that he had shown in Bradford. His methods were similar: more or less spontaneous attempts designed to cure problems that came to his notice were unleashed continuously; campaign after project, after scheme, each with its own time-table as target. He rated initiative high; his energy and drive remained unabated.

First were measures to examine the pastoral needs of specific areas: a Working Party was appointed in 1961 to consider the City of York with special reference to the future of churches likely to be redundant. It reported in 1964 and made recommendations as to new churches also, in which the Archbishop was always keenly interested. His forward-looking, optimistic outlook warmed not so much towards change, but rather new life, be it in the form of modes of worship, liturgy, translations of the Scriptures, young children, or buildings. The York survey was followed by that on Middlesborough, and in 1965 Donald Coggan set up a Commission to consider the pastoral needs, church buildings and parochial boundaries of Hull and its neighbourhood. It laboured for forty-five meetings, with 144 hours in session apart from visits on site, and issued four reports.

In November 1962 Archbishop Coggan appointed a Commission on Finance. The Report of 1964 contained the phrase that

> only a complete re-think on the whole question of Responsibility can increase parish revenue on any large scale – and this change of outlook is an essential part of a *spiritual revolution* facing anew the whole meaning of 'service', including the use of money and a good deal else as well.

It led the Archbishop into a project which became known as 'Opportunity Unlimited' which he launched at the diocesan conference of 30 June 1964 as a 'great forward move under the guidance of the Holy Spirit'. He stressed three things: first it was *not* a financial campaign, secondly it had not a rigid programme, and thirdly, it was not a clerical movement. He undertook a considerable personal part in the spade-work: he planned the outline of the operation, introduced it at a meeting of Rural Deans in June 1964, by a letter to all the clergy, at the diocesan conference, and in September 1964 to a special invited group of lay people of the diocese at Bishopthorpe. He appointed as Executive Officer Tony Smith, to co-ordinate effort in the parishes. From October to March 1965 the Archbishop visited every one of the twenty-seven Rural Deaneries. He met clergy and lay people, and spent part of each day in schools, factories, farms or hospitals. The recruitment of lay men and women as Archbishop's Messengers followed; over two hundred volunteered. At four services in York, Hull, Scarborough and Middlesborough, the Messengers were commissioned by Donald to go out in pairs, visiting parish meetings and parochial church councils in his name, to consult and discuss 'What belonging to the Lord entails and implies'. During the summer, the Messengers were trained in groups at various centres. A great service of offering took place at York Minster in November 1965.

During January 1966 Archbishop Coggan held three day-consultations with the clergy in the three Archdeaconries; an innovation which was repeated in subsequent years. After a celebration of the Eucharist, he gave two Bible Studies with open question-and-answer discussion sessions following and Evensong to complete the programme. As the result of his talks with lay people, the Archbishop prompted the preparation of a study course for Lent 1966 on 'Who is God?' in five sessions, to follow that on 'No Small Change' which had been designed on a national basis the year before. Donald announced that in June of that year he was calling a Conference for clergy, their wives, and lay workers at Butlins' Holiday camp at Filey 'to study anew the Christian Faith and nature and place of the ministry in the Church of God at this time'. This was repeated in 1970, when the purpose was the study of 'the Diocese in mission – today and tomorrow' (the Clergy Refresher Course at Scarborough was temporarily suspended that year only). The Archbishop's commendation was typical: 'the Church must be willing to let old ways die. God is calling us to new ventures'. New *means* were the watchwords, not overthrow of tradition. He was not a radical.

In May 1965 Donald set up a Commission under the chairmanship of the Hon. Richard Wood, MP (son of Lord Halifax) to examine some of the problems of Religious Instruction within the diocese of York, and to advise. He had already appointed his own special officer (Mark Green[74]) outside the Diocesan Council, to visit Church Schools for evangelistic purposes. Directly before the Clergy Conference at Filey in 1970, Donald called one under the title 'Look Out' for all involved in Children's work. He promoted the study of training for confirmation, and the consequent document, prepared by the Bishop of Selby (Douglas Sargent) and Mark Green, was sent to all clergy.

A small Commission to examine diocesan communications was set up by the Archbishop in 1967. The same year, prompted no

[74] 1917- ; Bishop of Aston 1972-85.

doubt by the Report of the Working Party which he and the Archbishop of Canterbury had set up under the title *Theological Colleges for Tomorrow*, he selected a team of twelve clergy who were prepared to preach on the ministry outside their own parishes, and offered their services to the diocese. A small consultative committee under the chairmanship of the Bishop of Whitby was charged with tackling the opportunities offered to the Churches by the creation of the new Borough of Teeside.

In the summer of 1968, Archbishop Coggan gave notice of his intention of making a Primary Visitation of the diocese the following year. He caused the Message of the Lambeth Conference to be read in all churches in September: 'God reigns; God loves; God speaks'. The words were the basis of his own confidence in the future. He also commended the popular Report of the Lambeth Conference for study by parishes in the coming winter.

The Primary Visitation of the diocese of York took place in April 1969; the Archdeacons were temporarily inhibited and the Archbishop delivered his Charge in six centres: York, Selby Abbey, Hull, Bridlington, Middlesborough and Pickering. Present were the clergy of the diocese, Readers, Women Workers, Church Army captains and sisters, Archbishop's Messengers, Church Wardens and two members of every parochial church council. Each address was delivered in the context of a service of worship. They were later published under the title *Sinews of Faith*[75], the Preface of which explained their nature:

> I saw these occasions as opportunities to share with my fellow-workers in Christ some of my concerns for the diocese of which we were all representatives . . . I have tried to put my finger on the things to which I believe we might address ourselves in the years of the new decade soon to open before us – things which, if neglected, will lead to slumber and death, but if put first in thought and action will lead to new life in and through the Body of Christ.

It was quintessential Coggan.

The visit of Donald George Snelgrove[76], Vicar of Hessle on Humberside, to St George's Windsor, the Church's staff college, in 1969, was instrumental in leading Archbishop Coggan to his most controversial undertaking during his time at York. Donald Snelgrove had chosen as his research project a study of how the fruits of

---

[75] Hodder and Stoughton 1969.
[76] 1925- ; Vicar of Hessle 1963-70; Archdeacon of East Riding 1970-81; Bishop of Hull 1981.

administrative technology could be applied to diocesan structures of management in the support they gave to the clergy in their spiritual and pastoral duties. When it was completed, he sent a copy of his thesis to Donald Coggan. As the result of subsequent discussions, John Adair PhD, of the Industrial Society, was invited by the Archbishop to carry out an investigation of the diocesan management scene, and make a Report. There was some opposition to the recommendations which followed, which were not carried out in their entirety. The main concern was to free senior staff, especially the Bishops, from their committees, so that they could spend more time on pastoral work. In the end much of the chairmanship devolved on the Archdeacons, and some new offices of Secretary were created. John Southgate[77], former Area Dean of Greenwich, was moved up from the diocese of Southwark to be Secretary for Mission and Evangelism. There were those who did not take kindly to the changes, and considered the upheaval a waste of time and effort; however, Donald Coggan was tenacious when he wanted to see something done.

By 1971 he had been Archbishop of York for ten years. On September 14 the diocese celebrated the event with a meeting of two thousand in the Guildhall. Donald and Jean, with Ann, were presented with a book inscribed and illustrated by many well-wishers from all walks of life. Contributions related to various aspects of the Archbishop's life, work and interests. Among the speakers was the Abbot of Ampleforth, Dom Basil Hume, to whom Donald had become a friend.

Much of the remainder of Donald's archiepiscopate at York was taken up with the Call to the North already mentioned, and the usual punishing routine which in July 1971 included preaching in the open air on three successive Sunday evenings in Scarborough, to huge congregations of several thousand holiday-makers. He continued to repeat the joyful messages which were characteristic of him: 'Lift up your hearts', he wrote in the York Diocesan Leaflet of February 1972, and found both a biblical text[78] and a quotation from Teilhard de Chardin to the effect that he regarded pessimism as a more insidious poison than atheism, to support his outlook. He wrote to Ruth in Pakistan in April 1974 'We share your anxiety (no, wrong word for a Christian to use) about staffing'. She was short-handed in her hospital.

---

[77] 1926- ; Archdeacon of Cleveland 1974-84; Dean of York 1984.
[78] John 16.33. 'I have conquered the world'.

Archbishop Michael Ramsey announced his retirement on 11 March 1974. There was inevitable speculation as to his successor, Donald Coggan's name being amongst those singled out by the media. He was summoned to Downing Street on 6 May, while staying in Cambridge for a week-end of sermons and dinners. Donald refused to give an immediate answer to the Prime Minister's request that he should allow his name to go to the Queen for nomination to the Archbishopric of Canterbury, but returned to Bishopthorpe for a few days. He and Jean had a medical check-up as a precaution. Jean wrote to Ruth on 8 May:

> F and I are taking time off tomorrow and going to Kettlesing (where they had bought a house for their eventual retirement). We will take a picnic lunch and perhaps go up on Blubberhouses Moor and then we can talk in peace and privacy before sending D's answer to the PM.

Later she wrote that the acceptance had been sent on 10 May, her birthday. The doctor 'couldn't find anything wrong with us' and there seemed no good reason for saying no[79].

There was widespread sadness locally at the news, for many had a deep respect for their Archbishop and it had been hoped that he would end his days in retirement in Yorkshire. The most abiding impressions he left were his transparent honesty and genuineness, lack of side or guile, professionalism as a bishop and consummate pastoral sense. He was competent at times of crisis. Countless people could relate instances of acts of personal kindness. His way of despatching hand-written 'chits' to those in trouble or distress became legendary. The clergy appreciated his unfailing concern, but they were a little afraid of him too. He tested them; his expectations were great, his efforts to stop them falling into a rut constant. Moreover, he was self-effacing to a remarkable degree; to some it resembled a defence against personal involvement which caused him to turn conversations about himself on to others. Despite his friendly manner and his humour there remained a reserve which made many wonder, although he left no doubt as to what he stood for, whether they knew him at all, whether beyond the forgiveness and compassion he showed, he was able in any profound sense to enter into their condition.

Donald Coggan was a private man in public life. To read the letters sent weekly and invariably from wherever he happened to be,

---

[79] Donald wrote to the Prime Minister: 'I feel I should be neglecting my duty if I did not accede to your invitation.'

to his daughter Ruth in Pakistan, is to know him better. Droll accounts of his exploits, sometimes told in Yorkshire dialect, were coupled with anecdotes which revealed kindly but sharp perception of mortal weaknesses, and, above all, with assurance of love and support. He addressed her, on passing the examinations for Membership of the Royal College of Obstetricians and Gynaecologists, as 'Dear MR COG'. There was a sense in which both parents identified themselves closely with Ruth's dedicated work; Jean especially because she had wanted herself to be a doctor, but it had not been permitted. She spent much time raising money for equipment for her daughter's mission hospital: piped water and a generator to provide electricity for air conditioning, as Ruth performed extensive surgery in a difficult tropical environment. For Donald there was a residual sense left in him that he would have liked to have continued to minister to the poor. The quality of the Coggans' own relationship also comes through: 'We return to York after tea today, driving ourselves and enjoying the opportunity of being together with no interruptions except traffic[80].

Donald Coggan's refusal to be a party bishop received general acclaim, but it also had its negative side. His intolerance of poor standards of worship made him equally restive whether he found lack of adequate planning of services by Evangelicals, or too great an emphasis on fussy minutiae in more catholic ceremonial. His preaching was strictly Bible-based, technically impressive and often appreciated. He owed much, so he frequently wrote and explained, to the Congregationalist divine, P.T. Forsyth[81]. Donald almost never drew, so it is said, from his own wells; he did not allow his preaching to take risks and become experiential. He spoke more of the experience of Hosea and Amos than of his own. Nor did it enter his written work. He published five books during the York period[82], which were precise and accurate, but neither intellectually profound nor works of scholarship; they were not intended to be, since they were for the most part based on his lectures and had a specifically didactic purpose, designed for popular consumption. Archbishop Coggan's letters in the monthly Diocesan Leaflet were sometimes criticized. Archbishop Garbett had taken infinite pains here, and Michael Ramsey had used this means to tackle difficult

[80] Letter of 12 September 1970.
[81] 1848-1921; in particular his book *Positive Preaching and the Modern Mind*, Hodder & Stoughton 1907; also see Donald Coggan, *Christian Priorities*, (Harper and Row 1963), pp.149-54.
[82] See Appendix 1, Publications.

theological questions. Shortage of time and a desire to appear friendly, inclined Donald to write in an informal manner; it was difficult to win all the time.

It was generally conceded that Donald Coggan at York had been overseer of a happy diocese. The most frequent criticism of his ministry was on the matter of an uneven level of consultation. As in the case of many able men, he liked to make up his own mind; mulling over issues struck him as a waste of time. (It was noticed that when he returned from an overseas tour he was loath to speak of his experiences; they were over.) That he tried to run the diocese from his staff meetings rather than through the diocesan network of Committees who did not consider themselves sufficiently consulted, was the subject of comment. This was another problem that was to follow him to Canterbury.

A disinclination to admit weakness was noted: a failing of long standing. The only chinks in Archbishop Coggan's armour had been occasional bouts of laryngitis when the pace had proved too great even for him, and he lost his voice. His very strength and measure of self-discipline seemed to separate him from the rest of mankind, as also the extent of his commitment and careful allocation of time. His wife and daughters were seen to have learnt to take these circumstances in their stride and accept with gratitude the time it was possible to spend together. Jean found herself useful and fulfilling roles in the local community, particularly in the sphere of mental health[83]. The staff who had served Donald with esteem and devotion smiled when the next Archbishop of York[84] announced one afternoon that he intended to down tools and have a game of tennis; a *frisson*, which recognized the winds of change, went through the office.

---

[83] She also became the first woman Lay Reader in the diocese.
[84] Stuart Blanch.

CHAPTER EIGHT *Canterbury*

Few Archbishops-designate of Canterbury have possessed advance knowledge of what the office, in practice, would signify. Randall Davidson, Archbishop 1903-28, may have been one of these exceptions. He had been chaplain to Archbishop Tait[1] and had witnessed daily the activity and problems within Lambeth Palace, and moreover had married the Archbishop's daughter. Donald Coggan was not in this category. One fact those who feel they understand the Church of England find certain: the Archbishopric of York does not carry with it a foretaste of Canterbury. The two functions are dissimilar, and different kinds of stewardship are called for.

Donald spent six months buffeted to and fro in a kind of ecclesiastical limbo, in receipt of alternate encouragement and discouragement, as he waited to assume the chair of St Augustine. Hundreds of letters, telegrams and cables flowed into Bishopthorpe from a broad range of people from all over the world; they included Christian and other leaders. Pope Paul VI offered his good wishes and assurance of fervent prayers for the new pastoral task in terms that recognized Donald's particular interests and outlook, and identified himself with them. The Pope wrote that he saw in him one who was no stranger to fruitful ecumenical collaboration with the Roman Catholic Church and other Churches. The renewal of fervour for evangelization embodied in the 'Call to the North' and in Donald's presidency of the United Bible Societies gave clear testimony of his concern for the spread of the gospel and his distinction as a contributor to the study of sacred Scripture. As he assumed his increased responsibility as President of the Anglican Communion, the Synod of Bishops of the Roman Catholic Church would be meeting in Rome to consider the theme 'Evangelization in the modern world'. 'Your record of pastoral work and of published statements gives us confidence that your brotherly interest, your thoughts and prayers, will be with them'.

Cardinal Suenens thanked the Lord for the 'providential nomination' and congratulated the Archbishop and his wife with 'deep

[1] Archbishop of Canterbury 1868-82.

pastoral affection'. The Cardinal remained 'very united with you in prayer to the Holy Spirit in ecumenical hope'. The Rector and staff of the English College in Rome cabled their good wishes. Various Jewish Communities expressed their pleasure. The Chief Rabbi wrote:

> I feel I must convey to you personally my great delight and warm felicitations on your elevation. As a cherished friend of our people, a Hebrew scholar of note and an outstanding champion of our common ideals, your election is a source of particular gratification to us.

Free Church leaders sent their greetings. There were letters which looked forward to an era of promise for the Church. The Prince of Wales wrote in this vein as one of 'the swelling ranks of your devoted admirers'. (Prince and Archbishop drew close in the next five years.) A correspondent made the request that the Archbishop should entertain the thought of issuing a call to England and so unite the Church in nationwide mission: to educate the man in the pew to tell the Good News to the man in the street. Billy Graham was convinced that 'this is of God'. Rosamund Fisher expressed her delight, both on her own account and Geoffrey's: 'To have an old friend, and a dear one, as Archbishop is most comforting'. There was a sprinkling of communications from the mentally sick, not all of it benign, though Donald enjoyed being reminded that he was following in office Archbishop Ramsey Macdonald. The main bulk of the correspondence was immensely supportive; much of it was answered personally.

Donald's initial experience with the press on his new appointment was, however, less cheering. Throughout his Canterbury ministry there were two counts upon which he received particular criticism; one was the old bogey of hesitation to consult, the other was a tendency towards insufficient preparation. Both factors came into play on this occasion. Mitigating circumstances were the usual chronic pressure and shortage of time, but the results were unfortunate; the future Archbishop of Canterbury did not do himself justice. His inherent goodness, trust, hope, keen pastoral sense, and dedication to the Kingdom of God and the gospel message did not transmit themselves readily by means of answers to questions put by the largely uncomprehending. The attempt to convey what came out of the interview in concrete terms in a newspaper column, was not found easy. As a result, those references he did make on specific topics were latched upon and accentuated, not for the last time.

Much was made of his remark that Britain would have a healthy society 'when it starts living by some rules again . . . and there is a lot to be said for the Ten Commandments.'

A particularly insensitive question at the first press conference concerned the reaction of the Archbishop's wife to the move: 'I know she is very domesticated, with knitting and even filing'. That his beloved Jean, with her responsible leading part in the work of hospitals and various charities, and adequate resident household staff, should be accounted a filing clerk, was nothing if not undermining. In fact, Jean's lack of interest in things domestic was one of the reasons why the Coggans set less store than others on entertaining. He replied, 'I think she is a marvellous person'; he did not think it would be possible to undertake the new assignment without her. An Archbishop had been appointed, it was declared, who would be sixty-five years old on assuming office; younger bishops were said to find him something of a conservative; the epithet 'caretaker' was applied. Donald Coggan was able to turn this to good account as he expressed himself happy to take care of the Church of God. It was, in fact, to become his crowning achievement, had his detractors but known it.

The general picture drawn of the next occupant of the see of Canterbury was of an ageing puritan, an example of the reactionary side of the Church of England. His remarks on 'the unacceptable creed of greed' were taken to imply criticism of the Trade Unions; there had been plenty of greed in earlier generations in the middle and upper classes. A television confrontation of 1961 with Adam Faith, the pop singer, cropped up again, in order to demonstrate the gap that had so patently existed between them. A gentle, friendly man, was one verdict, 'who should not be asked to confront real life'.

Later interviews with a more understanding questioner[2] took up the matter of the Ten Commandments. The Archbishop explained he had mentioned them earlier 'almost as an aside'. He had been haunted by them ever since. No, they were not the gospel; men needed to move from law to grace and new life in Christ. He spoke of the issues he cared about: a concern for world need, the place of God in history, help for agnostics, mission, efficiency in the Church, optimism, preaching. A more sympathetic picture of

[2] John Barton, then Religious adviser to Thames Television, now Chief Broadcasting Officer of the General Synod, in a series of talks at midnight in January 1975 during the week of the Enthronement.

Donald Coggan emerged as the result of longer thought and preparation.

His appointment to Canterbury was made public on 14 May 1974. Archbishop Ramsey had announced that he would retire on 15 November. The confirmation of the election of his successor was accordingly arranged to take place on 5 December; it would signal his assumption of the office. The Enthronement in Canterbury Cathedral would follow on the eve of the Conversion of St Paul, 24 January. One of Donald's first thoughts was to make sure that his complete family would be present. He wrote to Pakistan to ask Ruth whether she would consider making a short visit to England 'for this little event', if her patients could spare her; he would pay the fare. 'Lots and lots of luv, darling, and may the miracles keep on happening' was a typical close to his letters; Ruth's because she recognized her parents' interest, gave accounts of her surgery. It was agreed that she should come.

In June the second floor flat at Lambeth Palace, which had been occupied by Geoffrey Tiarks[3] and his wife, was inspected by Donald and Jean and found to be suitable for their occupation when re-decorated. The large reception rooms below, facing the garden, would only be used when there were guests. Because of pressure of work the Old Palace, which was to be their Canterbury home, remained unvisited until mid-September. Except for impossible and old-fashioned kitchen arrangements which could be altered, they liked the house 'under the shadow of the superb cathedral', though the garden was not a patch on the one at Bishopthorpe which had been such a solace; Donald's one real relaxation was the creation of bonfires. As Jean wrote to Ruth, fortunately the move was not until the worst time of the year, which would make the parting easier.

A fortnight in Sweden and Norway in August began as a complete rest, but the end was devoted partly to the planning of lectures: some for Canada in May 1975, and the Ashe lecture in Ashby-de-la-Zouche on 1 October. It was designed as a Retrospect and Prospect[4] – looking back on forty years of ordained ministry and ahead to the next stage at Canterbury, and is therefore not without interest. The reflections from the past that had suggested themselves were the *craving for God* which he saw as having been mani-

[3] Bishop of Maidstone and up until then Senior Chaplain to the Archbishop of Canterbury.
[4] See Donald Coggan, *Convictions*, pp. 17-24.

fested, the resilience of the Christian faith, a return to the New Testament, and a revival of worship. Prophecy of the future he thought rash, but 'expression of certain hopes' might be allowed. Two were offered in skeleton form: the first was that the Church be true to its divine Master's commission to feed his flock . . . to point men to *God* – only then would their thirst be satisfied; others could supply the social services. The second was that the Church would recover its joy; that he felt in recent years there had been something of a surfeit of ecclesiastical breast-beating. The Church had plenty to repent of, but on the other hand there were causes for joy and exultation in the Holy Spirit. Hope had long been the neglected member of the Pauline trio of faith, hope and love.

Donald concluded this talk by setting out his wish and prayer for the Church in the last quarter of the twentieth century; that she would turn to the world a face that reflected something of Christ. Later he was to be taken to task, particularly during his *Call to the Nation* in October 1975, for failing to draw sufficient attention to the disillusion that existed in regard to the Church. He saw the problem as imprisonment, which could be cured by more efficient administration as a start, rather than opposition. In the last words of the text of the Ashe lecture he had provided an answer to the problem, even if he did not show himself aware of the need to examine it.

On 8 October 1974 Donald Coggan addressed the Northern Convocation for the last time as President. He looked back to the last thirteen years in that office, asked for prayers and spoke of prayer. 'We will pray', he said, 'Thy Kingdom come; Thy will be done'; there was no greater prayer than that. And they would pray in a spirit of eucharistic joy. John Moorman, Bishop of Ripon, as the longest-serving bishop of the province, spoke of their benevolent and self-effacing President, of his feeling for evangelism, education, and social problems; his work for *Feed the Minds* and the *Call to the North*. The Prolocutor described Donald as a bishop who took enormous pains with people in trouble, particularly sick and elderly clergy: 'you can be sure of our love and affection'.

The farewell of the Diocese took place in the Minster on 24 October, when a congregation of two thousand joined in the Eucharist. Archbishop Coggan preached from St Paul's second letter to the Corinthians 13.11[5]:

> Finally, brethren farewell. Mend your ways, heed my appeal, agree with

[5] ibid., pp. 33-7.

one another, live in peace, and the God of love and peace will be with you.

He did not intend a note of rebuke that night, he said, although that was not to say that the Church in the diocese was perfect; there were areas where there was no progress, where few of the fruits of the Spirit were shown, where the first concern seemed to be survival rather than mission. But there were other places where worship was joyful and witness powerful. He was grateful for all that he and Jean had been given in the past thirteen years. He went on to speak of the need for love, for response to the love of God.

We often tend to overcomplicate religion and make it more difficult than it need be. When this note of responding love, of grateful indebtedness, is missing from our religion, the fire and love go from it.

Finally he spoke of peace, of tranquillity of mind that arose from reconciliation with God and the harmony in relationships, one to the other, that could spring out of it. St Paul's salutation, 'Live in Peace, and the God of love and peace will be with you', was his final message.

Six weeks of ministry in the North remained, which included a number of royal occasions. The Queen Mother visited York in November to open a Centre for old people that had been created from a redundant church; she lunched at Bishopthorpe. Ann Coggan who had followed her father by deciding to teach, came up from the Pilgrims' School at Winchester for what became a family occasion. There was supper with the Queen at the end of the month, and a valedictory dinner at No 10 Downing Street for Archbishop and Mrs Ramsey given by the Prime Minister. Archbishop Coggan presided at the General Synod's farewell to the Archbishop of Canterbury on 7 November, and made the first speech and presentation. Michael Ramsey replied, and finished with the words 'we shall all be praying that under the leadership of you, dear Donald, the witness of the Church will be courageous and joyful'.

At 9.37 pm on 5 December 1974 the last named wrote to Ruth. 'Wot a day it has been!' First had come the confirmation of his election to the see of Canterbury in the crypt of St Paul's Cathedral; 'a field day for the legal boys and a posse of senior bishops did their stuff'; then a lunch at the Mansion House with the Lord Mayor of London, where the only ladies were the Lady Mayoress and Jean; finally to Buckingham Palace to do homage, when he had had a longish talk with the Queen. He ended 'I beg to remain . . . with very much love, your devoted father Donald Cantuar'.

The Coggans spent their last Christmas at Bishopthorpe. Early in January, after the arrival of Ruth from Pakistan, they effected the double move into the flat at Lambeth and the Old Palace at Canterbury. Chad, their black labrador, (named after the second Archbishop of York b.672) came with them; also John and Margaret Bates who had provided living-in help in the Yorkshire household. Two other members of the Archbishop's staff, his driver and gardener, had earned their retirement.

For four days before the Enthronement the Archbishop and his wife stayed at West Malling Abbey, home of an Order of Anglican Benedictine Sisters. The fact that the service on 24 January became a large-scale police operation was a measure of the political, social and moral unrest that was characteristic of the year 1975, and the climate in which he assumed the Primacy. Terrorism, race-riots, hooliganism and violence, high rate of marriage breakdown, inflation, cost of living increases, and rising figures for abortion, were some of the symptoms. For the first time, members of the royal family, the Prince of Wales, Princess Margaret and the Duchess of Kent[6] who came from a Yorkshire family and of whom the Coggans had seen a good deal in the North, announced their intention to attend the service. The leaders of the three main political parties, Harold Wilson, the Prime Minister, Edward Heath and Jeremy Thorpe came also, with members of the Cabinet, of both Houses of Parliament, the Judiciary, the universities. Thus a considerable security risk had been created, and hundreds of policemen and women, dogs trained to smell explosives, barricades and cordons filled the Cathedral and Precincts, and had done for several days in advance of the event. Entry was by pass only.

The ceremony itself was one of great splendour, with 640 members of the congregation of 3,200 in the processions. The Dean and Chapter of York had presented their departing Archbishop with a cope on which the orphreys spelt out his *curriculum vitae*: embroidered were the arms of Merchant Taylors' School, St John's College, Cambridge, Manchester University, Wycliffe Hall Oxford, Wycliffe College Toronto, the London College of Divinity, the diocese of Bradford, the Provinces of York and Canterbury; also a mitre and stole. All these he wore. The Merchant Taylors' Company gave him a pastoral staff.

Particularly memorable was the representation from other Christian Churches; for the first time since the Reformation from the

---

[6] Her younger son, Lord Nicholas Windsor, was Archbishop Coggan's godchild.

Roman Catholic Church, in the persons of Cardinal Willebrands, head of the Vatican Secretariat for Christian Unity; Donald Coggan's old friend Cardinal Suenens, Primate of Belgium; Cardinal Marty, Archbishop of Paris; Monsignor Cyril Cowderoy, Roman Catholic Archbishop of Southwark and Monsignor Bruno Heim, the Apostolic Delegate. Members of other Christian Communions were also present: the Orthodox Archbishop of Thyateira, the Moderator of the Church of Scotland, the Moderator of the Free Church Federal Council. All these greeted the Archbishop of Canterbury on the steps of the nave, and representatives from the world-wide Anglican Communion gave their greetings at the High Altar. The choir sang *Expectans Expectavi* by Charles Wood at Donald Coggan's request.

He was enthroned twice: once as 101st Archbishop of the see of Canterbury into his episcopal seat in the Choir by the Archdeacon (his prerogative in respect of all enthronements in the Southern Province), and the second time as head of the Anglican Communion in the so-called Chair of St Augustine, placed for this occasion on the steps in front of the nave altar by the Dean. The Primate of Kenya, the Most Reverend Festo Olang, gave his blessing.

The new Archbishop preached on a text which might have been expected in the disturbed times: 'In the world you shall have tribulation. But be of good cheer, I have overcome the world'[7].

The pivot of the glittering occasion, surrounded by the great of the land and those for whom he cared most, Jean, Ann, Ruth, his sisters, the huge cross-section of men and women of all walks of life, Donald Coggan chose to give vent to an issue close to his heart. Television cameras which took the whole ceremony to much of the world, relayed his message, the main burden of which concerned the needs of the ordained ministry. He spoke of the realism that Jesus had shown in times of complexity and danger; of the confidence which Christians should show by means of hope based on the Resurrection. In recent years the Church had passed through – was indeed still passing through – a period in which loss of nerve had been a prevailing attitude. Against that background, he pleaded in particular for those fruits of the spirit of confidence and joy to address themselves towards two great needs: first for a steady increase in the numbers, which had been declining, of those coming forward for the ordained ministry. He made it clear that he was

---

[7] John 16.33. ibid., pp. 38-42.

addressing himself to men who would offer the whole of their lives, full-time:

> There is no finer life than that of a parish priest. Covet this calling. Train for it. Pour your best into it. Glory in it. Count yourself thrice-blessed, if you hear God calling you to it.

He ended with the second need: to look beyond divisions of denomination, nationality, economic grouping, and so achieve reconciliation on a world basis. 'We must grow till our arms get right round the world'[8].

The Church of England, as he implied, was undergoing its own ferment, some of it constructive and a sign of continuing life; some of it resistant to change. A mixed reception was given to the Archbishop's words. There were those who responded by offering themselves for ordination; others felt that he was guilty of a lack of the realism of which he spoke: how were these extra priests to be paid; were not the experiments in alternative forms of ministry, such as the training of auxiliary and non-stipendiary clergy, who were more closely in touch with the lives of lay people, the signs of hope for the future? The interplay of differing points of view that were to characterize Archbishop Coggan's ministry at Canterbury, had begun.

On the afternoon following the Enthronement he received at Lambeth Metropolitan Juvenaly, who had come to represent the Russian Orthodox Church. This was the Archbishop's first ecumenical visitor; the gesture was appreciated and bore fruit during the Primate's visit to Russia in the Autumn of 1977. In the evening Donald preached at Westminster Abbey, when he was welcomed as Archbishop of Canterbury at Evensong, on the text 'To me life is Christ'[9]. He spoke with familiarity on St Paul, whose feast it was, and since he had made so many of the Apostle's attributes his own, his words carried conviction and force. He reminded the congregation of the words of his predecessor at York, Archbishop Garbett: 'the Church of God is an army on the march in a hostile country, not a rest camp for the tired'. It was a salutary warning for those who were about to work with him. But the mellow side of him emerged also when he concluded with a quotation from Charles Raven[10],

He takes us and fills us with a life not our own, a life which is beyond

---

[8] Quoting General Booth of the Salvation Army.
[9] Philippians 1.21. ibid., pp. 43-8.
[10] 1885-1964; Regius Professor of Divinity, Cambridge University, 1932-50.

sorrow and romance, He takes us and in His grip we live abundantly, sharing for a moment the activity of His overwhelming love.

He ended: 'There is justification. There is holiness. There is unity. There is life.'

Before the end of January the House of Bishops met at Church House, Westminster for the first time under his presidency, followed next day by the (twice yearly) Bishops' meeting. It was to become a delicate area. Archbishop Coggan's relationships, as President, with the Bishops of the Northern Province had been dominated by the fact that, apart from the Bishop of Ripon[11], he had been the longest in office; bishops had been consecrated by him and had stayed at Bishopthorpe; he had had a hand in their appointments. His sense of exposure was therefore bound to make itself felt, as chairman of the larger group. Moreover, the question as to what issues should be presented to the House of Bishops, and which to Bishops' meetings, was in the melting pot, as also the constitution of the latter: whether suffragans, and if so how many, should be included. Some bishops favoured that meetings be more informal. (The extent of publication of the proceedings of the House of Bishops was also under consideration.) It would seem that general agreement accounted the new Archbishop an excellent chairman. There would be times, however, when disappointment would be registered as to the degree of consultation he prescribed, and his view of the principle of collegiality.

Some initial concern was expressed about Donald Coggan's experience of administration, particularly in regard to arrangements in the office at Lambeth. He had made it clear in press conferences that he understood the tasks of the two appointments at York and Canterbury to be 'very different'. His interventions in the debates on Crown Appointments[12] had indicated that he felt 'a bishop is more than an ecclesiastic'; he had spoken of the function of a bishop in the life of the nation. His greater participation in secular events once he was Archbishop of Canterbury, and the more specifically patriotic tone of many of his addresses in the future, were seen as the application of this outlook to his new role. Some of his staff who were responsible for the great volume of paper work, however, were heard to question whether their Archbishop was sufficiently aware of the contrast between the administrative demands of the two sees.

[11] Appointed 1959.
[12] 22 February 1973, *General Synod February Group of Sessions 1973 Report of Proceedings*, Vol. 4, No. 1, pp. 178-9.

It seemed to them that he was assuming that the Archbishopric of Canterbury could be managed in the same way as he had run the Archbishopric of York. In this area, the Northern Province was in no way a preparation.

From the beginning, the staff was amazed at the Archbishop's capacity for work. For the good of the Kingdom of God, his efforts knew no limit. Moreover the speed at which he worked was impressive; true to form, not a moment was wasted. There was a considerable backlog of material which required resolution when he entered his office at the end of January. He made it clear that he had his own way of operating, which did not involve leisurely discussions to become acquainted, or to get abreast of events and background. In fact, consultation was to become a difficult issue, and as a consequence, the whole matter of briefing and preparation also. Much of the decision-making, interviewing, correspondence, was handled by Archbishop Coggan himself. He wrote all his sermons and speeches, and at the beginning, dictated many of the letters. In some areas he worked independently of his staff.

Nearly all of them were inherited from the previous regime; two, Hugh Whitworth[13], the Lay Assistant and Barbara Lepper[14], the Archbishop's Personal Secretary, had been Civil Servants and familiar with administration at high level. John Kirkham[15] was Domestic Chaplain, Michael Moore[16] was Chaplain and Christopher Hill[17] Assistant Chaplain to the Archbishop, for Foreign Relations. David Moir Carey[18], a partner in the firm of Solicitors, Lee Boulton and Lee, of Westminster, was part-time Legal Secretary and Registrar. Geoffrey Tiarks, who had been Senior Chaplain to Archbishop Ramsey, returned to live in his area as Suffragan Bishop of Maidstone. Donald Coggan appointed Douglas Cleverley Ford[19] in his stead. There were, in addition, some junior secretaries.

A great pile of letters flowed daily into Lambeth Palace, many of which were personal pleas to the Archbishop; he was widely regarded as the final arbiter not only on spiritual issues, but on matters of welfare or morals, second perhaps only to the Queen. He

[13] 1914- ; MBE 1945.
[14] Lambeth MA; MBE 1980.
[15] 1935- ; Bishop of Sherborne 1976.
[16] 1935- ; Chaplain at Hampton Court Palace 1984.
[17] 1945- ; Joint Secretary of ARCIC.
[18] Lambeth DCL 1980.
[19] 1914- ; Hon. Director College of Preachers 1966-73.

was asked to put right alleged oppression by the civil authorities, or by the Church, for instance, questions of remarriage or baptism. Some requests were trivial: that a vicar be prosecuted for having allowed sheep or goats to eat flowers on a family grave. Many letters concerned the treatment of animals, some took up various causes to do with children. A proportion of them were hysterical, even paranoid. But there was a greater section of correspondence which dealt with personal and spiritual problems, from parents whose children were on drugs, men and women who were in danger of losing their faith or their way, prospective candidates for Holy Orders, wives whose husbands were in prison, the unemployed, and so on. These the Archbishop took very seriously. All received carefully phrased, constructive, personal replies which often continued after the initial contact. The files at Lambeth for the next five years would be filled with letters such as these. Moreover, personal interviews would be suggested. Those who watched shook their heads over the time that was occupied in this pastoral ministry which could have been delegated. Had he done so, the Archbishop would not have been Donald Coggan. Though he could be stern and authoritative, he was the least princely of men, who could not bear that anyone should feel he was too important to help them. All deserved answers; there must never be any sense of writing to the engine driver only to receive 'a wipe from an oily rag'.

The price that was paid for this outlook was the even further curtailing of time that could be spent on other business, particularly its preparation. The Archbishop was a believer in the value of friendly, spontaneous speech. Some of his utterances were to have repercussions that he did not expect, and of which he could have been warned. The tendency to misrepresent him he found saddening; when it was severe, the wickedness of it was a shock. Archbishop Coggan was in his Chapel at 7.15 each morning, and worked till late into the night, but still there was pressure. A life-long obsession that a team of few people worked more efficiently than one with many, and the need to economize, prevented him from pressing for more assistance.

One of the additional administrative hazards was the existence of the second home, at the Old Palace in Canterbury. The Archbishop, accompanied nearly always by his wife, would drive down on Friday evenings to spend time in his diocese over the week-end. Michael Ramsey had written, on Donald's appointment, 'diocesan work, whilst adding to the load, is in itself a lovely refreshment.' So he found it. His attachment to Canterbury and its surroundings became increasingly strong and began to surpass that to York. On Sundays he celebrated the Holy Communion in the Cathedral at 8 am then officiated in one or two churches of the diocese during the rest of the morning and afternoon, returning to Lambeth at night. A number of letters would have been waiting for him at the house in Canterbury; he would reply in his own hand or by way of tape recordings. When the telephone rang, frequently the Archbishop himself would answer and deal in person with the problem or request.

Eventually the Archbishop came to appreciate the confusion that these practices caused in the Lambeth office. Apart from a dislike of becoming audio-typists, his secretarial staff suffered from the inability to keep fully abreast of the Archbishop's movements and activities. Engagements became duplicated. He was still a very private man who liked to run his own affairs, make his own arrangements, keep his own secrets. His dislike of publicity and intrusion into his personal life made him exclaim, 'They'll be wanting to know the colour of my pyjamas'. But because Donald was fundamentally a reconciler, who valued good relationships and the application of humour to human situations, the problems became fewer. As mutual trust and respect increased, there were members of his staff on whom he knew he could rely who would receive some of his confidences.

There was still another big engagement before the end of Archbishop Coggan's first week since his Enthronement, and it was one that brought him much pleasure. His first Consecration to the episcopate in the South was of his colleague of long standing, John V. Taylor, formerly General Secretary of the Church Missionary Society, son of his former principal at Wycliffe Hall, to the see of Winchester[20]. Five days later he addressed the General Synod for the first time as President, and chose as his theme 'True Patriotism'[21]. He analysed the term not as one that implied 'my country right or wrong, its wealth and demands first to the neglect of the needs of other nations, including those of the third world'; that would be a travesty of its true meaning. As might have been expected, he turned to the Bible to examine three figures, Moses, Hosea, and Jesus, as the three greatest Hebrew patriots from whom present-day Britons could learn. Patriotism, he said, involved prayer, constant, deep and costly; and probably criticism of much

---

[20] 31.1.75; together with Ivor Colin Docker to be Suffragan Bishop of Horsham.
[21] Donald Coggan, *Convictions*, pp. 53-6.

that took place in public life and government policy. In the two examples he gave he reiterated his condemnation both of the inversion of the divine order to which he had often before made reference (self first, others next, God last), and also of acquisitiveness: 'we assent to the creed of greed'. He appealed for a charter of duties, rather than rights, and for the willingness to agonize over the destiny of the nation. From now on there was to be no respite for Donald Coggan; there was also to be some agonizing.

The activity of an Archbishop of Canterbury can be seen to exist on various levels: there are the single engagements that occupy a limited amount of time and are not necessarily repeated; also journeys and conferences abroad over a more extended period. Meetings, whether of the Bishops, the General Synod and the Standing Committee, the Church Commissioners, Diocesan Synod, Archbishop's Council, or those with his staff of Suffragans and Archdeacons, come round with unfailing regularity; as also letters from all quarters, including those from fellow Primates and members of the Anglican Communion. There are matters of long standing left over from a predecessor which stretch far into the new reign, awaiting development and resolution; successive Archbishops deal with them differently and leave their own imprint. Last come the initiatives which a Primate decides to take himself. And intertwined with it all are his relationships on a broad front: with the Monarch and her family, Members of Parliament and the government, his fellow bishops, the clergy, people of great influence and none, the men and women he baptizes, confirms, marries; the relatives of those he buries.

Archbishop Coggan undertook a heavy load of daily engagements. He had a concern to identify himself in what might have been thought purely secular and civic concerns, for he felt it was incumbent upon him to take the Christian gospel into all areas of life. Whether he managed to do so, is a matter of opinion. His own strong personal faith was obvious to all; his ability to translate it into terms that could stir the people of England was sometimes questioned.

The more important of the daily events will be recorded on a continuous narrative basis, as also the overseas journeys. The long-term questions that faced Donald Coggan included those of the ministry: the ordination of women, new types of ministry, the future of the theological colleges; matters of relations between Church and State, especially the appointment of bishops; certain social and moral issues, such as race relations and family problems;

the reunion of Christendom, which concerned not only future relationships with the Free Churches, but the shape of continuing dialogue with Rome. These will be examined as salient issues arise, and the survey will cover a long-ranging time span. Archbishop Coggan's own initiatives, the *Call to the Nation*, the *Nationwide Initiative for Evangelism*, the visit to Pope Paul, to the Oecumenical Patriarch and headquarters of the World Council at Geneva, and the Lambeth Conference, will receive similar treatment.

His immediate programme was one of infinite variety: interviews or meals with the Ambassadors of Egypt, Israel and Greece, the Lord Chamberlain, the Free Church Federal Council, an Armenian Bishop; a visit to Cardinal Heenan, at this time no longer well; talks to the Religious Press and the Parliamentary Press Gallery[22], a body of 120 men and women; lunch with Mrs Judith Hart, Minister for Overseas Development; back to York to preach at the Memorial Service for the Dean, Alan Richardson[23]; five visits to schools, three for confirmations; the installation of an incumbent in his own diocese. The BBC's private showing of the television coverage of the Enthronement was much enjoyed by the Coggans, particularly as Chad, the black labrador, could be heard barking as he reacted to police alsatians on his territory. Early in April came the first Easter at Canterbury, where the Archbishop preached to a full cathedral on Jesus the Carpenter, who repaired wood and human lives. Next day he mixed with some hundreds of young people on the annual youth pilgrimage. It was much busier, he remarked, than Easter at York.

Donald's first journey beyond England as Archbishop of Canterbury was a significant one for its impact upon him. In mid April he made a six-day visit to Northern Ireland and Dublin. True to form, he combined various of his spheres of interest: first came pastoral visits by helicopter to British troops in barracks at Londonderry, and in Bishop Street, when he viewed the Bogside and Creggan from the walls; he met Church and Community leaders there and in Belfast; a day was spent with the clergy of the Church of Ireland, when he lectured at their annual Refresher Course at Portrush on 'Preaching Today'. In Dublin he made a courtesy call on Cardinal Conway and the Roman Catholic Archbishop, Dr Dermot Ryan. His last engagement was to preach at Evensong in St Patrick's Cathedral on *Feed the Minds*. To Ruth, Donald wrote that Ireland had been strenuous and tragic, as he visited troops and casualties in

[22] Donald Coggan, *Sure Foundation* (Hodder and Stoughton 1981), pp. 73-5.
[23] Donald Coggan, *Convictions*, pp. 306-9.

hospitals, homes and shops; 'kindness all along the road, but oh, when will the slaughter end?'

The pace of life, once back in England, is illustrated by the events of a successive few days: a dinner in Lincoln's Inn, where he had been made a Bencher, was followed by interviews at Lambeth next morning and attendance by 2.15 in the afternoon at the General Council of the Church Missionary Society at Reading. At 4.30 pm he flew from Heathrow airport to Edinburgh for an address at 7 pm before 500 people. A night sleeper returned him to Kings Cross by 6.40 am. He celebrated the Holy Communion (Series 3) at 10.30 am in Canterbury, at the beginning of the Diocesan Synod, where he presided and gave an address. The following day (Sunday) was devoted to visits to two parishes; another full week began.

The British Council of Churches met two days later, for the first time under the presidency of the new occupant of the see of Canterbury. Next morning he preached at St George's Chapel, Windsor[24], lunched with the Queen, and later in the afternoon talked with the Prime Minister at Downing Street.

An article in the Times[25] that week declared, under the heading 'A Primate who stands for all Christians', that the Archbishop of Canterbury was the one figure in British church life who transcended denominational boundaries; the presidency of the British Council of Churches was the only visible sign of it. Dr Coggan, it went on

> because of his personal style as a man of the evangelical tradition, is particularly well suited to give this dimension of his office new life and deeper meaning. As Pope John brought alive the papacy, so Dr Coggan can bring alive the primacy . . . The Church of England has not yet woken up to the full significance of the primate's standing in the eyes either of the new-Anglican churches or of the unchurched masses in general.

From what was to happen in the autumn, it would seem the Archbishop himself was impressed by this line of argument.

On 30 April he flew to Canada with his wife and domestic chaplain, John Kirkham. He gave an address to the Convocation of Trinity College, Toronto, next day and talked at length during much of the following thirty-six hours with the Primate and Metropolitans of Canada, and the Presiding Bishop of the Episcopal Church of the United States, John Maury Allin, who had travelled

---

[24] Donald Coggan, *Sure Foundation*, pp. 165-8.
[25] April 21, 1975.

to Canada to confer with the Archbishop of Canterbury. At lunch on May 1 he addressed the prestigious Empire Club of Canada and Canadian Club of Toronto, under the title 'Waste in the West'[26]: pollution, waste of food, waste of life, particularly the destruction of the unborn, waste of youth, of university opportunities, of resources. It revealed his distress at what he saw as a nation-wide malaise, as also his belief that these issues were fundamentally theological and religious.

Donald paid a nostalgic visit to the huge St Paul's, Bloor Street, where he preached before flying West to Saskatoon. During the following four days he delivered four Bishop Martin Memorial Lectures on Preaching[27] at the College of Emmanuel and St Chad, in the course of which he laid some of the blame for the current 'moral chaos' on the absence of 'solid, systematic, down-to-earth and up-to-heaven teaching and preaching'. He bewailed the modern tendency to replace the pulpit by a folding *legillium*. The Old Testament prophet Hosea had in his time pinpointed his nation's defection as 'lack of knowledge'. The Archbishop proceeded to examine some of the prophetic figures of the Bible. What constitutes a prophet is exact, he said: the rigorous proclamation of what God does, of God's decision today. A prophet offers a living Word for the present. He offers a Word relevant to the actual situation of men, a Word which will be the solution . . . and which implies for man a strange renouncing of his own methods and policies and normal inclinations. He stressed the place of preaching in the life of Jesus as the climax of the prophetic line; the need to declare the Word as from God, and as members of Christ, as part of the Body of Christ. It meant that it was possible to rely not only on one's own experiences, but those of others. He acknowledged, once more, his indebtedness to P.T. Forsyth, who 'had written the greatest book on preaching in this century', and ended with various practical issues. A visit to the diocese of Kootenay which celebrated a seventy-fifth anniversary Eucharist, at which he preached, and a Provincial Centenary service for Rupertsland, back in Saskatoon, where he did likewise, rounded off the tour.

Concern over the growing number of abortions carried out in England was a subject to which the attention of the Archbishop was constantly being drawn. An invitation to preach at Westminster

---

[26] ibid., pp. 107-13.
[27] Later published under the title *On Preaching*, Toronto, Anglican Book Centre 1978.

Abbey[28] for the Order of the Bath in the presence of the Queen, at which the Prince of Wales was to be installed as Grand Master, gave him the opportunity to secure a wide hearing. In spite of a strong feeling towards renewal, there was a nostalgic streak in Donald Coggan and a respect for tradition, which came to the fore in the national ceremonies of the next five years. On this occasion he spoke of the protection that the Orders of Chivalry had traditionally offered to the weak; in the present context, this must, he considered include a defence of the unborn. He went on to define 'the enemies at the gate', influences which poisoned or led astray the minds of the young: pornography, acquisitiveness, those who sought to educate without faith. A fortnight later, he installed the Duke of Gloucester as Grand Prior of the Order of St John, of which he had been Prelate since 1967[29].

The agenda of the session of the General Synod of July 1975 included a debate on the ordination of women. The Anglican Consultative Council[30] had requested, as a result of the Lambeth Conference of 1968, that every national and regional Church and Province should study the question and report. The Church of England decided in July 1973 that the views of the dioceses should be sought, both on the matter of principle, and the desirability of further action. In thirty-three Diocesan Synods the motion was carried that 'there are no fundamental objections to the ordination of women'. On the second issue, fifteen dioceses resolved that the Church should proceed to remove the legal and other barriers which impeded such ordinations.

On 3 July the Archbishop of Canterbury vacated the Chair and in a long speech added his weight in favour of the removal of those impediments which precluded women's ordination. He reiterated the relevance of the Holy Spirit in this matter, on which the Bishop of Oxford[31] had touched when he proposed the motion. 'This is quite fundamental to our thinking and to the decisions which we must reach before the end of the day'. He did not feel that any very clearly defined or rigid pattern of ministry had evolved by the first century; there was a fluidity about it. Eventually, he said, the

---

[28] 28 May 1975. Donald Coggan *Sure Foundation*, pp. 73-5.

[29] In succession to Archbishop Fisher.

[30] A body established by the 1968 Lambeth Conference to take over the responsibilities of the Lambeth Consultative Body and the Anglican Council on Missionary Strategy.

[31] Kenneth Woollcombe 1924- ; Bishop of Oxford 1971-8; Canon Residentiary of St Paul's 1981.

pattern of the three-fold ministry emerged, 'by a process of Spirit-guided evolution, rather than by a divine dictate of the Master of the Church'. The Archbishop thought this was a pointer for the future. He asked the question what was it in the nature of a woman which made it impossible for her to function as a priest, and suggested that it would be the Church which would benefit if Women's Ministry be extended to include the sacramental aspects contained in priesthood. The Synod voted on the main issue as follows:

Bishops Aye:28 No:10
Clergy Aye:110 No:96 (2 abstensions)
Laity Aye:117 No:74 (3 abstensions)

A second motion was proposed and carried which invited the House of Bishops, when they judged the time to be right and in consultation with other elements in the Anglican Communion, to bring before the Synod a proposal that women be admitted to the priesthood.

A good deal of the debate centred upon the consequences of the ordination of women upon relationships with the Roman Catholic and Orthodox Churches. A third motion carried by the Synod requested the Presidents

(i) to inform the appropriate authorities of those Churches of its belief that there are no fundamental objections to such ordination; and (ii) to invite those authorities to share in an urgent re-examination of the theological grounds for including women in the Order of Priesthood, with particular attention to the doctrine of Man and the doctrine of Creation.

Archbishop Coggan felt sufficiently strongly on the importance of these issues, that he caused the foregoing figures and facts to be printed as his monthly letter in the Canterbury Diocesan Notes[32]. He then set out to communicate with the Pope and with the Oecumenical Patriarch.

The Archbishop's Assistant Chaplain for Foreign Relations[33] had gone to Rome in May, in order to seek the reaction of the Secretariat for Promoting Christian Unity to the proposed debate by the General Synod in July on the ordination of women to the priesthood. The matter had been discussed extensively with a full staff, with Cardinal Willebrands, the President, in the Chair. The Secretariat was anxious not to precipitate any action which could be

[32] August 1975.
[33] Christopher Hill.

construed as intimidating the Church of England in its decision. It was made clear, however, that in spite of individual comments by some theologians, the official attitude of the Roman Catholic Church was for the present clearly against such a move, and would be so for the foreseeable future. On the other hand, the Secretariat had come to the view that, if at all possible, the Church of England and Anglican Communion should be invited to enter into dialogue.

Before the Synod debate Archbishop Coggan wrote to Cardinal Willebrands for his views on the forthcoming issue. The Cardinal replied on 7 June to the effect that the ecumenical importance of the question under discussion was certainly not one to be neglected. The Catholic Church had recently been organizing a number of studies on the role of women in the Church; a Study Commission had been set up, while the International Theological Commission and the Pontifical Biblical Commission had embarked on the same field. While therefore it could not be said that the ongoing studies pointed to any prospect of change in tradition, they might well raise points on which useful exchange of views might take place. If some exchange of views seemed acceptable to the Archbishops, practical suggestions would be welcomed. It might be that a meeting such as that envisaged by Bishop Howe[34] to the Secretariat in the following November, might be a proper occasion for a first exchange of information. This idea was adopted. On 12 June Cardinal Willebrands wrote to the Archbishop again. In preparation for the feast of Pentecost, the Pope had addressed to bishops, clergy and people an apostolic exhortation on Christian joy entitled *Gaudete in Domino*. He enclosed a copy. It was a subject close to the Archbishop's heart.

Following the Synod's decision, the Archbishop wrote to Cardinal Willebrands once more and set before him what had taken place. The House of Bishops had been asked to keep the situation in mind, and to judge when to bring before the Synod any practical proposals. More significantly, the ecumenical dimensions and the Synod's wishes regarding consultation and possible re-examination of theological issues, was made clear. Bishop Howe might be the person to take this further. Since the matter affected the Archbishop as Primate of All England and President of the Lambeth Conference, he had thought it right to write a letter to Pope Paul VI.

He informed the Pope on the same date of the slow but steady

---

[34] John William Alexander Howe 1920- ; Bishop of St Andrews 1955-69; Executive Officer Anglican Communion 1969-71; Secretary General Anglican Consultative Council 1971-82.

growth of consensus of opinion within the Anglican Communion that there were no fundamental objections in principle to the ordination of women to the priesthood. At the same time there was an awareness that the matter could be an obstacle to further progress 'along the path of unity Christ wills for his Church'. The central authorities of the Anglican Communion had called for common counsel in this matter. Correspondence had been exchanged with Cardinal Willebrands, and he and Bishop Howe were to have discussions. It was the Archbishop's hope, he ended, that such common counsel might achieve a fulfilment of the Apostle's precept that 'Speaking the truth in love' we 'may grow up into him in all things, which is the Lord, even Christ'.

He wrote a similar letter to the Oecumenical Patriarch at Istanbul. The negative reaction of the Orthodox Churches was seriously to affect future discussions of the Anglican Orthodox Joint Doctrinal Commission.

Bishop Howe duly had his meetings in Rome in November. Later in the month a message was passed to him from Cardinal Willebrands to the effect that he did not consider that if Anglicans proceeded to ordain women, this would necessarily bring to an end the efforts of the two Churches towards unity. Bishop Howe requested corroboration of this important statement. The Cardinal agreed that the substance was correct, but added the rider that such ordinations would constitute a new and serious difficulty and obstacle in the joint search for unity. The Pope, he went on, had made the same points in his reply to the Archbishop (dated 30 November 1975). The Cardinal hoped that the Archbishop would see fit to make this letter of His Holiness public at a suitable moment.

The Pope had appreciated the setting of confidence and candour in the Anglican presentation: he set out the Catholic view and reiterated the element of grave difficulty which had been introduced. Obstacles did not destroy mutual commitment to a search for reconciliation, he ended, and he had learnt with satisfaction of the discussions which had started on the fundamental theological importance of the issue in question, with the Secretariat for Promoting Christian Unity.

Soon after the Archbishop's Enthronement, on 11 February, he had asked for a summary as to what had been the progress of the Anglican-Roman Catholic International Commission (ARCIC). Agreed statements on the Eucharist (Windsor 1971) and on Ministry and Ordination (Canterbury 1973) had been published.

The Archbishop received a description of the International Commission's preliminary study on Authority which had been issued as the result of a meeting in Venice in 1970, and of the ARCIC meeting in Grottaferrata in August-September 1974, when work on the first of two statements on Authority had been begun. This was to be continued at the next meeting of ARCIC at St Stephen's House[35] in Oxford in the Autumn of 1975. Archbishop Coggan paid the Commission a personal visit on 3 September with Bishop Howe, who introduced him to the nine Anglican delegates under the co-chairman, Henry McAdoo, then Bishop of Ossory[36], and the nine Roman Catholic theologians with their co-chairman, Alan Clark, Bishop of East Anglia.

In a subsequent letter to Bishop McAdoo, the Archbishop expressed the pleasure the Oxford meeting had given him. The level of debate and the friendliness of members had been impressive. He liked the concept of 'sister churches'. Sisters should share the family board; they had the right because they were sisters. 'We must not be content with, nor accustomed to, the abnormality of relationships now existing. There must indeed be an "ecclesiology of the unprecedented situation".'

Cardinal Heenan lay dying during the first week of November. Archbishop Coggan sent him messages of 'anxiety, sympathy and prayer at this time and over the coming days'. On the Cardinal's death he issued a statement as to their friendship which went back to the days at Liverpool and York; 'I have valued the opportunity of working more closely with him in various spheres of common Christian concern. I pay tribute to him as a warm-hearted friend and a leader, not only in his own Church, but also in the ecumenical realm. He will be greatly missed'. The Archbishop also wrote in this vein to the Pope and to the Apostolic Delegate, and arranged to be represented at the Cardinal's funeral, which was on the eve of his own departure for Nairobi.

The newly-elected General Synod met two days earlier, preceded by a Eucharist in Westminster Abbey in the presence of the Queen. Donald Coggan's mention of the late Cardinal during the biddings was particularly appreciated by the Roman Catholic community in England. The Apostolic Delegate, who was also present at the opening of the Synod, made history when he asked for an interview with the Archbishop on the subject of a successor for Westminster.

[35] An Anglican Theological College.
[36] From 1977 Archbishop of Dublin.

To return to the events of the summer of 1975, there was one item of significance for the future, before the Coggans left for their holiday. In response to a request for an interview on a radio programme entitled *Sunday* in mid July, Archbishop Coggan indicated the kind of questions to which he wished to suggest answers. They concerned the economic crisis through which the nation was passing: whether the problems were a symptom of spiritual weakness, or due to disruptive elements within the economy and industry; whether a 'generation nurtured on affluence and materialism could be asked suddenly to stop wanting more'. What lead could Christians provide? It was clear that he was giving thought to how he might personally involve himself in the situation.

During the last days of July, Donald and Jean crossed from Southampton to Cherbourg with their car for a fortnight's holiday in Normandy, driving themselves. The first week had been booked in a country hotel, for the second they wandered at their will; their main objective was not to be recognized. Thereby fortified and back at home, the Archbishop made the final plans for his *Call to the Nation*. He was clear that it should be personal in nature, a call from the Archbishops to the country at large; not necessarily to Christians, but to 'all men of good will' who were concerned for the welfare of the nation and who 'realized that we are drifting towards chaos'. There had been times in the Spring when he had been considering a call for the evangelization of England; but this he realized needed mature consideration and planning by all the Christian Churches, so it was laid temporarily aside[37]. Consultations were held with Archbishop Blanch of York, who agreed to issue a joint Pastoral Letter to be read in all churches in both Provinces on Sunday 19 October 1975. It was much on the same lines as the general *Call*, but within a Christian connotation. Other bishops were informed of the event, as also the heads of other Churches in England, but no further consultation took place; time for preparation was short. The Archbishop had decided to move swiftly, and apart from the co-operation of his fellow-Primate, and certain giants of the press, alone.

The *Call* was to be sounded through the media. Archbishop Coggan arranged to meet leading Editors in Fleet Street who agreed to give him press coverage. His Press Officer, John Miles[38], asked for television and radio time for the Archbishop, and seven opportu-

---

[37] See p.211
[38] Also Chief Information Officer of the General Synod.

nities were created for him to appear or speak on various programmes within five days of the opening announcement. On 15 October Donald held a press conference to launch the campaign; the news of his intentions had been embargoed until that date. He did not offer, he said, a blue-print as a way out of the troubles he felt faced the country, which appeared to him to be drifting without an anchor. A materialistic answer was no answer; there were moral and spiritual issues at stake.

One of the main burdens of his message was that whereas an individual might think himself powerless to effect changes of attitude, this was mistaken: individual opinion and action were important. He invited individuals and groups to face and study two questions: 'What sort of society do we want, and what sort of people do we need to be in order to achieve it?' If anyone wanted to write to him, they could do so. He received 27,000 letters before the end of the year[39].

When in later months questioners asked the Archbishop how he came to frame the *Call*, he replied that from his arrival at Lambeth, he had received letters and deputations which made him feel that although he had gone to the see of Canterbury without a set programme, the time had come for him to give a personal lead in the present climate. The *Call* provoked a variety of responses. The thousands of letters that poured into Lambeth Palace were opened by a team of volunteers, but the Archbishop read most of them. To those who asked, a prayer card was sent:

> God bless our nation,
> Guide our rulers.
> Give us your power,
> that we may live cheerfully,
> care for each other,
> and be just in all we do.

By Christmas, 75,000 cards had been despatched; some correspondents had asked for several copies. The letters that called for a personal answer were put on one side. Many were moving, some tragic, and told of unhappy, lonely, fearful lives.

There were some disparaging letters, mainly on two accounts. The first type echoed criticism of a sort that had been directed towards Archbishop Coggan since his appointment: that some of his utterances, particularly on economic issues, were inaccurate, simplistic or failed correctly to identify the fundamental problems.

[39] See John Poulton, *Dear Archbishop*, Hodder and Stoughton 1976.

He had been censured to such an extent by a politician in a public speech that a fellow-bishop had written to suggest, with some diffidence, that it might be well to have 'the very best advice to guard against misquoting facts and figures'; people in top positions of leadership were not always served too well in this way; 'An unofficial censor on statements you plan to make' might be useful. (It is pertinent to recall that Archbishop William Temple ran into much the same problem, to which Archbishop Garbett drew attention. 'Temple had aired his theories on banking and the issue of credit, which created a considerable flutter in financial circles.' After Garbett had spoken subsequently in a House of Lords' debate on Planning, the Lord Chancellor commented, 'It is a pleasure to hear an Archbishop speaking on a subject he knows'.)[40]

A second body of opinion deprecated the *Call* because it was felt to lack content, to be a moderate, muted, moral appeal, without hard-hitting specifically Christian elements. The Archbishop had applied a Kingdom-type theology which was part of the teaching of Jesus, so much was recognized, but, it was alleged, had omitted its costly challenges. Other critics contrasted the *Call* unfavourably with the Call to the North, with its long and careful preparation and ecumenical nature.

Soon after the *Call*, a survey of the mood of the nation was published by the British Council of Churches in preparation for their meeting on 28-29 October. It supported the Archbishop's contention that a profound crisis had come upon the people of Britain in regard to moral and spiritual ideals, but it gave a different diagnosis of cause and cure in a highly structured society: not so much greed and envy, as insecurity, anxiety, disillusionment. Affluence was fragile, social justice elusive, order threatened. So far as cure went, emphasis was on the future, not recovery of the past.

Mervyn Stockwood[41], Bishop of Southwark, became a leading critic of the Archbishop's *Call* when he wrote[42] that he wished Dr Coggan had not issued it in its present form. The Bishop contended that 'a man's character, be it good or bad, is partly, if not largely determined by his environment, by the social and economic circumstances in which he is placed.' Bishop Stockwood's intervention had the effect of prolonging the debate and sharpening the points at

[40] Charles Smyth, *Cyril Forster Garbett*, (Hodder and Stoughton) p.293.
[41] 1913- ; Vicar of Great St Mary's, Cambridge 1955-59; Bishop of Southwark 1959-60.
[42] *Morning Star*, 31 October 1975.

issue. Groups to debate them sprang up. Archbishop Coggan extended the impetus of his initiative himself with a series of radio programmes on social and economic topics, in company with the Chief Rabbi, entitled 'You don't have to be Jewish'. If discussion had been part of the Archbishop's objective, it had succeeded.

The Lord Mayor's Banquet early in November, when both the Archbishop and the Prime Minister, Harold Wilson, had been invited to speak, gave Donald Coggan the opportunity to answer some of his critics. He agreed that much of the blame for personal predicaments could be laid on society, and proceeded to make some suggestions as to how the community might seek to help repair the damage. In doing so he ran into a new lot of trouble; some of his solutions were too personal (i.e. that highly-paid individuals might give up some of their salary[43]) to find general acceptance.

In the midst of the publicity surrounding the *Call*, Donald and Jean Coggan celebrated their ruby wedding. He had confided to Ruth that he intended to buy his wife a piece of jewellery. She described it in a subsequent letter: a brooch in the shape of a flower with four small rubies in the centre, one for each of the ten years. They drove down to the Old Palace at Canterbury and spent the wedding anniversary house-hunting, for it had been decided that their Yorkshire house should be sold. Retirement, when it came, might well be in Kent. Prince Charles came to stay a few days later. He had become Chairman of the trustees of the Cathedral appeal and was in Canterbury to make a documentary film in this interest[44]. 'Very natural and easy,' Jean wrote to Ruth, 'and welcomed a lot of serious conversation'; they had enjoyed his sense of humour. She could not remember a busier time, she continued, than the previous two months.

There were some blows that autumn: the first had been the death of Chad: tourists had left the gates of the Old Palace open and he had escaped, gone down to the railway line, and been electrocuted. Secondly, John Kirkham, the Domestic Chaplain, was knocked from his bicycle by a taxi in London, and quite badly hurt, especially about the head and face. He was to have accompanied the Archbishop to Nairobi for the Fifth Assembly of the World Council of Churches. The Coggans left England for Africa in mid November; Anglican Primates were to meet before the Assembly

---

[43] He had already done this.
[44] The Archbishop had launched the appeal on 6 December 1974, the day after the confirmation of his election.

itself. A first class ticket on the aircraft was booked for the Archbishop, to give him more rest and privacy, and some sections of the
press commented savagely on this privileged treatment – an
insensitive gesture towards a man of continuously frugal habits.

Fifteen Primates met together for four days at Trinity College,
Nairobi, with Donald Coggan their new chairman. They followed
no set agenda. The first twelve hours were spent as a Quiet Day,
praying together, led by Bishop Eric Nasir of Delhi, Moderator of
the Church of North India. For the remainder, each spoke briefly on
his own Province. Donald's relationship with his fellow Primates
was always personal; he saw them as individuals rather than as
representatives of their Churches, as a fellowship, a mutual support
group. He seemed to expect personal opinions rather than a résumé
of the general opinion in a particular Province, and gave his own
view in return.

On 23 November the Fifth Assembly of the World Council
opened, with the theme 'Jesus Christ frees and unites'. For the first
time the Archbishop of Canterbury was not one of the Presidents;
Donald Coggan had declined to be put forward. As President of the
United Bible Societies, however, he collaborated with the musician,
Donald Swann, in a well-received dramatic presentation of the story
of the prodigal son. Archbishop Coggan acted as a skilful compère;
Donald Swann wrote the lyrics and provided the music. 747 delegates met in Nairobi appointed by the 271 member Churches of the
Council. Among sixty guests were for the first time representatives
of other faiths, Buddhists, Hindus, Muslims, Jews and Sikhs.
Around 2,300 people (the rest were advisors, stewards, staff and
translators, etc.) gathered in the Jomo Kenyatta Centre. Archbishop Coggan led a workshop on Spirituality with a group of
twenty-five members from various Churches; also a Bible Study
which 'played a valuable part'[45].

The theme of the Fifth Assembly lent itself to the examination of
all aspects of human rights, racism and the theology of liberation. It
was a turbulent session[46], but one from which the English participants agreed they learnt much. During the course of the debate on
the Report from Nairobi in the General Synod[47], one of the aspects
which presented itself was that of the relationship of the struggle for

[45] Paragraph 8 of the Report of the Church of England Representatives to the
Assembly (GS 285).
[46] See Kenneth Slack, *Nairobi Narrative*, SCM Press 1976.
[47] 24 February 1976, *General Synod February Group of Sessions 1976 Report of
Proceedings*, Vol. 7, No. 2, pp. 366-88.

universal brotherhood to the specific message of the uniqueness of Christ which Christians had to offer to the world. Here was further encouragement to the Archbishop towards the formulation of another initiative; this time for mission and evangelism.

During the meeting of the WCC at Nairobi Donald Coggan absented himself for a day, and flew eighty miles north to Embu for the inauguration of the new Anglican diocese of Mount Kenya East on 7 December, before a rally of 20,000 Christians. The new Bishop, David Gitari, had been consecrated and the diocese created in July. The Church in Kenya had grown to such an extent that it was calculated to consist of 8.4 million baptized persons, out of a population of 12 million. The Archbishop's sermon was translated into Kiswahili by a member of the Kenyan government. He flew straight back to Nairobi to preach (broadcast) in the Cathedral the same evening. His words (on the combatting of racism) reached the English national press. This was from now on to be common practice, wherever he might happen to be; a fact he did not immediately realize. Shortly after his arrival back in England, he received a letter from Archbishop Edward Scott, Primate of Canada, who had been elected Moderator of the new central committee of the WCC.

> . . . just a note to say how great I felt your contribution was to the Fifth Assembly. You helped focus attention in many key issues in a way that was helpful.

Donald Coggan's clear mind in discussion won him another accolade that autumn. The matter of Anglican jurisdiction in Europe had been much debated during 1975. Gerald Ellison, Bishop of London, wrote to congratulate him on the way he had chaired a decisive meeting which reconciled various interests. It was a process in which he showed skill; he believed wholeheartedly in the underlying principle. The Archbishop showed similar eirenic powers in relation to pressure from certain elements in the House of Commons as to the Synod's intention to introduce measures held to be inimical to 'the interests of private citizens' (the example then under discussion was an attempt to deal with the matter of patronage).

The year ended with events which showed that Archbishops are not exempt from the problems that assail private citizens. John Kirkham returned to the household at the Old Palace just before Christmas. Two drunks broke into the garage, stole his car and wrecked it by driving into the 16th-century brickwork of the Christ Church gate to the Precincts. A few days later the Archbishop surprised a stranger inside the house, who first pretended to seek spiritual counsel and then flew into a rage at being asked questions. After his angry departure, Jean's modest collection of jewellery was found to be missing. As might have been expected, she saw the event in proportion: the ruby wedding present was gone, but its donor was safe. 'Only things', she wrote to one of her daughters; 'so grateful Father was not hurt'.

The year 1976 began with Donald Coggan's first visit as Archbishop of Canterbury to the United States. He landed in Boston in intense cold and was met by Charles Minifie[48], Rector of Trinity Church, Newport, who drove him to a meeting of the clergy of Rhode Island, whom the Archbishop addressed. Any expectations that the Archbishop of Canterbury would be a proud, remote figure were dispelled by his natural friendliness and insistence on carrying his own luggage. A Service at Trinity Church to celebrate the 250th anniversary of its foundation followed. Archbishop Coggan preached to a large congregation: he spoke first on worship, then holiness, which he said was likeness to the Lord Christ. The Gospels showed Jesus on earth; the Epistles what he is like everlastingly. Passages of the New Testament revealed his reflection in the lives of his followers; some biographies do the same; the Spirit of God can be seen alive in contemporary people. He ended with the outreach of the Church. It existed to make mankind like Jesus; it had something to say to the world.

Such heavy snow fell that night that the possibility of the Archbishop's departure next day for New York, where he had a full programme, at one time seemed unlikely. Snow-ploughs cleared a way, however, and he took off in 'a horrid little six-seater plane' in still extreme wintry conditions. The New York schedule included engagements for the American Bible Society, a visit to the United Nations and talk with Dr Waldheim, a sermon to a congregation of 2-3,000 people at the huge Riverside Church and two lectures to 600 clergy at the Trinity Institute, which was also celebrating a 250th anniversary. A long interview with the Columbian Broadcasting System of America was devoted to what was referred to as the 'theology of enough'. He spoke of the 'have' nations and the 'have-not' Third World which was fast becoming the Two-Thirds World, where there was illiteracy and if not actual starvation, such under-nutrition as to create lassitude in large sections of the population. The Archbishop said he thought there was scope for both personal

[48] Later Warden of the College of Preachers in Washington.

response, in giving up a proportion of income, and political pressure on governments in order that world economic structures could be reordered. Men's values in the West would have to be changed to make that possible. He went on to describe some of his experience of Africa where the Church was growing fast, his views on materialism, the ordination of women and the future of the ecumenical movement. Was there sufficient unity in the Anglican Communion for it to reunite with Rome at some point in the foreseeable future, he was asked. The Anglican Communion, the Archbishop replied, was broad, but held within it great tensions. That was the difficulty in the Anglican/Methodist debate. It was defeated because the two dissentient extremes joined together and prevented the adoption of the scheme. On the question of authority depended the future of the unity of the Churches: it pervaded them all.

At the end of January the Archbishop addressed Members of both Houses of Parliament on the subject of his *Call to the Nation* in a meeting summoned by Lord Beswick. It was followed by an address at a luncheon given by the Foreign Press Association which provided him with a further opportunity to speak of the divide between the opulent and semi-starving. The world was threatened by three Ps, he said, population explosion, pollution and poverty; then added the problems of unemployment and high abortion rates. He ended with his reasons for making the *Call*, and its results in terms of the creation of opinion and discussion.

Before the House of Lords that Session was a Private Member's Bill, introduced by Baroness Wootton on the legalizing of euthanasia, one of the many moral issues which was raised that year. Archbishop Coggan attended the debate (which was lost by 85 votes to 25); he also made a visit to St Christopher's Hospice for the terminally ill, in Sydenham, under the direction of Dr (later Dame) Cicely Saunders. The President of the Royal College of Physicians had invited him to give an endowed lecture at the end of the year and had chosen the subject of 'Dying'.

Another interview with the Prime Minister in Downing Street took one step further the discussions which he had been having for almost a year on Church-State relations, particularly on the matter of the procedure governing the appointment of bishops. It was debated at the July Session and finally resolved at the November meeting of the Synod.

The February Session was the next event of significance in the winter of 1976. The Archbishop's initiative with the *Call* had resulted in a Report by the General Synod's Board of Social

Responsibility, to which was added a discussion paper by David Edwards[49], then Canon Residentiary of Westminster, entitled State of the Nation. During the debate, Donald Coggan scored a small victory in that it was admitted that the Church should demonstrate its commitment to the nation in its dilemma; the issues to be seen as falling within the mission of the gospel. A Report on 'Dying Well', which raised many of the issues debated in the House of Lords, was also presented. Emphasis was placed upon the need to improve standards of care for the dying; it was concluded that legislation designed to legalize the deliberate killing of those near death would cause greater evils than it would remove.

There was at this time another spate of correspondence on matters concerning relationships with other Churches; a most important issue was the decision that Archbishop Coggan should make a visit to Rome to talk with the Pope during the spring of 1977. The statement from the Vatican Congregation for the Doctrine of the Faith regarding Sexual Ethics which was issued late in 1975, received a poor reception in England, both in some Roman Catholic, and in other sections of the press. In an interview which the Archbishop gave to the Roman Catholic *Tablet*, he was reported as having said that he thought the statement somewhat lacking 'in pastoral guidance and tenderness towards those who find these problems quite agonizing'. 'On the question of birth control,' the report of the interview went on, 'we differ pretty radically from the Roman Catholic position, as we made clear in statements . . . from the Lambeth Conference.' Pope and Archbishop had exchanged letters at Christmas. On 10 February Archbishop Coggan wrote a further letter which was taken to the Vatican by the hand of Bishop Howe, who conveyed it to his papal audience on 16 February. The Archbishop drew attention to the fact that ten years had elapsed since the visit of Archbishop Ramsey; he referred to the goal 'which we jointly seek' as 'that visible unity of the Church for which Christ prayed'. He referred to the discussions within the Anglican Communion on the ordination of women in terms of diversity in unity: 'We believe this unity will be manifested within a diversity of legitimate traditions because the Holy Spirit has never ceased to be active within the local churches throughout the world'. The Pope in his reply looked forward to their meeting as 'a great blessing'.

The Apostolic Delegate gave the Archbishop prior warning of the appointment of Dom Basil Hume, Abbot of Ampleforth, old friend

---

[49] 1929- ; Dean of Norwich 1978-82; Provost of Southwark 1982- .

of York days, to the Archbishopric of Westminster. Donald Coggan's delight was expressed in a press statement.

The report of the Oxford meeting of ARCIC asked the Archbishop for his comments, prior to a full meeting of the Commission at Venice in August. In giving them, he wrote to Henry MacAdoo, Bishop of Ossory:

> I wish it were possible to say something about receiving Holy Communion at each other's altars. I believe it is already happening in various places.

That he felt strongly on this subject he was to make clear in his visit to Rome. He put his signature on the completed Authority Statement after the Venice meeting and gave directions for it to go before the Lambeth Conference in 1978, with the two earlier documents on the Eucharist and the Ministry.

There had been talks between Archbishop and representatives of the Orthodox Churches at Nairobi; informal consultations took place at Istanbul in December with the Oecumenical Patriarch. In the new year, the Archbishop of Canterbury and Archbishop Athenagoras of Thyateira and Great Britain[50] met on several occasions.

The third meeting of the Anglican Consultative Council was arranged to take place in Trinidad at the end of March 1976[51]. Archbishop Coggan decided to combine visits to Anglican dioceses in the Caribbean. Before he left, he issued a commendation on keeping the problem of abortion in mind during the Season of Lent:

> Within another few weeks one million abortions will have been carried out under the 1967 Abortion Act. Though I believe that a number of these were unavoidable, and indeed necessary to save the mother's life or health, yet the total is horrifying. There is something deeply wrong in a society which allows such a figure to be reached.
>
> I therefore commend all those who during the Season of Lent are combining to make the week of the 20-28 March a time for repentance and prayer with Abortion in mind – *repentance* for our own failure to live up to the great positive Christian ideal of family life and family love, and prayer that this ideal may become a reality to the community at large.

Donald and Jean and his domestic chaplain set off on 15 May for Barbados. He preached there twice and addressed clergy; a helicopter took them to Tobago, then back to Trinidad for the Consultative Council. Jean had her own programme of visits to schools and

---

[50] Died 1979.
[51] The first meeting was at Limuru, Kenya, in 1971; the second in Dublin in 1973.

Homes; her interest was particularly in the education of physically and mentally handicapped children. She gave a number of talks, chiefly to women's groups. During the latter years at York she had developed an interest in painting; such leisure as her overseas journeys or life at home gave her was devoted to this new and absorbing pursuit.

The agenda for the ACC was heavy; two items only are of direct present concern. The first was the Lambeth Conference. Donald Coggan made it clear that the final decision as to whether, where and when a Conference be held rested with the Archbishop of Canterbury. He asked, however, that the ACC should give its advice. The debates on the issue are not without relevance, since their substance was reiterated in some opinions after the 1978 Conference. The first formal step was taken at the ACC Standing Committee Meeting in August 1975. A long debate showed a narrow majority in favour of a Lambeth Conference to which should be invited all diocesan bishops and some assistant bishops. An *ad hoc* Committee, with a membership from several continents, met in Trinidad a few days before the full ACC, to prepare a paper for discussion. Some misgivings were expressed as to finance and how a Lambeth Conference was to be paid for, but a recommendation emerged that a Conference be held; that it should be residential and take place in Canterbury or the Canadian West Coast. It proposed an option of two kinds of Conference: one with a restricted membership of 300; the other with the traditional pattern of all diocesan bishops and some assistants. The majority favoured the first and less costly.

The subject was debated by the full ACC on 30 March. A majority of forty were in favour, and five were against[52] a Lambeth Conference in the foreseeable future. Delegates from Africa, Asia and South America were unanimous that all diocesan bishops be invited. Although the cost of a larger Conference would be heavy, finance should not be a decisive factor. A few were less confident that this was a right use of so much money. Members of the minority were heard to say that the 1968 Conference had been a disappointing experience, and that in the present state of Anglican development it was no longer fitting that bishops, on their own, should deliberate matters of Anglican policy.

The following evening the President, the Archbishop of Canterbury, told the Council of the decisions at which he had arrived. The

[52] There were 5 absentions, which included the English members who felt they should not express an opinion.

main points were: that there would be a Lambeth Conference in 1978 which would be residential, probably in Canterbury, and would last three weeks; that the accent would first be on prayer, waiting on God, with an emphasis on understanding episcopacy such as might also make the Conference an occasion of training. This would relate to an agenda covering the bishops and the People of God, theology and the 20th century, the nature of and contemporary structure for, the Anglican Communion, the relating together of Lambeth Conferences and the ACC. He was still considering the size of the event; there was obviously a clear majority in favour of the larger gathering, comparable to previous ones. The Secretary-General of the ACC, Bishop John Howe, would serve as Secretary to the Conference.

The second issue of consequence to the present study was the debate on methods of Joint Consultations as an expression of what the Dublin ACC had named 'Partnership in Mission'. That Council had stated that:

> the responsibility for mission in any place belongs *primarily* to the Church in that place. The universality of the Gospel and the oneness of God's mission, however, mean also that this mission must be shared in each and every part of the world, with their distinctive insights and contributions. If we once acted as though there were only givers who had nothing to receive, and receivers who had nothing to give, the oneness of the missionary task must now make us all both givers and receivers.

Archbishop Coggan's whole-hearted acceptance of this ideology, which he had held since his declamation of the MRI document at Toronto in 1963, he was to demonstrate in his leadership at the 1978 Lambeth Conference. At Trinidad, discussion was to take the subject of Joint Consultation several steps further: for the first time, it was considered, local churches were meeting as equals, and a deepened sense of relationship between autonomous churches within an Anglican family had begun to develop, where previously it had been on a mission-agency basis. Among points requiring further attention were difficulties in maintaining the balance between the spiritual and material. Archbishop Coggan's addresses on his journeys overseas were to show his constant reflection on these issues. He returned home via St Lucia, Guadalupe, St Croix, Virgin Islands, Puerto Rico, the Dominican Republic, Haiti and Miami.

Back at Lambeth, he set into motion the implications of the Trinidad Council. Bishop Howe was officially appointed Secretary of the forthcoming Conference and asked to draw up preliminary plans. Before Easter at Canterbury, the Coggans stayed at Windsor Castle as guests of the Queen, when the Archbishop confirmed Prince Andrew and David, Viscount Lindley, son of Princess Margaret, in St George's Chapel. The Three Hours' devotions in Canterbury Cathedral on the seven words from the Cross on Good Friday, were led by the Archbishop, who later headed the procession of witness through the streets. On Easter day he preached a sermon of which some elements, concerning the building of a wall by Nehemiah[53], had lain dormant since a diary entry in Canada in July 1939.

There was a back-log of engagements resulting from the Archbishop's absence abroad. A sample of the events of the following weeks illustrates their range: a reception by the Prince of Wales at St James's for the Cathedral Appeal, a State banquet at Buckingham Palace for the state visit of the President of Brazil, a speech to the Cutlers of Sheffield, dinner with the Speaker of the House of Commons, a sermon in the Episcopal Church of Scotland in Inverness, dinner with the Chief Rabbi, lunch with the Governors of the BBC, a visit to the residents of Canterbury Prison, a meeting with an Arab delegation and subsequent visit to the Islamic Arts Exhibition in the Royal Festival Hall.

An article by the Archbishop in an unusual setting appeared in May[54]. The Communist *Morning Star* had taken note of some of his statements of opposition to racism, and had indicated that words of his in this view would be welcome. Whitsunday was spent back in Canterbury. Before the 8 am Holy Communion he confirmed a solitary adult candidate in his private chapel at the Old Palace; this was a not infrequent occurrence. The remarkable feature was the degree of interest that he maintained with the men and women in question. His sermon that morning once again had a theme which ran from Old to New Testament, a favourite device: a contrast between the tower of Babel and the scenes of Pentecost.

Archbishop Coggan had given notice of his intention to open a debate in the House of Lords, a rare event. He called[55] for a Minister for the family; for action to strengthen family life, the bulwark of a stable society. He spoke of the factors which constituted a major menace: bad housing, unemployment, too early

---

[53] Nehemiah 2.7. Donald Coggan, *Sure Foundation*, pp. 37-40.
[54] 29 May 1976, under the title 'The Battle for a Healthy Society'.
[55] 16 July 1976. Donald Coggan *Sure Foundation*, pp. 80-90.

marriage, trivialization of sex, and pleaded for better education in relationships, counselling for couples under stress, play facilities, more work and better living conditions.

The July Session of the Synod contained a debate on Crown appointments. The Chadwick Commission on Church and State had reported in 1970; one of its major proposals had concerned a change in the system whereby bishops were appointed. The General Synod debate in July 1974 had put forward the view that in order that the Church should have a more effective voice in this matter, a small body composed of representatives of the vacant see and members of the wider Church should submit a name to the Crown. It was resolved that the Archbishop of Canterbury with Sir Norman Anderson should consult with the Prime Minister. On 13 July 1976 the Standing Committee Report was presented by Sir Norman. In the debate that followed, differences of opinion emerged as to whether the Church's position was sufficiently safeguarded. The Archbishop made a forceful appeal[56] against any action that would reduce the Church-State connection, or might prolong the deliberations: 'We must dither no longer but must have the courage to make up our minds.'

> To direct our energies from the great task of evangelism and outreach, witnessing to the Church in a needy England and further afield a needier world . . . would, I think, be a tragic course for the Church to pursue.

He made one more plea in preparation for the debate in November. In his view the proposed body envisaged by the Chadwick Commission was too large rather than too small; a characteristic observation. 'The matter of confidentiality is a very difficult one,' he continued; he saw danger here.

The Ten Propositions of the Churches' Unity Commission Report of January 1976 also received a hearing. Member Churches were asked for a 'provisional first response' to an extremely complex set of propositions. Most speakers found them imprecise. On a suggestion from Dame Betty Ridley, it was agreed that formal reference should go to the dioceses, and all of the Ten Propositions be considered before any voting took place.

During the Question period of the Synod, reference was made to the Archbishop's remarks on evangelism at the past November Session. Would plans be made to debate the evangelistic mission of

---

[56] *General Synod July Group of Sessions 1976 Report of Proceedings*, Vol. 7, No. 3, pp. 743-5.

the Church while the *Call* was fairly fresh in mind? The matter thus raised, gives an opportunity in the present work to examine the whole matter of Donald Coggan's thinking in the field of evangelism over the previous year.

In 1943 Archbishop William Temple, with Archbishop Garbett of York, had set up a Commission on Evangelism under the chairmanship of Bishop Chavasse of Rochester. Its report *Towards the Conversion of England* was published in 1945, one of its recommendations being the setting up of a Council on Evangelism. This the Church Assembly declined to implement: the initiative, it was claimed, belonged to the dioceses. In 1967 Cuthbert Bardsley[57], Bishop of Coventry, persuaded the Archbishop of Canterbury, with the support of Donald Coggan, then Archbishop of York, to set up an unofficial body, the Archbishops' Council on Evangelism. Its members (about twenty) were drawn from various walks of life, both clerical and lay, and known for their evangelistic sympathies. Its finances came mainly from private benefactions; John Poulton[58] became its full-time Executive Secretary in 1969. He operated from the start from his own home in Guildford, but at the time of the *Call*, his services were diverted to the office at Lambeth Palace, so that he could be at the Archbishop's disposal for the next phase. From then on they worked closely together. Certain problems were presented, since the Archbishops' Council on Evangelism was an unofficial affair, and the various Boards of the General Synod did not find it easy to deal with non-synodical bodies. There was a residual feeling that the Archbishop was attempting to operate by way of his own machinery.

Donald Coggan was obviously injured by the insinuation that the *Call* should have been interpreted as less than Christian, and that it had avoided the main issues behind the Church's existence. It was his constant preoccupation that the Church should put its house in order, with the aim that it would be better equipped to proclaim the gospel with all its strength. Moreover, he had been turning over in his mind what form a national evangelistic campaign should take. At the opening of the newly-elected Synod in November 1975, he asked that prime attention be devoted 'to making Christ known'. During 1976 a good deal of the Archbishop's own attention was devoted to considering how this might be done on a national basis.

He made strenuous personal efforts in a series of meetings to

[57] 1907- ; Bishop of Croydon 1957; of Coventry 1956-76.
[58] 1925-87; Canon Residentiary of Norwich 1978-87.

bring together heads of other Churches, an Interdenominational-Evangelical Working Group who were themselves planning to mount a national mission (Let my People Grow), the relevant section of the British Council of Churches and the Anglican Bishops in England. By the middle of the year it seemed that a celebration or festival of the faith, as an evangelistic exercise, might be a possibility. The Archbishop wrote to the General Secretary[59] of the British Council of Churches on 17 May 1976:

> It does seem to me that the Spirit of God has been directing us towards some major national outreach for Christ in 1978 or 79. I like the 'festival' note which you struck in your letter to the three Evangelical leaders – the note of 'celebration'. If we strike this note we shall no doubt be accused of triumphalism, but if we triumph in Christ, crucified, risen and reigning, we cannot go far wrong.

This proposal for this kind of evangelistic effort on a national basis, in two or three years' time, was put to Church leaders and the Anglican Bishops by the Archbishop of Canterbury in the Autumn of 1976. Although there were some replies which showed support, the general response was cool: the project 'lacked substance', the need was for prayer, teaching in the faith, passing on the experience of healing; for the ordinary person to see the relevance of Christianity in their own lives, not a 'sloppy demonstration without real thought'. One Bishop remarked that he celebrated constantly. Some admitted that they found difficulties in the present climate, in seeing clearly the way forward in the field of evangelism, but this did not seem to be it. The planners, with the Archbishop at their head, needed to go back to the drawing-board for a fresh set of initiatives. This they did.

It was made clear to Donald in the summer of 1976 that he should enter hospital for an operation for hernia. He did so with the minimum of fuss. He cancelled a number of engagements, but worked on till half an hour before being admitted. After a busy week, he and Jean drove to Royal Lodge, Windsor on the 17 July, to spend the week-end with the Queen Mother; several other members of the Royal Family, notably the Prince of Wales and Princess Margaret, were there also. The Archbishop preached in the Chapel in Windsor Great Park next day. On Monday the 19th he left early for Lambeth Palace for a staff meeting with his Suffragans and Archdeacons all morning, received Monsignor Torella, Vice President of the Vatican Secretariat for the Union of Christians at 3.30

[59] The Reverend Harry O. Morton.

pm, and entered King Edward VII's Hospital at 5, under the name of Curran, so that there should not be any national alarm. He was particularly amused to discover the name of his anaesthetist – Michael Ramsey. Some weeks of convalescence in Canterbury and with the Anglican Sisters of the Love of God at Bede House, Staplehurst, were followed by a holiday with Jean in Greece. There were some meetings with Orthodox clergy, among them the Abbot of a monastery on the Island of Patmos and the Bishop of Rhodes.

The first major engagement on the Archbishop's recovery was his second visit to the United States that year. Part of the itinerary was concerned with the bicentennial celebrations; an important item was his attendance at the three-yearly General Convention of the Episcopal Church; he also undertook some engagements connected with the appeal for the restoration of Canterbury Cathedral.

A packed first week, which began in Princeton and Washington, included a sermon in Washington Cathedral at a Eucharist attended by the President, Gerald Ford, his wife and son. President and Archbishop met briefly. In Bethlehem, Pennsylvania, one of several events was the award to Donald of the honorary degree of Doctor of Divinity from the Moravian College; later he left for the diocese of Long Island and then on to Minneapolis where the Triennial General Convention was in session. Some crucial issues were being debated which threatened to split the Church, namely the ordination of women and revision of the Book of Common Prayer. When the Archbishop arrived, the House of Bishops had voted in favour of the ordination of women; the result of the voting in the House of Deputies came at 7 pm; also in favour.

The Archbishop of Canterbury spoke to each House next day (17 September 1976)[60]: 'I come to you at a very critical time in your deliberations,' he said; the decision on the ordination of women had been taken, and 'now soon you will be launched into a very important debate on the liturgy'. He went on to express his profound thankfulness for the spirit in which the debate had been conducted: a spirit of love, courtesy and prayer. His theme developed along the lines that, beyond tension and wounds, if there be penitence and understanding, healing can come. The American Church expressed itself warmly in its reception of his sensitive and telling address; he had struck a profound note and engendered a spirit of reconciliation. His hearers recognized that he had felt it important to distance himself from his own strong opinions on the

[60] Donald Coggan, *Sure Foundation*, pp. 250-4.

17 Archbishop Coggan with Len Murray, General Secretary of the Trades' Union Congress, in the Precincts at Canterbury on the Kirchentag, 14 May 1977.

18

19

21

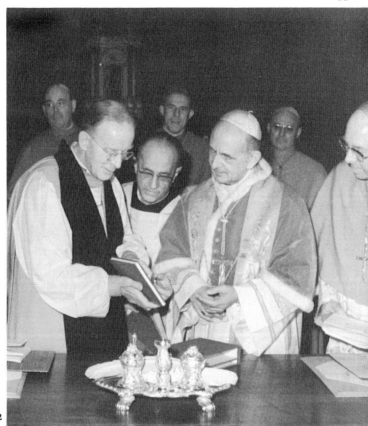

22

23 Archbishop Coggan laying a wreath on Mahatma Gandhi's Samadhi, Delhi, 26 October 1976.

25 On the Moscow underground, Archbishop Coggan and Bishop Robert Runcie of St Albans, September 1977.

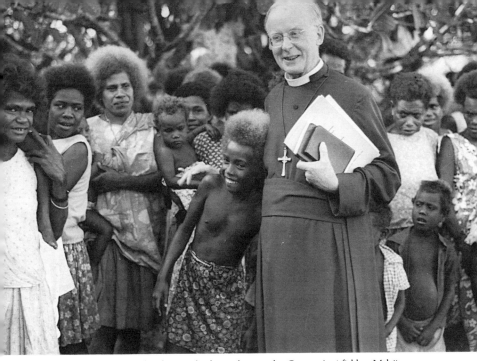

24 The Archbishop with Solomon Islanders on his arrival at Gwanaru'u airfield on Malaita, one of the four dioceses of the Church of Melanesia, March 1977.

26 Archbishop Coggan at the wheel of the Whitstable lifeboat, with Jean Coggan and David Painter, July 1979.

28

29

27 The Archbishop in the dress of an Honorary Paramount Chief after a ceremony at Gobaru in southern Sierre Leone, March 1979.

28 Anglican Primates' Meeting, Ely, 26–30 November 1979. From left to right, *back row*: Bishop John Howe, Bishop Robert Runcie, Archbishop M. Kahurananga, Bishop — Woodroffe, Archbishop Elinana Ngalamu, Archbishop Coggan, Archbishop Trevor Huddleston, Archbishop Silvanus Wani, Bishop B. Ndahura, Archbishop D. Hand, Archbishop E. Scott, Archbishop A. H. Johnstone, Archbishop Marcus Loane, Bishop Alastair Haggart, Archbishop A. Ratz, Archbishop M. Scott; *front row*: Archbishop G. Hla Gyaw, Bishop T. Nakamichi, Archbishop G. Simms, Archbishop Norman Palmer, Bishop T. Olufosoye, Bishop H. Dehqani-Tafti, Bishop Colin Bazley.

29 Archbishop Coggan's seventieth birthday, Lambeth Palace, 9 October 1979, with past and present chaplains and their wives, and household staff. From left to right, *back row*: Jim Scott, Michael Turnbull, Michael Escritt, John Kirkham, John Bates; *middle row*: Douglas Cleverley Ford, Olga Ford, Colin Still, Mary June Scott, Brenda Turnbull, Margaret Escritt, David Painter, Margaret Bates; *front row*: Jean Coggan, Donald Coggan, Ann Coggan, Jean Barling.

30 Donald and Jean Coggan on the eve of his retirement as Archbishop of Canterbury, January 1980.

31 The wedding of HRH the Prince of Wales with Lady Diana Spencer at St Paul's Cathedral, 29 July 1981. The Reverend Harry Williams CR before the royal couple; Lord Coggan, the Moderator of the General Assembly of the Church of Scotland and the Cardinal Archbishop of Westminster stand in front of the high altar; Archbishop Runcie and his chaplain to the right.

30

31

32 Family portrait on the Coggan's golden wedding, –October 1985. From left to right:
Ruth, Jean, Donald, Ann.

points at issue. A man whose basic humility was impressive, it was said; he did not clamour for power, but could assume it when necessary. Donald's firmness in removing camera-men from strategic positions and quelling noise before services and sermons, was as much applauded as his open friendliness with members of congregations.

In New York there were more sermons, including one at the Cathedral, and a visit, insisted upon by the Archbishop, to Harlem. (No English national newspapers were interested in the subsequent photographs.) His efforts on behalf of the Cathedral at Canterbury, which culminated in a 7 am interview on the programme *Good Morning America* the day he was leaving, raised a great deal of money. Although he was critical of some aspects of American life, like the amount of food consumed and the waste of it, the noise at parties, he was invariably exhilarated by the warmth of his reception and the vigour of so much of the Church. John Miles, his Press Officer, and his Domestic Chaplain, John Kirkham, came back exhausted by the intensity of the visit; Donald Coggan, despite his recent experiences in hospital, appeared unperturbed.

There was no peace once at home: the General Committee of the United Bible Societies met for three days in London, twenty-four hours after Donald's arrival; he led the prayers throughout and held a reception at Lambeth Palace for the members. He had given notice of his intention to resign as President after nineteen years; it took effect from this meeting when he was elected honorary President. His work for the UBS was to continue, particularly after his retirement from the Archbishopric, though at a less intense level.

After a week-end at Dartmouth speaking to the Royal Naval Cadets, the Coggans, with John Kirkham, and for the first part of the journey, John Miles, left England on the 4 October 1976 for a tour of the Sudan, Pakistan, Afghanistan, India, Bangladesh, Malaya and Singapore. There were two noteworthy features: first, they met a high proportion of statesmen, government leaders and politicians as well as Christian leaders and congregations. Secondly they saw Ruth *in situ* at her hospital at Bannu.

Six days of constant activity were spent in the Sudan. One of the main reasons for the visit was almost thwarted: the Archbishop was to inaugurate the new Province[61] with its headquarters at Juba in the South. An outbreak of lassa fever had stopped all communica-

[61] Formerly the Episcopal Church of the Sudan, part of the Jerusalem Archbishopric.

tions; several victims had died. At a tea party with the President in Khartoum, he offered the Archbishop the use of his private plane. He and Jean left for Juba at 6 am the following morning and received a great welcome; they returned to Khartoum at 11.15 pm to find a huge meal with hot marmalade pudding thoughtfully provided for the English visitors.

During a five-hour wait at Jeddah, on the way to Pakistan, their luggage was lost and passports disappeared. There were engagements at Karachi and Lahore arranged by the Bishops, which included a service of Christian witness and a retreat for Bishops and clergy at Sialkot. They flew to Rawalpindi (Islamabad) for more services and a call on the Prime Minister before the flight to Peshawar. A drive of 200 miles through wild, barren country (the road at times almost disappeared), took them to Bannu where the Coggans were reunited with Ruth at the Pennell Memorial Hospital. The Chaplain became ill with fever for the next forty-eight hours, which he was obliged to spend in bed; the Archbishop, unscathed, preached at the local church, with interpretation. A mere two days later they left, with Ruth, to return to Peshawar, and a drive in cars from Embassy sources in Kabul for Afghanistan, through the Kyber Pass and spectacular scenery; nomads with their camels and flocks passed them. Attempts to take photographs resulted in a hail of stones.

Donald Coggan was the first Archbishop of Canterbury to visit Kabul. He celebrated the Holy Communion for the small Anglican community at 7 am and gave a brief meditation. He preached at Evensong for a wider Christian congregation and called on the Deputy Foreign Minister. Next day he flew to Delhi. Jean returned to Bannu with Ruth for a fortnight.

In India, the Archbishop visited Christian and political leaders: he had an interview with the President, with Mrs Indira Gandhi, the Prime Minister, and laid a wreath on the Mahatma's tomb. There were several services before he left for a heavy programme in Calcutta and various parts of Bangladesh (where he met the President). In Malaya and Singapore a great deal was expected of him by both civil and religious communities. He arrived home tired, just in time for the November Session of the Synod.

The Patriarch of the Assyrian Church, Mar Kinkha, was present and gave a message in Aramaic which the Archbishop was able to translate for the benefit of members. One of the opening debates concerned theological training; a report from the House of Bishops was presented by the Archbishop of York: it was a sensitive area, for the opinions of bishops and theological college principals could not be guaranteed to coincide, particularly at times of economic stringency, like the present. Archbishop Coggan was to chair some crucial meetings.

The debate on Crown Appointments was resumed: Bishop Woollcombe of Oxford voiced the Archbishop's fears on the undesirability of creating a large Commission for the appointment of bishops, and called for a reduction in the proposed number of members. This the Archbishop reiterated in a subsequent speech, but he did not carry the Synod with him. The decision created a Crown Appointments Commission of twelve plus four local members in the vacant see.

A few events of consequence took place before the end of the year. John Kirkham was consecrated Bishop of Sherborne on 30 November, and David Painter[62] came to be Domestic Chaplain in his stead. The Queen visited Canterbury to see the work on the restoration of the Cathedral, and had tea at the Old Palace; most important of all was Archbishop Coggan's Edwin Stevens Lecture for the Royal College of Physicians on 13 December, with the title 'On Dying and Dying Well'[63]; it won him general acclaim for its sensitivity, scope and evidence of reading, experience and deep, fresh thinking. His sermon in the Cathedral at Canterbury at Christmas[64], in the context of the family, spoke of the ideal which finds inspiration in the home at Nazareth. By the afternoon the Archbishop had no voice left; he had spent himself to the uttermost; it was several days before he could speak again.

The pre-eminent theme of the first days of 1977 was theological training. A meeting of the principals and staffs of theological colleges took place in London, addressed by the Archbishop, who called for more prayer, depth, trust and self-giving. The following day a Bishops' and Principals' Conference was held at Church House, Westminster. Bishops' Meetings later in the month continued to pursue the subject. Donald Coggan let it be known that he was not in favour of some of the expedients that were being put forward: for courses to be shortened, or the development of regional centres, for example. He remained rigorous, as he had always been, on the need for long and thorough theological education on a firm, preferably residential basis. 'I am not myself afraid of sounding a

[62] 1944- ; Curate of All Saints', Margaret Street 1973-6.
[63] See Donald Coggan, *Sure Foundation* (Hodder and Stoughton 1981), pp. 90-107.
[64] ibid., pp. 45-8.

note of challenge to discipline', he said; 'there is little of it in certain clerical circles'[65]. A printed letter[66] calling attention to the fact that in 1976 the number of men ordained to the stipendiary ministry was the lowest for twenty-five years, was despatched to all clergy in the Church of England by the Archbishop of Canterbury. He asked for their help in the fostering of vocations. In doing so he did not deny that the pattern of ministry might change: 'In our complex missionary situation new concepts and forms of ministry are developing;' but 'the Church's strategy will continue to be based on a full-time stipendiary ministry, and men of high calibre are needed as priests'.

The Prime Minister, James Callaghan, agreed to meet a delegation of Church leaders, which included Archbishop Coggan, in order to discuss a higher form of national insurance which the government had announced its intention to impose on certain categories of employment; the clergy were included, which would add a great sum to the salaries bill. As a result of the discussions on 21 January, it was agreed that the matter would be sympathetically investigated[67].

Back in the diocese, the visit of the Archbishop to the deep Betteshanger mine near Deal, caught the attention of the press. He descended to the coal face and spent one-and-a-half hours speaking to men who were working underground, and later, after a bath, had more talks with the representatives of management and unions. Next day he was conducted round a housing estate in Lambeth where he noticed evidence of a good deal of vandalism.

The February meeting of the Synod included the inevitable debate on theological training; also on the Ten Propositions, which had not gone to the dioceses since the Churches Unity Commission had been asked for further clarification. During the course of the Session, the Archbishop of Canterbury heard of the violent death in Uganda of Archbishop Janani Luwum. In his speech to the Synod, Donald Coggan drew particular attention to the late Archbishop's great qualities of courage and gentleness; to the fact that he had in a Christmas broadcast expounded the Christian theme that the only true victory was that of suffering love, only a few months before his public arraignment, sudden arrest and almost immediate death at

---

[65] To the Principal of Oak Hill College, 10 January 1977.
[66] 25 January 1977.
[67] From 1 April 1978 the clergy were regarded as employees of the Church Commissioners, and not self-employed as heretofore.

the hands of the security forces. The Apostolic Delegate and the Pope sent messages of condolence to Archbishop Coggan to whom the death of one of his fellow Primates had been a considerable grief.

1977 was a year when the heavy burden of primatial and diocesan duties did not lighten, but were accompanied by a particularly heavy programme of overseas journeys: to Anglican dioceses in Australia, New Zealand and islands in the Pacific; then to Rome, Istanbul and Geneva; Canada, and finally Russia and Armenia.

The visit of the Archbishop of Canterbury to the southern hemisphere lasted from 21 February until 25 March 1977. Jean Coggan's estimate at the end of the tour was that they had slept in twenty-seven different beds and flown in twenty-one aeroplanes, almost without a break. Moreover, calculations never seemed to allow for rest either before or after any of their travels. The programme fell into two distinct parts: the first, somewhat formal types of engagement, were to cathedrals, universities, cities and towns in Australia and New Zealand; hospitality was lavish, usually at Government House or its equivalent; the second kind, rich with spontaneous, unexpected happenings, took them to more recently established but vigorous churches on the Pacific Islands; travelling was sometimes by boat.

The flight to Sydney via Bahrain, Bangkok and Singapore took twenty-six hours. After only an overnight stop at Sydney, the party rose at 4.30 in the morning to fly to Port Moresby in Papua New Guinea which they reached by 9.30 am. A tumultuous welcome greeted them: garlands of flowers, dancers in traditional dress, the Bishops of the South Pacific Anglican Council, a guard of honour and the National Anthem; the heat was almost insufferable. After a full day and evening in Port Moresby a plane took them in the morning to Goroka and then on to Fiu over the 8,000-foot Dalau pass for the Archbishop to lay the foundation stone of a new Anglican Church. It was a remote area which the first Europeans had seen only twenty-five years before. A member of the congregation told the Archbishop he had been a cannibal, but was now a Christian. A significant event took place at an evening Eucharist back at Goroka. Members of other Churches, including the Roman Catholic, attended and many communicated; a Roman Catholic Bishop embraced Donald Coggan with tears in his eyes because he felt he could not yet do so: 'Next time you come, please God, it will be different'. A sermon which Archbishop Coggan was to preach in Rome owes something to this episode.

Another early morning start brought the Archbishop's party to

Lae and then Popondetta, where they were met at a remote airstrip by an Archdeacon in a landrover and conveyed to a centre of population with a church, and a most spirited welcome. After the Archbishop's address he was showered with gifts, the most beautiful of which was a pectoral cross made of shells. The Governor-General's six-seater plane lifted them to a bumpy airstrip at Dogura, the capital, where the landing was hair-raising and all thought they would end up in the sea.

The climax of the visit was the inauguration on the following day, in the Cathedral at Dogura, of the new independent Province of Papua New Guinea. Felix Arnott, Archbishop of Brisbane, relinquished metropolitical jurisdiction, which passed to David Hand, formerly Bishop, who became the first Archbishop of the new Province. The Archbishop of Canterbury preached during the ceremony, which lasted three hours. The first Anglican missionaries had landed in 1891, he said:

> You have grown to become a Province of five dioceses, with five bishops, 500 priests and over 120,000 Church members within 100 years, and have maintained warm and close links with Christians of other denominations, working for the spiritual, educational, medical and social good of the people of your country. At the same time, it is to be hoped that many of the unique customs and much of the culture of the Papua New Guinea people will continue to flourish hand in hand with the spread of enlightened Christianity.

He wore his new stole, given to him at Popondetta, made of Tapa cloth (bark) and inlaid with animal teeth and shells. There was no air-conditioning nor fans. The atmosphere of joyous expectation and the remarkable singing with natural harmonies, however, helped to offset the temperature of over 100 degrees. Donald Coggan took it in his stride, as also the lizards, toads and scores of insects in his sleeping quarters. He visited a priest in hospital who had lost both feet in a road accident. His clan, following tradition, made to take revenge on the clan of the offender, but were prevented by the victim. Archbishop Coggan commented on the acceptance it revealed of the Christian principles of forgiveness.

He, with his wife, Chaplain and Press Officer left for the Solomon Islands next day, and arrived at Honiara by the afternoon. The welcome included some wild men in traditional garb thrusting spears at the Archbishop; it was an ancient custom which required the newcomer to declare his business and that it was of friendly intent. Gifts and dancing followed. The same pattern greeted them, after an early start, at Auki. After a Eucharist in the Cathedral, the

Archbishop addressed the clergy of the diocese of Malaita; then a big open-air gathering to which some of the congregation had walked many miles, and lastly a catechetical school where men, under conditions of great simplicity, were trained as teachers for the villages.

The Provincial ship the 'Southern Cross', with the Archbishop on board, made the most moving landfall of his tour on 2 March, just as dawn was breaking at Ysabel. He was rowed ashore with his companions in a fleet of canoes bedecked with flowers and arbours of branches. The clergy of the diocese in white cassocks received them on the shore, with children singing and clapping, as they were carried on wooden seats among the cheering crowd. The Archbishop preached at a Eucharist, then members of the congregation re-enacted the martyrdom in 1871 of Bishop Patteson[68]. During the last days back in Honiara time was spent at the theological college, with clergy, and with members of Religious Orders, both men and women.

It would seem important not to underestimate the effects of visits such as these upon Donald Coggan. Not only did the enthusiasm and resolution shown in the new Provinces draw from him qualities of endless encouragement and support, but it raised his expectations of what it should be possible to achieve elsewhere in the Anglican Communion. It provided a yardstick by which to measure dedication and sacrifice; also of warmth of attitude towards the Archbishopric of Canterbury. His visit to the Soviet Union, later in the year, likewise gave an insight into the price which some Christians paid for their faith.

On arrival at Brisbane from Honiara on Sunday 6 March, Archbishop Coggan first faced a press conference which tackled him on the situation in Uganda following the death of Archbishop Luwum. He had commented on affairs in that country which he knew well, earlier on his tour:

> This is the Church of Martyrs and you will recall that only a few days ago a very dear friend of ours laid down his life and became the last of that long list of martyrs who have loved our Lord even to death.

He asked for prayers for the Church in Uganda, for those Africans in the hands of 'a very cruel and pagan tyrant'. Everywhere he was required to address himself to international, rather than local,

[68] 1827-71; John Coleridge Patteson, First Bishop of Melanesia. Murdered 1871 on the island of Nukapu, in revenge for the kidnapping of some inhabitants by Europeans, some months earlier.

issues. That evening, inspired no doubt by the events of the past weeks, he preached at a vast Eucharist of 5,000 people in the Festival Hall, probably the most striking sermon of the tour, and one that received a warm response. With Martin Luther King's words, 'I have a dream', the Archbishop spoke of his own dream for a united and Christlike Church.

The tour extended to Melbourne, Adelaide, Perth, and to the diocese of North West Australia, which with 720,000 square miles is second only to the diocese of the Arctic in size; some clergy came 500 miles to hear the Archbishop. Then on to Darwin in the Northern Territory by night plane which left at 2.30 am. Darwin Cathedral had been destroyed by the cyclone of Christmas Eve 1974. The Archbishop consecrated a new building in a modern style, and preached; he also laid the foundation-stone of the chapel at Nungalinya College, a joint theological centre for white Australians and Aborigines.

A single-engined plane flew him and his party to a CMS mission station at Oenpelli where a community of about 400 Aborigines was served by twelve white Australians; there was a short service, before spending the night there, and a Eucharist early next day which was nearly the Archbishop's last. The weather was bad for the return flight to Darwin: the airstrip waterlogged, visibility low, pouring rain; however, the connection was achieved for the onward journey back to Sydney. During the programme in Sydney, Canberra and Newcastle, the Archbishop visited the Prime Minister and Governor-General, and gave a lecture in the University of the last named on 'The Bible and Contemporary Society'.

The following week was devoted to an arduous itinerary in New Zealand: Auckland (with the best cathedral choir of the tour) Rotorua, where the Archbishop met members of the Maori community, and on to the South Island. The Queen Elizabeth II stadium, built for the 1971 Commonwealth Games, was the site for a large open-air Eucharist for 8,000 to whom Archbishop Coggan spoke. (1,500 pigeons were released from cages at the end, to signify freedom in the gospel; some of them declined to fly off, which as the chaplain remarked later, would 'provide admirable material for a sermon one day'.) After forty-eight hours in Wellington and a return to Auckland, the Archbishop flew to Fiji, with a brief stop at Tonga on the way. Here his lecture[69] in the Cathedral at Suva on 'The Bible and Social Justice', showed his ability to respond on

[69] Donald Coggan, *Sure Foundation*, pp. 141-58.

different levels; he had walked barefoot a few hours earlier up a muddy track in pouring rain to a corrugated iron hut to visit a poor, devoutly Christian family, with whom his rapport was remarkable. A Fijian ceremony of welcome of some complexity, which is the highest honour that can be given to a visitor, attended his arrival at Levuka, the ancient capital, on another island. He was offered the Kava, a drink in a wooden bowl, which has to be swallowed without pause. After the return to Suva, and more singing and prayers, the Archbishop boarded an aircraft for Honolulu, Los Angeles and London, where as usual a heavy load of engagements awaited him.

Only a few of these were significant enough to be noted. A service in St Paul's Cathedral for members of the Guilds of the City of London[70], two thousand of the wealthiest and most influential men in England, was one of them. He was well aware of the responsibility he bore in his address, for he mentioned it to his daughter. He spoke briefly of the *Call*, but more specifically of the Cross,

> For there on the Cross, God was in Christ, reconciling himself to a world which had got itself all tangled up, which thought that power and money and possessions and position were things that really mattered.

He incorporated some experiences that had come to him in his travels, but not many, and always in terms of the reactions of others; on this occasion the gratitude which a Sudanese Christian had expressed towards Europeans for having given him, not modern technology, but the Bible. The sense of contrast in his life must have been considerable, but he seldom mentioned this in personal terms; he kept his own reflections in the background. The contrasts continued: from a sermon at a meticulous service of Mattins at the Royal Military Academy at Sandhurst, to the musical splendour of Easter at Canterbury; the Archbishop preached to a crowded congregation in the Cathedral Eucharist. At the usual cheerful youth pilgrimage on Easter Monday, he answered questions put by young people in the Cloisters. The same afternoon he received Chiara Lubich, foundress of the Focolare, a lay apostolate movement dedicated to the practice of the gospel in everyday life. She had just received the Templeton prize for 1977, given for 'progress in religion'.

Two more journeys out of London had to be made before the start of the next arduous tour abroad, beginning with Rome. The first was to Nottingham to the second National Evangelical Anglican

[70] ibid., pp. 61-5.

Congress, following that at Keele in 1967. In inviting the Archbishop to speak, the Congress's Secretary[71] had written that most Evangelicals were anxious that they should not appear to be entrenching themselves as a party, but rather 'that we may be seen to be reapplying the essential tenets of evangelicalism to the whole situation in the Church and the world today'. The notes provided for the Archbishop set out that the Congress intended to be bold in restating evangelical understanding of the Bible, of mission and ministry, of the need for deep involvement in helping to create the *mores* of tomorrow's world. 'All these demand of us a purified faith, strengthened by being *our* faith in *our* world, not yesterday's faith in a world gone for ever'. This was very much his own standpoint: the word 'evangelical' was used in the way that he had long used it, not in an exclusive sense, nor qualified by additional terms.

The Congress's final statement was to press these examples of coalescence even further. It reflected an atmosphere of repentance and hope: repentance that the handling of Scripture in the past had 'often been clumsy and our interpretation of it shoddy'; for past indifference and ill-will towards Rome; for backwardness in facing social issues. Narrowness of outlook was also admitted, and resolution made no longer to tolerate low standards in worship and apathy in spiritual life. The need was for 'a costly identification with people in their alienation'. It was not enough to care for the casualties of the social system; there had to be a quest for better structures.

But in the event there were some problems. It was agreed that Archbishop Blanch of York should give the opening address and Archbishop Coggan should preach at the final service of Holy Communion. Two thousand people crowded into an aircraft hangar for this occasion. David Sheppard, Bishop of Liverpool, was the celebrant. The Archbishop's office had given his proposed sermon[72] to the press and an embargo had been placed on its release until it had been preached, but the contents had been leaked. The Archbishop was greeted by disappointment when it became known that he intended to present a view that, great though he thought the current spiritual emergency to be, he did not consider that an evangelistic campaign planned centrally on a national basis to be the way forward. He and his committees were planning, rather, a nation-wide initiative on evangelism which would stimulate local efforts and enterprise to this end. He agreed to a few alterations

---

[71] Raymond Turvey, 31 January 1975, from St Paul's Onslow Square.
[72] ibid., pp. 232-6.

which made his view appear less conclusive, but it was a hard road as he sought to reconcile diversities of outlook.

Ironically enough, little more than a week later he was to experience the problem from the opposite end, as he struggled to retain reference to the urgent need for evangelism in the Common Declaration that he made with the Pope. A week-end in the diocese of Lincoln, and it was time to make the momentous journey to Rome, Istanbul and Geneva.

Many of the arrangements for the meeting of Archbishop Coggan with the Pope were of long standing. Following Bishop Howe's papal audience in February 1976, he and Christopher Hill paid a visit to Rome that November for consultations with the Secretariat for Unity as to the shape the visit might take. It was decided that there should be one public occasion with Pope and Archbishop together, since two were now too much for the Pope's strength. This would be on the second full day, as a result of talks at a private meeting during the previous twenty-four hours. The private session would not be simply a greeting, but would represent a sequence from the meeting with Archbishop Ramsey in 1966, and the agreement signed on that occasion; as a result of the encounter, broad direction and commitment should emerge for collaboration towards a goal of unity. A significant outcome of the private discussions between Pope and Archbishop would be the preparation of an agreed statement which both would sign on the public occasion.

Subjects which they might wish to discuss, and which would appear in the Common Declaration, were then examined, it having been decided that some work would need to be done beforehand and submitted to the two participants for their comments. Two possibilities were, first the commending of the three ARCIC documents on the Eucharist, Ministry and Authority I to the two Churches for study; and secondly the matter of Evangelization, which they felt the Archbishop would particularly like to discuss with the Pope, following the latter's issue of an Apostolic Exhortation 'to all the faithful of the entire world' entitled *Evangelii Nuntiandi* of December 1975.

On 5 April 1977 Cardinal Willebrands called to see Archbishop Coggan at the Old Palace at Canterbury to discuss the programme of the Rome visit in further detail; he brought with him a draft text for the Common Declaration. It was a version prepared by the Secretariat for Unity, based upon that written by Anglican drafters, which the Archbishop had amended. This was not discussed in

detail; Archbishop Coggan was to scrutinize it and make emenda-
tions, but it was agreed that it would be possible to make changes at
the private meeting at the Vatican on the first full day of the visit.

Two Anglican occasions had been included in the itinerary: for
Donald Coggan to celebrate the Eucharist on the morning following
his arrival in Rome at the English church of All Saints in the Via
Babuino; and secondly for him to preach at the American Episcopal
Church of St Paul in the Via Napoli, when he would also dedicate
some new doors which had been specially commissioned to commemorate the visit of Archbishop Fisher to Pope John XXIII in 1960.

The Archbishop of Canterbury left London airport on 27 April
1977 accompanied by a small entourage: Bishop Howe; Bishop
Edward Knapp Fisher[73]; John Satterthwaite, Bishop of Fulham
and Gibraltar, in whose jurisdiction were the English Anglican
Chaplaincies in Europe; John Trillo, Bishop of Chelmsford,
Chairman of the Committee for Roman Catholic Relations of the
Board of Mission and Unity; and David Painter. Henry McAdoo,
Bishop of Ossory, Co-Chairman of ARCIC, had a few days earlier
been nominated Archbishop of Dublin in the Church of Ireland and
was awaiting the confirmation, and was therefore unable to come.
Three press representatives accompanied the party, John Miles,
Gerald Priestland of the BBC and David Murphy of the Catholic
Truth Society.

During the flight Bishop Howe was surprised by the Archbishop's wish to discuss the substance of his forthcoming private
conversations with the Pope; it appeared that Donald had not, up to
that point, fully made up his mind on the items he might introduce.
It was an example of his approach to such events and demonstrated
not so much his lack of preparation, as his belief in spontaneity, and
his conception of the ways of God the Holy Spirit and trust in him.
Already in Rome awaiting the Archbishop on the Anglican side,
were Christopher Hill, Ervine Swift, Bishop for American Episcopal Churches in Europe, and Harry Smythe, Director of the
Anglican Centre in Rome.

Archbishop Coggan was greeted on his arrival in Rome by
Cardinal Benelli, Deputy Secretary of State, Cardinal Willebrands,
other members of the Secretariat for Unity, the British Ambassador
to Italy, and the British Minister to the Holy See. There was a great
concourse of photographers and reporters. A police escort accompa-

---

[73] 1915- ; Bishop of Pretoria 1960-75; Archdeacon of Westminster 1975-87; Member
of ARCIC.

nied the Archbishop's party to the English College in the Via Monserrat where they were to stay. Known locally as the *Venerabile*, 'the Venerable English College' was originally an English pilgrims' hospice. In the sixteenth century it became a seminary for Englishmen studying for the priesthood; its current Rector was Monsignor Cormac Murphy O'Connor[74].

The Archbishop and Cardinal Willebrands spent an hour or so that first afternoon examining the draft Common Declaration which had already undergone several further revisions; its nature demanded mutual agreement. Christopher Hill and Monsignor William Purdy[75] were called in to assist. There were two problem areas at that stage: the first was the future of the ARCIC documents. The original draft had spoken of their being referred to the two Churches for the expression of views; the revision suggested referral to theologians and then back to the Commission; this was felt inappropriate; the Commission would have done its work. Secondly, an important passage commending *action* in regard to evangelization had been removed. The Archbishop put the phrase back. An important element in Anglican minds was the avoidance of platitudes. Agreement was reached on the text which would be discussed with the Pope the following day.

That evening, after a sung Office and supper, Archbishop Coggan answered questions put to him by students; some were penetrating and difficult: the ordination of women, the Establishment in England, the status and privilege of the Church of England, Inter-communion. His frankness was remarked upon with admiration. Next morning he celebrated the Holy Communion at All Saints', assisted by the Bishop of Gibraltar, the Archdeacon of Malta and the Anglican chaplain in Rome. Though there was a large congregation (some well-wishers had travelled from England to support him), coupled with the presence of many Italian photographers, the calm of the Archbishop permeated the atmosphere. After breakfast at the English College, a fleet of cars with SCV number plates came to take the Archbishop and his companions across the river to the Vatican. The Tiber was in spate; the churned-up waters like wet cement. St Peter's Square came into view from the long Via della Conciliazione; they entered further into the Vatican City through an archway on the left of the Basilica, and drove round the back of it to the Cortile

---

[74] Now Bishop of Arundel and Co-Chairman of ARCIC.
[75] An English secular priest; for many years specialist on Anglican affairs at the Secretariat for Unity; joint Secretary of ARCIC.

San Damaso where a red carpet had been laid on the steps. The procession made its way through endless corridors to the *ante-camera* of the Pope's library. In Pope John's time, the walls had been covered with red silk; now it was grey velvet.

Archbishop Coggan's private talk with the Pope in his library lasted one hour and twenty-three minutes, which was longer than the interview of Geoffrey Fisher with Pope John XXIII, and that with Michael Ramsey; and a good deal more lengthy than any audience for some time past, because the Pope tired easily. The Archbishop of Canterbury was accompanied, on the Anglican side, by Bishop Howe and Bishop Knapp Fisher; Cardinal Willebrands and Monsignor Ramon Torella were present also. The exact content of the conversation has not been disclosed, but it was known that some discussion on the Common Declaration took place. Pope Paul was 79 years old and frail; his health was poor and he was in recurrent pain from arthritis. The strength which he had shown in a pontificate of great difficulty was beginning to ebb; there were signs that he did not find it easy to maintain concentration. Only his eyes remained bright and he smiled wanly. But he received the remainder of Archbishop Coggan's suite with kindness and made a short address.

He referred to Saint Anselm, native Italian, Abbot of Bec in Normandy and Archbishop of Canterbury, whose feast had been kept a week before; also to earlier discourse between the Catholic Church and the Anglican Communion. In particular he spoke of the conversations at Malines and the paper written by Dom Lambert Beauduin of Chevêtogne which referred to 'the Anglican Church united not absorbed'. He ended with a reference to evangelism, clearly because he felt it was a subject dear to his guest.

> You yourselves, Brethren, are concerned that the Gospel should be translated into deeds, and renew its significance for a society of Christian tradition. As our predecessor Pius XI put it, 'The Church civilizes by evangelizing.' That Gospel is the heart and soul of your Christian living and it is equally our inspiration.

In his reply Archbishop Coggan spoke of the two visits of his predecessors and the work of ARCIC, of growing warmth of relationships and of the increasing pastoral co-operation between the Churches in many fields. Personal gifts were exchanged; a water colour of Canterbury Cathedral by a Kent artist from the Archbishop. A visit was made to the Vatican library, where an exhibition of documents relating to England had been assembled. Lunch at the

British Embassy with the Ambassador to Italy and the Minister to
the Holy See as joint hosts followed.

That afternoon the Archbishop attended a service at the neo-
Byzantine American Episcopal Church of St Paul, and dedicated the
commemorative bronze doors already mentioned. With the Archbishop in the glittering apse, with its blue, green and gold Burne-
Jones mosaics sat Cardinal Willebrands and members of his Secretariat. It was a sight impossible to have foreseen a few years before.
The Archbishop's sermon on this occasion has been the subject of a
good deal of comment, both at the time and subsequently, so it is
important to examine its substance in detail. Almost the whole
sermon was devoted to the theme of evangelism. He chose as his text
part of a verse from St Paul's first letter to the Corinthians[76], in the
New English Bible translation: 'A great opportunity has opened for
effective work, and there is much opposition'. He spoke in the
context of the founding of the Church at Corinth and at Ephesus,
and of the difficulties:

> the work of evangelism, of the preaching of the gospel and of the winning
> of men to its allegiance, must go on, not in spite of the difficulties but
> because of them.

There were difficulties in the twentieth century. Tactfully, he
warmly welcomed the publication of the Pope's Apostolic Exhortation *Evangelii Nuntiandi* on evangelism; also the decrees of the
Second Vatican Council which dealt with the Church's missionary
activity.

'We find ourselves' he continued 'faced with an evangelistic task
whose size escalates with the multiplying of the millions and whose
strength is debilitated by our divisions – 'Talk to us about reconciliation' says an unbelieving world, 'when you yourselves are reconciled, and we will listen'. At the very end of his sermon came the
lines that were to cause controversy.

He spoke of a matter of, to him, great importance and great
urgency: the outcome of ARCIC he hoped would be studied at
grass-roots level, lest there be too large a gap between the thinking
of the theologians and that of the people in pews. 'To this world the
Lord of the Church sends us with His divine commission "Go forth
. . . make all nations my disciples".' This being so, was it not time,
when such a measure of agreement on so many of the fundamentals
of the gospel had been reached, that a relationship of shared

[76] Corinthians 16.9. ibid., pp. 117-22.

Communion be encouraged 'by the leadership of both our Chur-ches?' Joint evangelism, he suggested, might well be seriously weakened

> until we are able to go to that work strengthened by our joint participa-tion in the Sacrament of Christ's Body and Blood. The day must come when together we kneel and receive from one another's hands the tokens of God's redeeming love and then directly go, again together, to the world which Christ came to redeem.

Archbishop Coggan ended by suggesting that in many places in the world, 'as those of us who travel know perfectly well', intercommu-nion was already taking place. It would take place increasingly 'whether official sanction in the highest quarter be given or not'. His final words called for the search for the truth, not the blurring of issues on which agreement had not yet been reached: 'the evange-listic task of the Church must go on. And both must go on together.' He believed that greater success would crown effort if it was possible to say

> We do not want indiscipline in the Church of God. We desire that all things be done decently and in order. We can no longer be separated at the Sacrament of Unity. We are all sinners in need of the forgiveness and strength of our Lord. We will kneel together to receive it.

Reactions were of several kinds; they were not all negative, as sometimes suggested. Some felt that the Archbishop had been courageous and had acted according to the dictates of his conscience, whatever the price; that what he said needed saying. Why should the baptized not share Communion together? Reports in the press concentrated on the Intercommunion issue and, moreover, removed it from its setting of evangelism which had occupied so much of the sermon. He was interpreted as having made, not a call for common cause in evangelism, but a call for shared Communion *per se*, placed in the context of an irregular situation. This was regarded by the adverse lobby as naive, unrea-listic or ignorant; at best tactless. Archbishop Coggan was unpre-pared for the degree of shock he caused; his object, as always, was to further the cause of the spread of the gospel by removing hindrances.

Those who suffered most were the members of the Secretariat for Unity, whose efforts for ecumenism were sometimes carried out against considerable odds. Cardinal Willebrands, who was required to speak directly after Archbishop Coggan, had a particularly unenviable task. For he was unprepared for what had gone before.

The text of the sermon had been released to the press, but the Secretariat were taken by surprise. By this failure to communicate what he was proposing to say, the Archbishop was not playing the game according to the rules. Donald had written the sermon comparatively late; since the visit of Cardinal Willebrands to Canterbury on 5 April. He had sought a degree of consultation at home beforehand, and had received warning that it would be a mistake if what he said was seen as condoning or even encouraging indiscipline, for such was not his intention. He was construed in some quarters as having reminded an authoritative Church, at its centre, of the weakness of its authority. But it would appear that the episode had a much less harmful effect than some tried to make out. The Archbishop was well pleased with his private conversation with Paul VI; and the impression he himself created, of a friendly, well-intentioned, dedicated man, lacking in malice or guile, who was trying to do good rather than harm, won him a number of allies.

However, the difficulties of the day were not over. After a large reception in the ballroom of the Doria Pamphilj palace, the Archbishop left for the Anglican Centre in the same building, for a small private dinner party with Harry Smythe, its director. Bishop Howe was there also. Later in the evening a message came from Cardinal Willebrands; certain sources at the Vatican were anxious to make further revision of the Common Declaration to be signed on the following day[77].

Cardinal Willebrands called at the English College early next morning; a meeting with the Archbishop and his senior advisers followed. The public ceremony with the Pope, when the Common Declaration would be signed, was to take place in the Sistine Chapel at 11 am. The clause which had caused difficulty was that concerned with the transmission and reception of the ARCIC documents. Archbishop Coggan expressed himself unable to depart from his previous position: for the ARCIC documents to be kept to the Commission only, was unacceptable; the Churches must be involved. Alternative forms of wording were discussed. At one point the Cardinal had two telephone lines open to the Vatican. At 10.20 am the reply came; a change had been agreed: the phrases in question would read

> We now recommend that the work it [ARCIC] has begun be pursued, through procedures appropriate to our respective Communions, so that both of them may be led along the path towards unity.

[77] ibid., Appendix I, pp. 314-17, for final version.

The moment will shortly come when the respective Authorities must evaluate the conclusions.

No collaboration was implied in this process, but the improvement was accepted. At 10.30 am the Archbishop, Cardinal Willebrands and their accompanying clergy, left for the Sistine Chapel.

There had been discussion as to whether the ceremony should be within the setting of the Mass, but it was decided that such a course would be more divisive than the alternative, 'a sacred celebration of the Word'. The Sistine Chapel was crowded and brilliantly lit. The Pope and Archbishop entered side by side, the Pope made a slight indication of his hand to slow down the pace. They took up their places on two gilt chairs, with their backs to the altar, facing the congregation. Readings and prayers of thanksgiving and intercession followed, with a brief allocution from each. Pope and Archbishop then exchanged the kiss of peace to *Ubi Caritas est vera, Deus ibi est*. Finally there came a joint Blessing. During the singing of the hymn 'Praise to the Holiest in the Height', the procession moved from the sanctuary to the Pauline Chapel where the Common Declaration was signed. Monsignor Purdy read the document; the signatures followed. None of the subsequent reports captured the emotional nature of the event: William Purdy completed his reading only with difficulty; a papal chamberlain remarked to him that he himself had been similarly moved by the significance of the occasion. It was considered by many, despite, or perhaps because of the difficulties, an occasion of progress towards the reconciliation of Christians still divided. One final observation; as Archbishop Coggan took his pen to put his signature to the Common Declaration, he was seen to make a slight addition to the text. In the hurry of redrafting at the last moment, a set of quotation marks to close a reference to a passage of Scripture had been left out; he put them in.

Farewells to Pope Paul were moving also; there seemed small likelihood that any of the Englishmen would see him again in this life[78]. The remainder of the visit was taken up with social occasions and ancient sites; lunch with the Abbot Primate of the Benedictines at San Anselmo, dinner with Cardinal Willebrands and the Secretariat; a tour of some catacombs and the excavations under St Peter's Basilica. Accounts of the ceremony in the Sistine Chapel filled the Italian papers, but few appreciated the possibilities which the common commitment to evangelism might bring. It revealed once

---

[78] He died the following year, during the Lambeth Conference.

again the danger of expressing important truths as vague, somewhat generalized, pious hopes; a reference in specific terms such as that introduced at the end of Archbishop Coggan's sermon, received more attention. On the morning of 30 April he left Fumicino airport for Istanbul.

Donald Coggan arrived in Turkey to find his new suite awaiting him. (His Rome entourage, apart from Bishop Howe, Bishop Satterthwaite and David Painter who had travelled on with him, had departed for London; Christopher Hill went on to Geneva). Robert Runcie[79], Bishop of St Albans and Chairman of the Anglican/ Orthodox Doctrinal Commission, headed the Archbishop's advisers. The Commission had been formed in 1962 as the result of the visit of Archbishop Ramsey to the Oecumenical Patriarch. Bishop Runcie had been Chairman since 1973 when the full Commission had met in Oxford and work spread among sub-committees. Their findings had been presented to the second full meeting in Moscow in 1976; agreement was reached on a number of topics. No reference was made to the ordination of women in the final statement, but a separate note, which was added, said that the Commission's Orthodox members felt obliged to put on record that the ordination of women by Anglican Churches would 'create a very serious obstacle to the development of our relations in the future'. A few of these members felt so strongly that the suspension of Conversations for three years, to 'test sincerity', was proposed. Others, led by Archbishop Athenagoras of Thyateira (based in England), were determined that the talks should continue, so that points of view in all frankness could be put, in the hope of influencing Anglican decisions.

A problem that needed to be solved concerned the publication of the Minutes of the Moscow meeting. There was a difference of opinion as to whether this should include all the Minutes, or a résumé. The Oecumenical Patriarch had asked that the matter be dropped until the Archbishop's visit. It was hoped that the presence of Archbishop Coggan would encourage the continuation of the Conversations, and lift the ban on the publication of the Moscow statement; thereby allowing the Commission's work to become known and to further Anglican/Orthodox co-operation.

Michael Moore, Archbishop Coggan's Chaplain for Foreign Rela-

[79] 1921- ; Principal of Cuddesdon Theological College 1960-70; Bishop of St Alban's 1970-80; Archbishop of Canterbury 1980- .

tions, was at the airport to greet him, accompanied by what looked like a bevy of laymen in collars and ties. They were in fact Orthodox clergy, one of them a bishop, who were not permitted by the Turkish authorities to wear clerical dress in public. The Archbishop's party were exempt from the ruling, since they were visitors. Before any meetings with ecclesiastics, Donald Coggan and his companions made a courtesy call on the Vali, or Mayor, of Istanbul. Then they made their way to the Phanar, home of the Oecumenical Patriarch, Demetrios I. On the death of his predecessor, the great Athenagoras in July 1972, the Turkish government had blocked the original nominations to the Patriarchal throne. The result was the election of the then unknown Metropolitan Demetrios of Imbros and Tenedos, islands at the mouth of the Dardanelles, the most junior member of the Holy Synod. Donald Coggan was the fourth Archbishop of Canterbury to visit an Oecumenical Patriarch; the first was Cosmo Gordon Lang in 1939; then Geoffrey Fisher in 1960, followed by Michael Ramsey in 1962. Donald Coggan had paid Patriarch Athenagoras a visit himself, as Archbishop of York.

The initial reception of the Archbishop of Canterbury by the Oecumenical Patriarch, greeting, and discussions, took place on the first day. In the evening, the English party crossed the Bosphorus into Asia to a reception by Metropolitan Meliton of Chalcedon, Dean of the Holy Synod, who was expected to be chosen as Oecumenical Patriarch, when it was prevented by political means. Next day, Sunday, the Archbishop and his companions attended an Orthodox Liturgy of great length in the Cathedral of St George. Both Archbishop and Patriarch spoke; the Patriarch first: he referred to the 'formation of new problems' and the 'introduction of novelties'; the movement towards the ordination of women he considered 'anti-apostolic'. Archbishop Coggan referred to the previous visit and those of his predecessors; he issued an invitation to Canterbury. He spoke of the valuable work of the Anglican Orthodox Doctrinal Commission and rejoiced that the Moscow statement was being printed and how much he hoped it would be widely studied. On the issue of the ordination of women, he explained that the action had already been taken in certain parts of the Anglican Communion, but that,

> We do not seek to impose this on any part of the Church of Christ. Nor, indeed, do we ask your church to do so. But we hold that those who see this action as being right should be free to do so; and it is our duty within the Anglican Church to live in love and peace with those who take this action.

He concluded by expressing the wish that 'brotherly dialogue should continue'. A joint declaration on these lines resulted[80]. A discussion on the *filioque* clause[81] followed in which Bishop Runcie eventually suggested that the West, by putting in the clause meant much as did the East by leaving it out. On this eirenic note, the proceedings drew to a close. Donald Coggan made a short call on the Armenian Patriarch, which excursion turned out to be full of danger. It was May 1, Labour Day; riots broke out in Istanbul; 34 people had been killed in the streets by nightfall. Gerald Priestland of the BBC, who was in the press party, was soon in the thick of the fighting and broadcast later that 'there seemed little of the 'Western' concern for life in that city'. The Archbishop celebrated and preached at the service of Holy Communion in St Helen's Chapel in the grounds of the British Consulate in the evening. During the later reception at the Consulate, police forbade guests to leave until the situation had become safer.

Next day the Archbishop left for Geneva. A certain nervousness had been felt at Lambeth at the news that Dr Philip Potter, General Secretary of the World Council of Churches, had booked Archbishop Coggan into an expensive hotel, on account of the reception given to the matter of the first class ticket to Nairobi. But Dr Potter refused to change his plans, and accepted the responsibility.

The first engagement was at the Orthodox Centre at Chambesy where the bells of the modern church were rung in honour of the Archbishop. His host was Metropolitan Damaskinos. In his reply to the speech of welcome, Donald Coggan assured him of Anglican determination to pursue dialogue, in spite of the divergence of views over the ordination of women. There was some discussion on the question of a Common Easter.

At a formal dinner given by the WCC to the Archbishop he spoke again on women's ordination, which he said he was anxious to remove 'from the emotional and sentimental into the realm of the intelligent, and the study of the whole way of the Spirit in the history of the Church. We cannot finish this question with the year 100 and put a full stop there'. During the next twelve hours he celebrated the Eucharist in the Chapel of the Ecumenical Centre, and took part in a session on Spirituality, visited the Centre for

[80] ibid., Appendix II, pp. 318-19.
[81] 'And the Son'; the double procession of the Holy Ghost; added by the Western Church to the Creed after the words 'the Holy Ghost who proceedeth from the Father'.

Ecumenical Studies at Chateau Bossey, attended Evensong at the Anglican Church in Geneva and spoke at length to various staff members of the World Council. He also answered countless questions at a press conference. Later, there was some private conversation between the Archbishop and Philip Potter, who expressed the hope that the Church of England would be able to play a stronger part in the life of the World Council. Archbishop Coggan, for his part, invited him to send an observer to the Lambeth Conference in 1978. As might be imagined, there were engagements of a civil and cultural sort in this city of the great Calvin. In the Cathedral, where the Archbishop met local clergy, Bach's G Major Prelude and Fugue was being played; the atmosphere of the visit was sufficiently informal for David Painter to be allowed to extemporize on the magnificent new organ.

So ended eight of the more momentous days of Donald Coggan's life, the outcome of which it is still too early to tell. He had let it be known that diversity was part of the unity for which he prayed; respect for diversity, agreement to differ, would enable unity to come. He pressed this attitude with friendliness, but with firmness too, as one who was sure of his ground.

Three days of residential meetings of the Standing Committee later, he was in Truro to celebrate the centenary of the diocese, which had been carved from that of Exeter in 1877. After preaching in the Cathedral he and his wife drove to Bodmin Moor to a vast outdoor Eucharist to which all the parishes in Cornwall came. The Archbishop was almost mobbed as he moved among the people afterwards with great affability. Next day he opened a new Church primary school, named after Archbishop Benson, one-time Bishop of Truro and one of Donald's predecessors as Archbishop of Canterbury. The enthusiastic, relaxed attitudes of the children were a reaction to his remarkable gift with young people of this age group. The Archbishop opened another primary school in his own diocese at the end of the same week, with the same happy results.

Further visits to dioceses took place that summer; to Portsmouth later in May for the fiftieth anniversary there, and to St Albans in June for its centenary. On none of these occasions, placed as they were always in the midst of a heavy programme elsewhere, did he give an impression of boredom, of having done it all before, or of tiredness. Neither he nor his wife spared themselves in their efforts to meet the maximum number of people; all of which became a personal encounter, not a mere formality. The desire to put others at their ease and an absence of superiority was an endearing feature of their relationships. Diocesans, who might consider him magisterial at Bishops' Meetings, found him delightful company in their own homes. It would be a mistake, however, to imply that there were no occasions where mettle would emerge. The Principal of a College visited by the Archbishop that spring would be unlikely to forget his omission of a service of Holy Communion on Ascension Day. During the singing of the opening hymn at a Confirmation in his own diocese, Donald was equally firm as he stopped organist, choir and congregation, and told them to effect some improvement.

A *Kirchentag* on the German pattern, in the Cathedral of Canterbury, designed to help 2,000 members of the diocese to renew and study their faith and to worship, included a group on the Family, run by the Coggans. Len Murray, General Secretary of the Trades Union Congress, discussed Christianity and industrial relations. Donald's diary for that day, 14 May 1977, showed an entry in his writing: 'Climb Cathedral scaffolding with J. Brasier (the head verger).' There is no reason to suppose he did not do so.

One important engagement lay ahead before the events of the Queen's Jubilee: a visit to the General Assembly of the Church of Scotland which he had been asked to address. He took care to identify himself with the ideals of that Church, even in his choice of jokes. It appeared that the Assembly had experienced problems with speakers failing to announce their names and numbers. When he rose, the Archbishop announced 'My name is Coggan. I haven't been told my number, but I think it must be 666'[82]. The biblical quip was well received in the land of the Book.

> I long for the closest possible unity between our two great Churches; pre-eminently because I believe this to be the will of the Lord of the Church, but also because of the need of a world which has something of a right to say: We will listen to you with your message of reconciliation when we see you reconciled among yourselves.

It was an echo of what he had said in Rome, but he made some different emphases too, with an eye to his hearers: the distinctive contribution which Scotland made to the World Council of Churches; the element of reciprocity that should exist between Christian communities, receiving as well as giving. He spoke of joint evangelism and the results, perhaps unexpected, it might have. He called for recommencement of official joint negotiations for the Union of their two Churches.

---

[82] The number given to the second beast in the Book of Revelation, chapter 13. For text of address see Donald Coggan *Sure Foundation*, pp. 123-127.

I would like to see a little group of theologians . . . who would engage on very informal but very deep theological work together. I would like to see them become a closely-knit family who would meet and live together periodically, engage in leisurely prayer and honest discussion, pressing back behind the controversies which have engaged us in recent centuries, back to the basic biblical documents and the writings of the early Church. I confess that, in putting this forward, I have in mind the kind of fellowship, the kind of depth of praying and theologizing, which marked the members of the Anglican-Roman Catholic International Commission, and which issued in the publication of the three Agreed Statements . . . It might well be that . . . the members would come across issues or produce documents which they would wish to bring to the notice of our official assemblies. They would see how the Spirit led them. But their labours would ensure that theology, sound and deep, was being done, and done jointly.

He ended by asking for various forms of joint activity in other fields; the religious education of the young in particular, a sphere of concern in Scotland[83].

The year 1977 marked the twenty-fifth anniversary of the Queen's Accession. Among the celebrations to mark the event was an act of worship at St Paul's Cathedral on 7 June, when Archbishop Coggan was asked to preach and give the blessing. Early that morning he broadcast on the BBC's 'Thought for the day' programme on dedication; he reiterated what he had said at the time of the *Call* – 'God first, others next, self last', and spoke of responsibilities rather than demands. The glittering occasion took place seemingly without a hitch. A special service had been devised: the choir sang, the Archbishop of York and Archdeacon of London (Canon in Residence) read the lessons, Samuel Cutt, minor canon, led the prayers; all were Anglicans. Other Church leaders, including Cardinal Hume, were present, but took no verbal part. The Archbishop took his text from a verse in the second lesson: 'Every one that heareth those sayings of mine and doeth them, I will liken him unto a wise man which built his house upon a rock'.[84] Taking firm foundations as his theme, he spoke of the Queen's dedication and self-sacrifice; that she had built her life upon the rock of religious faith and a stable family life. He touched on the self-seeking nature of materialism and sectional interests; on reconciliation and understanding, for which many had come to see the need, but which by itself 'does not provide a foundation strong enough to resist the

[83] Donald Coggan, *Sure Foundation*, pp. 123-7.
[84] Matthew 7.24. ibid., pp. 169-71.

storms which assail it in personal, family or national life'. Penitence, dedication, and thanksgiving, that was what mattered. He elaborated on the ends to which each should be directed: penitence for past evils; dedication to God for the future; thanksgiving for twenty-five years of service faithfully given; for God's goodness and redemption of the world by Jesus Christ; 'for the means of grace and the hope of glory'.

Next day, reactions began to flow into Lambeth Palace. A great deal of criticism directed towards the Archbishop referred to matters which were none of his doing (he had had no part in the drawing up of the service): the fact that no members of other Churches had taken part; that no new translations of the Scriptures had been used, no modern hymns; only the choir boys had been under fifty; the changes that had taken place during the Queen's reign went unnoticed. Some criticism of the sermon on these lines came in too, though the more traditionalist liked it. Too much concentration on Old Testament qualities and not enough challenge to 'the vain traces of earth' that were 'on almost unparalleled display', was a comment, though he had mentioned the hollowness of a way of life built on materialism.

Two days later, the Queen and Duke of Edinburgh, who had travelled up the Thames in the Royal Barge from Greenwich, alighted at Lambeth Pier and came to tea with the Archbishop and Jean Coggan. Their daughter, Ann, brought her form of seven-year old boys from her school in Winchester to provide an unofficial guard of honour outside the gate of Lambeth Palace. Ruth was there also, home on furlough. Too cold and wet to be held in the garden, the small informal tea party took place in the large drawing room; the Queen stayed about an hour. It was the kind of occasion at which the Coggans excelled, with its cheerful, unassuming family atmosphere. The Queen's Private Secretary wrote later to express her thanks for the haven of calm and relaxation that had been provided, and how pleased she was to meet their daughters.

Less than a week later, the Archbishop took part in a very different event, but one in which he showed an equal talent, a visit to Maidstone prison. He made an impression on staff and prisoners, most of whom were friendly and talkative. The climax came when Donald spent about an hour with ten men serving life sentences, in the company of the prison chaplain and David Painter; the discussion was frank and relaxed. One man was one of the great train robbers; another had killed a girl under the influence of drink;

when, at the close, the Archbishop, with naturalness and simplicity, prayed for them all and their families, they were much moved.

The repercussions following the Jubilee service had hardly subsided when another bombshell landed at the Archbishop's feet: a volume entitled 'The Myth of God Incarnate', a symposium of ten essays by seven different authors and edited by Professor Maurice Wiles, formerly Chairman of the Doctrine Commission, was published on 1 July. The General Synod met a few days later when the Archbishops of Canterbury and York received an application that the Synod should have an opportunity to debate, or hear a statement about, this publication. Archbishop Coggan answered:

> We fully understand the concern and anxiety of many Christian people, but while we regret the title of the book, with its unfortunate implications for people who are not familiar with theological language or with the theological debates of this century, we think that it would be irresponsible to engage in discussion of a book, published only last Friday, which few of us can have read[85].

He drew the attention of Synod members to a response to be published the following month. Much alarmed correspondence on the subject arrived at Lambeth Palace. A stock letter sent in reply drew attention to the points indicated above, and added that the intentions of the authors of the essays, were not to damage the witness of the Church, but to interpret the doctrines of the incarnation in such a way as to make the Christian faith 'easier of acceptance for modern man'.

> The Archbishop does not believe this to be the case. He sees the Catholic creeds as the safeguards of the Apostolic preaching and this alone conveys the message of eternal salvation.

He made it clear that it was not the Church of England way to engage in any form of heresy hunting, but rather 'to leave matters such as this to the faith and good sense of the whole body of the Church and to the judgement of time'. In addition to the book mentioned in the Synod, a recent book by Professor C.F.D. Moule, *The Origin of Christology*, which defended the orthodox view, was also recommended. Needless to say, there were those who did not agree with this attitude.

The Coggans' Summer holiday took the form of a relaxed fortnight in Canterbury at the beginning of August, followed by a

---

[85] *General Synod July Group of Sessions 1977 Report of Proceedings*, Vol. 8, No. 2, p. 511.

strenuous return to Canada for the celebrations at Wycliffe College to mark the hundreth anniversary of its foundation. The most illustrious former member of staff was required to lead the programme of reunions of old students with plenty of speeches. Jean Coggan gave an address to the wives of Wycliffe alumni, gathered from all parts of Canada, at a large luncheon in a Toronto hotel. She spoke with some authority on the sphere of the clergy wife.

Donald Coggan had attended the Lambeth Conferences of 1958 and 1968; in the second he had taken a major part in leading discussion and reporting, but not in the planning operation. If he had any illusions of its being moderately straightforward, he was to be disappointed. After the Wycliffe celebrations, Archbishop Scott, Primate of Canada, and Bishop Allin, Presiding Bishop from the USA, met with the Archbishop of Canterbury in Toronto. He was asked whether he would see some Canadian Bishops the following day, and he agreed.

There had been murmuring for some months as to the design of the Lambeth Conference scheduled for 1978 (preliminary papers for which had been circulated), which had been reflected elsewhere in the Anglican Communion among bishops of what might be called Western European origin. Bishop Howe had already become aware of it, because he and, to a lesser extent, the Archbishop of Canterbury, had received letters on the subject. One bishop wrote that he thought

> the theme of episcopacy and its exercise today did not give a wide enough expression to the essential concerns which ought to bring Bishops together.
>
> We fully realize that under the new arrangements, Lambeth 1978 is designed to be a learning experience for the participants and not a place of pronouncement . . . We feel, however, that the content of learning needs to be based on a concern for the present moment in world history, rather than what appears to be an internal Church question.

Another Bishop wrote:

> We are coming very close to abdicating our episcopal responsibilities and in fact turning them over to the Anglican Consultative Council. One interpretation of the pattern which is revealing itself for the upcoming Lambeth Conference would be that it reveals a nervousness and lack of confidence in our role as the chosen and consecrated leaders of the People of God . . . In spite of sharing in the current turmoil and reaction to all leadership, it has become quite obvious that the 'ordinary' people of the parishes look to the Bishops for leadership.

An Archbishop from Australasia expressed his disappointment that the Lambeth Conference was to be kept 'low key' and 'have nothing to say to the world'.

The Canadian House of Bishops discussed the Lambeth Conference at their meeting at Cochrane, Alberta, from 5-9 August 1977, as did also the Canadian General Synod from 11-18 August. It was in the light of their deliberations that a talk between the Archbishop of Canterbury and some Canadian Bishops had been requested. It took place in Toronto on 30 August. A great deal of the discussion was reported in Archbishop Scott's subsequent letter of 8 September to Bishop Howe in London, a copy of which went to the Archbishop of Canterbury. All were concerned that the Lambeth Conference should be a

> focal point in the renewal and enrichment of the Anglican Church in its mission throughout the world. We recognize, however, that simply wanting this to happen will not automatically make it come to pass.

Their first worry was the amount of pressure which the planning placed upon both the Archbishop of Canterbury and Bishop Howe; the Canadian bishops offered help in any way possible. Although some bishops had tended to reveal expectations of the old style of Lambeth, with a lot of emphasis on resolutions and a report on wide-ranging concerns, they themselves recognized, and the Archbishop had confirmed the fact, that his expectations for the Lambeth Conference were different. To be able to achieve the hopes of the Archbishop, however, some way would have to be found to help bishops to get a clearer focus of the purpose of the Conference, to make it possible to identify and deal with issues and expectations which they would 'in fact' bring with them, whatever the stated purpose. The view presented by the Canadian bishops gave as the first essential the determination of key agenda concerns, which called for imput from all Provinces. Secondly there would be need for a broadly-based design group and steering committee to keep an eye both on central purposes and to see that other issues, as they came up, were identified and dealt with.

Archbishop Scott said that he felt it important to recognize the increasing complexity of the dynamics involved in world gatherings. The experience of Canadian bishops in *Partners in Mission* events had made them deeply aware of that, as also that 'designing' meetings was a very complex task and one that involved particular skills and cultural sensitivities. There had been a tendency among bishops to think of the Archbishop of Canterbury as a 'college professor' rather than an archbishop, and of the Lambeth Conference as a series of college classes. He ended that the desire to help was deep; it was felt that unless broadly-based support staff was forthcoming, no real solution to the pressure would be found.

Archbishop Coggan replied[86] with thanks for 'your care and for the thought that you are giving to the Conference'. He would give careful consideration to the points raised; he was just off to Russia, and would speak with Bishop Howe on his return.

Here was the crux of the matter: the pressure on the Archbishop from many quarters was so extreme that opportunity for either detailed or overall planning was simply not available. The preparations had begun late; a bare two years before the event was insufficient. Despite, and sometimes because of, the strictest stewardship of time, discussions between the Archbishop and Bishop Howe never completed the agenda on points needing resolution; subsequent engagements invariably broke in.

The Russian journey over, Donald Coggan returned to the issues talked over in Toronto. He wrote to Archbishop Scott on 20 October: he was arranging for a small pre-Lambeth Conference meeting of bishops; (it took place in January). 'I hope you will feel that the arrangements we have made meet the points that you had in mind'. He felt, he said, that this would be a very fruitful gathering. The Canadian House of Bishops, at their next meeting in November, pressed on with their objective: they looked forward to a 'new style' Lambeth, but one that would be accompanied by design and 'flexible and creative processing'.

> There are people, we understand, with particular skills in this matching of form and content. We would recommend that such resources be consulted both in the strategic designing of Lambeth and in the day-to-day tactics of its arrangement.

A resolution was carried that 'a skilled person be present at the January meeting to aid in the continuing designing of the Lambeth Conference'.

A few days before his departure for Russia, the Archbishop devised one of the most successful events of his office at Canterbury. The active clergy of the diocese, retired men, full-time lay workers, clergy wives and widows, were invited by him to take part in a day of celebration and fellowship in the Cathedral. Archbishop Coggan spoke first for an hour on the Ministry, to great effect. Though he

[86] 19 September 1977.

rarely did so, he allowed his own sense of commitment, aspirations, concept of ministry and long experience, to emerge; the results were found spell-binding. It was cold and wet in the cloisters during the lunch break, though it was only September, but this did not break the spell; the Archbishop had created a warmer climate. There were further talks in the afternoon by others, on the mission of the Cathedral. A recital by the Cathedral Organist led into a Eucharist for the 600 people present, celebrated by Donald Coggan who, it was generally agreed, had given much encouragement and good counsel.

The visit to Russia and Armenia which began on 22 September had several aspects: one was the series of discussions held with the leaders of the Orthodox Church, in which the Archbishop did not take so prominent a part as some of his advisers who had the advantages of a common language with their hosts, and specialized knowledge of the Eastern Churches. Secondly, and here Archbishop Coggan took a strong lead, was the opportunity the visit provided to visit religious communities under duress and to press their case with the authorities. Thirdly, though doctrinal agreement probably did not advance to any extent, attempts were made to promote greater mutual understanding; on the Anglican side to try to demonstrate the position of a Church in a free society. In an exercise of this kind, Donald Coggan was invariably a good ambassador, for his sincerity and straightforwardness shone through linguistic and cultural differences.

When Metropolitan Juvenaly, head of the Foreign Relations Department of the Moscow Patriarchate, came to England for Archbishop Coggan's Enthronement, he gave an interview to the BBC for their External Service. He spoke of a tendency among certain circles in England, supported even by some officials of the Anglican Church, to present a biased and one-sided picture of Orthodox life in Russia. In talks at Lambeth Palace, he elaborated on these points; one of the areas of grievance was Keston College, a centre for the study of Religion and Communism, of which the Archbishop was patron and Michael Bourdeaux, an Anglican priest, the Director. It was anti-Soviet, the Metropolitan asserted. An attempt was made to disabuse him of this view: the Centre's objective was to reach an all-round picture, fair to all opinions. This was difficult for him to understand; as also was the freedom of the press. The *Church Times* had offended the Russian Church, and the fact that this periodical was not under ecclesiastical, or indeed civil, control, and that newspapers were free to publish at will, was greeted with incredulity. All these issues came up again on the Russian visit.

Archbishop Coggan was accompanied by Robert Runcie, Bishop of St Albans, as Chairman of the Anglican/Orthodox Joint Doctrinal Discussions, who for the remainder of the tour and beyond was to be known as Albanski, which was his description on all the Russian documents. Also with the Archbishop was John Arnold[87], Secretary of the Board of Mission and Unity of the General Synod, who was a Russian speaker, as was Michael Moore. Patrick Gilbert, General Secretary of the Society for Promoting Christian Knowledge, came in his capacity as a provider of religious books for Russian seminaries; and John Miles, press officer, and David Painter completed the group. They stopped for an hour in Paris to change planes, and narrowly missed being consigned to Montreal, but reached Moscow safely at 4 pm, to be met by Patriarch Pimen, Patriarch of Moscow and All Russia, also Metropolitan Juvenaly, already mentioned, who spoke with warmth of his visit to Lambeth, Metropolitan Nikodim, Bishop Melchizedek of Penza and Saransk, and an interpreter by the name of Mystyslav. Accommodation was initially at the Hotel Sovietska. The programme had been left fairly fluid and no objections were raised when the Archbishop made some requests, such as to visit Baptists or a synagogue. On the first evening the English visitors, including the Archbishop, made a journey on the Moscow underground to see Red Square. Donald was keen to meet some ordinary Russians and observe their way of life.

The next three days were devoted to formal greetings and receptions, also some dialogue. The Patriarch, a tall bearded figure with white jewelled headdress, a cross on the top, and long black robes, treated the Archbishop of Canterbury with great cordiality, and a friendly relationship was established. A first attempt at discussion was somewhat stilted and the difference in starting-points obvious; the notion of developments in religious belief and practice was an alien concept to the Russians; the question of the ordination of women came up, as did the grievances against the BBC and Keston College. Both the Archbishop and Bishop Runcie reiterated the independence of the two bodies. The intention to draw up an agreed statement was decided upon.

Next day, a Saturday, the Anglican group visited a Moscow synagogue and joined for a while in the service on the Sabbath,

[87] 1933- ; Dean of Rochester 1978.

having been provided with big black silk hats as head coverings. Donald Coggan spoke in Hebrew with the Jewish leaders and was concerned for the shortage of rabbis; only fifteen were in training, he learned, throughout the Soviet Union. The rabbis answered him in Russian; Hebrew was not permitted, since it could not be monitored. The English visitors were then conveyed by car to Zagorsk, to the largest monastery now surviving, and nearby Orthodox seminary; sleet was beginning to fall, herald of the Russian winter. Archbishop Coggan addressed the students, all with close-cropped hair and pale, solemn faces, with the help of an interpreter, though he found the method difficult; he depended much on the element of spontaneity. One of the students faced the ordeal of having to give a practice sermon in front of the visitors, and dried up during the course of it. Archbishop Coggan made to reach him with words of encouragement, but the seminarian was whisked away. Vespers at the monastery chapel was full of people; there followed another service at the seminary, both with beautiful music and choirs singing antiphonally, incense and candles everywhere.

After an Anglican Eucharist in the Archbishop's room on Sunday, he and his entourage attended the Patriarchal Cathedral for the liturgy, during which they were invited to go behind the iconostasis[88] and were given unconsecrated but 'blessed' bread and wine. An exchange of speeches and gifts took place amidst the glare of television cameras, full of friendship on the Orthodox side apart from a sentence about the ordination of women, 'an unsurmountable obstacle' in the quest for unity. Archbishop Coggan's reply reminded the Patriarch that the word 'impossible' did not exist in God's vocabulary. He then gave a short biblical exposition to the congregation via an interpreter, reminding them how the two disciples found Jesus on their road to Emmaus – or were found by him – in a way which they would not have believed possible, and recognized Him in the breaking of bread. It was afterwards conveyed to the Anglicans how impressed the Russian congregation had been with the simplicity and sincerity of the Archbishop's words in a presentation new to them.

During the same afternoon Donald preached in a Baptist church in Moscow where the average age was lower than at the Cathedral and there were several children and young families. Bishop Melchizedek preached there also; an unusual occurrence for the Orthodox. The traditional waving of handkerchiefs marked the time to leave.

---

[88] In Anglican churches, the rood screen would be the nearest equivalent.

Evensong at the British Embassy, with the Archbishop preaching once again, was the last service on that day. He prayed with the English party at the tomb of the unknown soldier on the wall of the Kremlin next day, and laid a wreath. Then there was a tour of churches and cathedrals in the Kremlin. During a visit to the Minister for Religious Affairs, the Archbishop took with him a list of names of those he thought to be prisoners of conscience. The Minister became rather angry and spoke of distortion of facts about the Soviet Union in the *Church Times* and BBC World Service.

Joint Communiqués summing up agreement that had been reached, were read at the Patriarch's residence, first in Russian, then in English, and signed. Despite differences, conversations would continue. A huge lunch of seven or eight courses was provided in a restaurant, followed by speeches. In the Archbishop's, he gave the warning, heard often, of allowing too large a gap to appear between theologians, hierarchy and laity. It received applause from the great gathering of clergy and some laymen, but the Patriarch was heard to say that there was no such gap between hierarchy and laity in the Orthodox Church 'because the people had been taught obedience'.

The beginning of that evening was spent at a vigil at the Novodevichy Convent in Moscow which was to persist during the night. After a very warm and friendly speech by Metropolitan Juvenaly and reply by Archbishop Coggan, it was soon time to leave for the railway station and night train to Kiev. Here the ground was already covered with snow. Metropolitan Filaret was there to meet them. There were several receptions and services, including a Eucharist, celebrated by the Archbishop for the handful of Anglicans in the city, who were visited only infrequently by a chaplain and were overwhelmed by the visit and the interest and courtesy, typical of Donald, shown towards them. It was easier for the visitors to make their own way round in Kiev; they saw Orthodox and Baptist churches and managed, as the result of Archbishop Coggan's persistence, to visit the church where Georgi Vins had been pastor before his expulsion to Siberia. Donald had already taken part in protests in England on Vins' account, mounted by various organizations and Members of both Houses of Parliament. The church lay at the end of a muddy lane on the outskirts of the city. A crowd of about forty had gathered in the dusk. The Archbishop asked questions as to the present whereabouts of Pastor Vins; he assured the assembled company of Anglican prayers for him, in fact the prayers of the Churches of the West. Donald and his companions sang Bunyan's hymn, 'He who would valiant be'; the Baptists responded with a hymn of their own, the Archbishop prayed aloud and the sad gathering broke up.

There was one more call, this time to another synagogue, where two or three officials met the Archbishop and spoke in Hebrew. His concern for the persecuted and neglected brought forth in him spontaneous gifts of great quality.

The journey to Armenia by plane took less time than had been expected; the Anglicans were early at Yerevan with Mount Ararat (traditional final destination of the Ark of Noah) in the background, and the Supreme Catholicos of the Armenian Apostolic Church had not yet arrived at the airport to greet them, to his considerable eventual consternation. Archbishop Coggan replied 'I couldn't wait to see you' and embarrassment was forgotten. It was the first time an Archbishop of Canterbury had come to Armenia, although the two men had met before elsewhere. They went at once to Etchmiadzin, the Holy City. The Church was not Orthodox, but non-Chalcedonian, which meant that it had split from the rest of Christendom at the Council of Chalcedon in AD 451.

Several days of warm and informative dialogue produced the possibilities of a Common Declaration and for a Continuation Group for Anglican/Armenian relations. One of the most emotive occasions during the visit was when hosts and guests stood on a mountainside encircling a large flat round monument to the many Armenians massacred in 1915, in the middle of which was a burning flame, the sack-like hooded robes of the Armenian clergy interspersed with Anglican cassocks. The Supreme Catholicos prayed aloud, and without prior arrangement invited Archbishop Coggan to do likewise; without a moment's hesitation, he spontaneously made an invocation to God the Holy Spirit in words all found moving, and flowers were strewn on the ground.

It had been a visit of promise. A Common Declaration was achieved; and Archbishop Coggan's idea that mention should be made of hope through suffering (from the Epistle to the Romans) in relation to Anglican sympathy for Armenian genocide during the present century, was well received. There was also talk of an Armenian observer at the forthcoming Lambeth Conference.

At Heathrow the Archbishop heard the news that the Duchess of Kent was ill and had lost the child she was expecting and tired as he was, he went straight to see her. The Duke, who was in Canada, had left immediately he heard the news and would be arriving at the airport early next morning; Donald was there to meet him.

Although the Russian journey was over, its repercussions continued. The Archbishop became more involved even than before in the appeals for help for prisoners of conscience, although he refused to be drawn into any condemnation of the Russian régime. The Chief Rabbi[89] wrote:

> May I greet you on your return from your historic visit to the USSR and express to you, both personally and on behalf of the Jewish community, sincere appreciation for the interest you evinced in the situation of our Jewish brothers and sisters . . . we were particularly heartened by the visit you paid to the Moscow Synagogue and to Babi Yar in Kiev[90].

One visit abroad was left before the end of the year, a calm affair in comparison with what had gone before. On 27 October Archbishop Coggan and his wife left for Normandy to spend a few days at the Abbey of Bec, and a few hours at Caen and Bayeux. There were long-established links with the area, for no less than three of Donald Coggan's predecessors as Archbishop of Canterbury had been monks of the Benedictine Abbey of Bec Hellouin: Anselm, Lanfranc and Theodore. The particular occasion for the visit was the 900th anniversary of the dedication of the Abbey by Lanfranc. The Coggans travelled from Newhaven to Dieppe by car ferry: part of the crossing was spent on the bridge of the vessel. Officials of the ferry company wrote later, 'They were a real hit with the officers and crew on board at the time. They are still talking about our VIPs and how kind and sincere they both were'. They were driven across north-west France, Christopher Hill and David Painter accompanying them. At dusk, as they arrived in the secluded wooded valley where the Abbey stands on the banks of the Risle, candles had been lit at every window of the Abbey and church and the great bells of Bec were rung in salutation, as the Community gathered to greet the Archbishop of Canterbury. There followed three memorable days of liturgy, Word and music shared by the Community and Anglicans, many of whom had travelled to Bec for the Archbishop's visit. He preached at the Mass of Dedication on the Epistle and Gospel of the day. On the last evening he visited the Sisters of St Francoise-Romaine in whose *monastère* nearby Mrs Coggan had stayed; he sat with the Community round a log fire while they asked him questions, before Compline in their Chapel. At Caen the Coggans saw the Abbaye aux Hommes and met French Bishops; at Bayeux, they

---

[89] Dr Immanuel Jakobovits.
[90] A memorial to the dead of Hitler's war; many of them Jews, where Archbishop Coggan laid a wreath.

were received by the Chapter of the Cathedral and saw the celebrated tapestry of the conquest of England by William of Normandy
in 1066.

The November Synod provided an opportunity to make known
the progress of the Nationwide Initiative for Evangelism. Bishop
David Brown, Chairman of the Board of Mission and Unity,
disclosed the state of plans. The Initiative would comprise three
stages: stage one would take place immediately and evaluate local
evangelistic efforts, encourage new ones, and explore the convergence of evangelical and ecumenical attitudes towards evangelism;
stage two, which would take place in 1980, proposed a National
Assembly on Evangelism 'to reflect on the results of work undertaken in stage one and to assist British Christians to grow together in
the common task of bringing the gospel to the nation'. Stage three,
to be carried on throughout the 1980s, would, it was hoped, see 'the
emergence of more concerted and informed ecumenical evangelism'. Bishop Brown's reminder that 'we should remember that the
Planning Group at Lambeth did not quickly reach unanimity about
the proposals it should make' was an understatement. Although the
Churches in England recognized the importance of mission and
evangelism, the securing of assent to methods had not only taxed all
the planners, but had laid a particularly heavy burden on their
chairman. To the Archbishop fell the main responsibility for
achieving a workable agreement.

The structures which were to carry through the Initiative underwent revision during the following year, 1978. The Archbishops'
Council for Evangelism ceased to exist; the Council of Reference for
the NIE, consisting of representatives of the Churches, chaired by
the Archbishop of Canterbury, received assistance by the formation
of an Initiative sub-committee. It was fortunate that Donald
English[91], President of the Methodist Conference, agreed to be
chairman of this new and also ecumenical body.

The baptism at Buckingham Palace of the son of Princess Anne
(daughter of the Queen) and Captain Mark Phillips, provided
another royal occasion for the Archbishop just before Christmas
1977. Even this event was not without problems for him. He
received a number of letters, and there were articles in the press,
which pointed out that what the Prayer Book used to call 'the
Publick Baptism of Infants', the Church had for some years tried to
make into more of a congregational affair, with the new Christian

[91] 1930- ; Methodist Minister; President of the Methodist Conference 1978-9.

received into the fellowship in the context of a Sunday service. Why then the private ceremony? Some commentators even suggested that it would not be valid; all such ill-founded rumours had to be put right by the Archbishop. Neither was the baptism itself trouble-free: the baby cried without ceasing, drowning the voices of the Archbishop, the treble chorister in his solo, and the choir from the Chapel Royal. It was the last public occasion of a very crowded year, apart from Christmas events within the diocese of Canterbury. 1978 was less eventful because it contained a single very important event – the Lambeth Conference and meeting of all the bishops of the Anglican Communion.

At the end of 1977, Archbishop Coggan put into motion the promptings of the Canadian bishops in regard to certain aspects of planning the Lambeth Conference. He invited a small group of Primates to help him in preparing his own thoughts for the event. Also it seemed to him timely to explore generally future directions and development in the Anglican Communion. The meeting took place at Allen Gardiner House, Tunbridge Wells, Kent, from 10-12 January, 1978. Archbishop Edward Scott, Primate of Canada, Archbishop Allen Howard Johnston, Primate of New Zealand, and Bishop Howe joined Archbishop Coggan. Bishop Arthur Kratz, Primate of the Episcopal Church of Brazil, was prevented since he could not secure a visa; his place was taken by Bishop John William Flagg, formerly Presiding Bishop of the Anglican Council of South America. Archbishop Moses Scott, Primate of West Africa was also unable to leave at the last moment; Archbishop Festo Olang, Primate of the Province of Kenya came in his stead.

Archbishop Coggan's notes for the discussions provide an indication of his thinking; always the note of hope and trust was there. The Lambeth Conference would keep a balance between problems and God who is above and within problems. Problems and duties had accumulated; recent writings had suggested that the propagation of the gospel 'had been transformed into a burden'. 'Lift up your eyes' he wrote. A balance of devotion, theology and 'practice' was called for, in what Barbara Ward[92] had called 'these troubled and hopeful times', or rather practice infused by, illuminated by, devotion and theology.

The notes continued: 'What does the Anglican Communion do when faced by controversies which bid fair to divide it? What is the

[92] 1914-81; (Lady Jackson), an economist on a world scale who gave one of the major addresses at the Lambeth Conference.

state of ecumenism today? Have fires died? Are we lapsing into content with getting on nicely without full organic union? What are charismatics saying to us – or God through the Church? Are we too proud to listen?' South America was obviously much on his mind: 'Continent of tomorrow?', he wrote; 'what is our role? Since previous Lambeth Conferences, what picture of episcopacy has it for us?'. There were notes also for the discussion of relationships between Anglican and Roman Catholics, the Orthodox and the World Council of Churches; the relationship between 'the episcopate – guidance, and synod – government'.

In addition to their debating the shape of possible policies in the future, for the immediate present the small group of Primates helped to arrange a day-to-day steering committee for the Lambeth Conference and settled its composition. There would also be an overall steering committee composed of Primates.

The Archbishop of Canterbury returned to Lambeth Palace to find that the Thames opposite his home had risen to within a few inches of the emergency level. His engagements during the next months did not contain much beyond what was the normal high rate of routine business; although there were a few new features. He had been asked by the Editor of the Communist newspaper the *Morning Star* for a New Year message. He gave it as follows:

> What I should most like to see achieved in 1978.
> I should like to see people in increasing numbers asking two questions:
> 1. I am determined in 1978 to give all I can to the good of this nation and to the community I live in. How can I do this?
> 2. I am determined to find out whether it is possible for a thinking adult to hold the Christian faith. How do I find this and what would be its implications in my everyday living?
> To ask these questions would involve abandoning a lot of preconceived ideas and beliefs carried over from childhood. But it could well lead to a revolution and Britain could do with that.

Still anxious to maintain his vocation as a teacher, Archbishop Coggan undertook to preach on four successive Sunday evenings in Maidstone parish church on fundamental tenets of the faith. He began on January 1 with a talk on 'Who is God?' In the same interest, he flew to Leeds by helicopter to make a series of short talks for the Independent Television network for the programme *Stars on Sunday*, and on his own initiative made another set of consecutive talks on basic Christian teaching, entitled 'Simple Faith', for the BBC for evenings in Holy Week. He also recorded a set of sermons for an American broadcasting company. A viewer rang Lambeth

Palace to register disapproval of one of the Archbishop's program-mes; it was thought that a decanter and cigarette box could be seen in the background. For such criticism to be levelled at Donald Coggan, with his simple life-style and lack of self-indulgence, was ironical indeed.

During the week of prayer[93] for Christian unity, the Archbishop of Canterbury was for the first time invited to preach at Westminster Cathedral. He sent the script in advance to Cardinal Hume, and asked for his comments: 'I am your guest', he wrote[94], 'and you are my host, and I would not like to say anything that would be in any way discourteous to you, or unwelcome.' He said he would not release the sermon to the press until he had heard that it was acceptable. This assurance he received.

In this sermon Archbishop Coggan made what was described in a press report as 'one of the most urgent and emphatic appeals for Church unity ever heard'. Much of what he said was a repetition of his words nine months before in Rome. He began, once more, within the context of evangelism. 'Two great longings burn in my heart,' he said. The first had been admirably summed up in the Apostolic Exhortation *Evangelii Nuntiandi* quoted in the Common Declaration signed by the Pope and himself the year before. The Pope had referred again to it in a letter of last October[95]. Donald Coggan had taken the matter up again in his Christmas letter, 'in the light of the meteoric rise in world population and of the spread of materialistic philosophies of life in many parts of the world'. By such joint evangelistic work,

> Such spreading of the light of Christ in the menacing darkness of our world, is not and cannot be, brought about by resolutions agreed to by Church leaders.

Agreement to 'periodical joint meetings and consultations on pastoral problems of evangelization in the modern world' had been reached ten years earlier, but the process was too slow, in view 'of the speed with which forces inimical to Christianity press on with their programmes'. He felt that 'the whole people of God, in their own communities and areas, must together take counsel, *and act*, in

---

[93] 18-25 January each year. For the text of the sermon, see Donald Coggan, *Sure Foundation*, pp. 128-133.
[94] 19 January 1978.
[95] In which he thanked the Archbishop for his good wishes on the occasion of Pope Paul's eightieth birthday.

being torch-bearers of the Light.' This seemed to him a matter of mere obedience to the Lord of the Church.

Secondly, he made a further plea for 'our joint participation in the Sacrament of the Eucharist'. Once again he argued how the impact made on the world was pathetically feeble, witness muted, vision blurred by division at 'the deepest point of unity'.

> We recognize one unity in baptism; we persist in disunity at the Eucharist. So we go to our mission weak, where we should be strong and invigorated by joint participation in the Supper of the Lord.

He spoke of sheltering behind differences of doctrine, of expression, of explanation of being heirs of those who committed atrocities against other Christians. He asked for forgiveness of his Roman Catholic friends for coldness, and suspicion, even contempt, in the past. 'And should not that confession of sin be sealed in joint participation in the sacrament of Holy Communion?' He ended with St Paul's words[96] which tried to heal separated age-long barriers:

> Gentiles and Jews, he has made the two one, and in his own body of flesh and blood has broken down the enmity which stood like a dividing wall between them.

Reactions to the sermon were not slow to arrive. Some were favourable, from both Anglicans and Roman Catholics; some the reverse. A Roman Catholic theologian, Adrian Hastings, Lecturer in Religious Studies at Aberdeen University, had supported the suggestion made by Donald Coggan during his visit to Rome that the leaders of the Anglican and Roman Catholic Churches should now encourage their members to share together in the Holy Communion, in a sermon which he preached in Westminster Abbey on Sunday 1 January 1978.

The Winter Session of the General Synod opened on 31 January; the following day, Cardinal Hume was invited to speak. Like the Archbishop, he started from the point of view of mission to the world; he mentioned the Agreed Statements prepared by ARCIC on the Eucharist, Ministry and Authority, then, with the utmost charity, he rejected the proposal made by Archbishop Coggan on Intercommunion when he said

> The Roman Catholic Church holds, as you know, that for our Church to share in Holy Communion at the altar of another Church is the 'sign and expression of that full unity which the Eucharist of its nature signifies' and should not be 'regarded as a means to be used to lead to full ecclesial

[96] Ephesians 2.14-16.

communion . . . we believe that this sharing presupposes not only the same belief in the reality of Christ's presence in the Sacred Species, but also a common faith in general.

One of Donald Coggan's letters of encouragement after his sermon had been from Arthur Macarthur, General Secretary and Clerk of General Assembly of the United Reformed Church in England and Wales. In his reply[97] the Archbishop showed clearly his attitude towards the Free Churches in the matter of union. He would be sad, he wrote, if anything that he said on that occasion was construed by anyone as

indicating any lack of concern on my part, or that of the Church of England, in regard to unity with the Free Churches . . . You know how deeply saddened I was by the failure of the Anglican-Methodist negotiations. We must continue to work and pray for the favourable progress of the Ten Propositions. How easily these negotiations and conversations get bogged down. May the Spirit who is wind and fire liberate us from ourselves.

To the Bishop of London he wrote[98]:

A mass of correspondence has resulted from the Westminster Cathedral sermon, some of it from Roman Catholics warmly welcoming my action, some of it from people who feel that I am on my way to the pit! They either do not know the changes which are taking place within Roman Catholicism, or else cannot come to terms with it.

Also on the Synod agenda in February was, once again, the matter of theological training, but in a more positive and hopeful form than in recent years. The Working Party under Bishop Oliver Tomkins had reported, and made some recommendations which were well received. Archbishop Coggan, in his contribution, suggested that the number of men coming forward to the sacred ministry was at last increasing; he emphasized, once again, his belief in the principle of a ministry exercised full-time. Though planning for experimentation would go on, it was important not to let standards drop; if money were forthcoming, it would not be wasted.

In that same month the Archbishop carried out Sunday engagements of an interesting sequence: he preached at the City Temple, a United Reformed Church, in the morning, a sermon in the evening at Chelsea Old Church to commemorate the 500th anniversary of the birth of Sir Thomas More, before a large ecumenical congrega-

[97] 1 February 1978.
[98] 9 February 1978.

tion, among whom were the Lord Chief Justice of England and Apostolic Delegate. After a dinner at the vicarage, Archbishop and Chaplain walked round to a hostel for discharged prisoners a few streets away, some of them in a sad condition. As usual, Donald was able to find something to say, as he prayed with them and gave them his blessing. A visit to the Conference for Catholic Renewal at Loughborough on 30 March saw the Archbishop in association with churchmen of a tradition not his own. He chose to do what he did best, a biblical exposition, and took the second half of Ephesians 1; the writer's prayer that his readers' eyes might be opened. He spoke on vision, with warmth and hope; he and his words were well received.

He made a short tour to Belgium that Spring to visit the Head-quarters of the Supreme Headquarters of the Allied Powers in Europe; also a brief call on his 'dear friend', as he invariably began his letters, Cardinal Suenens. He met military personnel who belonged to NATO and various Christian allegiances at a series of services. He visited Dublin a few days later for the 100th anniversary of the restoration of Christ Church Cathedral. He called upon the President of the Republic of Ireland, Patrick Hillery, and met the Roman Catholic Archbishop. Archbishop Coggan preached twice in the Cathedral: once at the Eucharist, when Archbishop McAdoo celebrated, and again in the afternoon when the heads of the Roman Catholic and Anglican Colleges (University and Trinity) read the lessons. The visit gave pleasure, for Archbishop Coggan was shown much warmth and friendliness.

Another royal confirmation, on this occasion of Prince Edward, Lady Sarah Armstrong-Jones, Lady Helen Windsor and James Ogilvie, took the Coggans once more to stay with the Queen at Windsor Castle before the service in St George's Chapel. On 22 April the Archbishop spoke in the House of Lords during the debate on South Africa[99]; he said that the information which missionaries who were in close touch with the people of Southern Africa were bringing out gave his deep anxiety in respect of education and human rights; he drew attention to the number of prisoners who had died in prison.

Archbishop Coggan was now sixty-eight years old and beginning to turn over in his mind when he should retire. He told his domestic chaplain just before the Lambeth Conference, that he had decided to leave just after his seventieth birthday, probably early in 1980. He

[99] *Hansard*, Vol. 390, No. 68, pp. 1823-7.

and Jean had bought a 17th-century house and good garden in Kent, in the village of Sissinghurst. A certain amount of repair was required, but a base had been established. In the meantime, it was his staff who became ill. Douglas Cleverly Ford, the Senior Chaplain, came back from SHAPE in a serious condition with pneumonia, and was away from Lambeth for several weeks; soon it was David Painter's turn. The Archbishop continued resilient as ever, as countless evidence showed.

After a heavy week, on a Friday evening in mid April, Donald Coggan and his chaplain drove from Lambeth Palace to institute a vicar into a parish in the diocese of Canterbury. The new incumbent, besides other gifts, was well known for his ability to drive a motorcycle at 100 mph; the church was crowded and there needed to be receptions in two halls afterwards. Archbishop Coggan as usual spent much time talking to parishioners. It was late when they reached the Old Palace at Canterbury; David Painter was exhausted and confided to his diary that how the Archbishop kept his strength up, he did not know.

It was the Archbishop who brought up the chaplain's meals and celebrated the Holy Communion in his room when, two weeks later, it was diagnosed that he had infective hepatitis, and was not well enough to go at once to the home of his mother. Donald and Jean behaved as if they were his parents. Having been deprived of one chaplain, the Archbishop was now without the other, and the Lambeth Conference was only two months away.

But worse was to come. The Coggans took a short break in Scotland before the Conference. During the course of the holiday, Jean had symptoms of what might have been a serious illness. Her stature was revealed in that her main thought was of the distress this would cause her husband at a crucial time. But the crisis passed; a minor operation proved that fears could be laid aside.

The July Session of Synod held at York was one of importance. The Archbishop spoke in several critical debates, and Bishop David Brown moved the reception of the Report on the Ten Propositions: they offered a path along which 'we and other Churches may journey towards a more truly catholic Church in the future'.[100] Archbishop Coggan spoke of the effect that acceptance of the Ten Propositions and of the Covenant would have on future relation-

[100] *General Synod July Group of Sessions 1978 Report of Proceedings*, Vol. 9, No. 2, p. 536.

ships with Roman Catholics[101]. Two recent statements from Roman Catholic theologians were at variance from each other on that matter. He felt that

> The wind of the Spirit is blowing through all our Churches and it is our responsibility to respond as faithfully as we can to his promptings . . . I believe that we may do so without jeopardising our growing relationship with the Roman Catholic Church which we value so highly.

The Synod, 'noting the overwhelming support of the Diocesan Synods for continued consultation towards covenanting with other Churches on the basis of the Ten Propositions', declared by a large majority in all Houses its readiness to proceed.

The Archbishop spoke on the future of the ministry, but more significantly on the Report[102] of the General Synod's Marriage Commission which had been established in 1975 under the Chairmanship of Kenneth Skelton, Bishop of Lichfield. In moving the Report, Bishop Skelton described the Churches' dilemma in cases of marriage breakdown where Anglican partners wished to remarry after divorce. What should be the Church's response? There were three possibilities; to adopt the Roman Catholic procedure and extend nullity, to recommend civil marriage, or thirdly for the Church to revise its regulations so as to permit the marriage of some divorced persons in church. This last was the majority view of the Commission,

> to enable the Church, freed from the embarrassment of its present apparent obsession with divorce, to witness to the importance of marriage, to which we feel not only the Church, but also the state gives too little attention.

The Archbishop of Canterbury said he had administered the current discipline of the Church in these matters for twenty-two years without a single exception, although sometimes with a heavy heart. He could not free himself from a fear that the effect of lifting the regulations on second marriages in church after a divorce would be 'to give the impression that the Church was bending to the wind of current laxity in regard to marital faithfulness'. He said he longed to accommodate Church people who were 'deeply serious about entering a second marriage, and it is a matter of some agony to me to have to register my own decision against this'. The motion for

---

[101] ibid., pp. 555-8.
[102] *Marriage and the Church's Task*, pp. 780-4.

changing the regulations was lost by a small margin. It would seem that the Archbishop's intervention was unexpected, and that he had not discussed his point of view with the Commission. On the other hand, it could hardly have been a surprise to find he thought as he did. There was a leak of the Commission's findings to the press before publication, which upset him a good deal; lack of security was one of his big bugbears. He wrote to the Chairman that a severe rebuke was needed to the culprit. 'We are living in days when honour is at a premium'. It is open to conjecture whether the Archbishop's vote against the motion had a decisive effect.

Directly after the Synod he wrote personal handwritten letters to the Free Church leaders who had worked on the Churches' Unity Commission, telling them of his pleasure in the way that the vote on the Ten Propositions had gone. He looked forward to the covenanting in two years' time.

Three weeks later, on Sunday 23 July, the Lambeth Conference began. The opening service in Canterbury Cathedral was made more memorable than before, partly because of the development of the Anglican Communion and creation of new sees: 407 Bishops, nearly all diocesans (few suffragans as heretofore) processed in Provinces led by a standard-bearer carrying the provincial designation. And also because, most thrilling of all, the presence of a Caribbean steel band lifted the ceremony from its bonds as a staid European occasion. The Archbishop of Canterbury sat in the Chair of St Augustine and preached[103]; John Sepeku, Archbishop of Tanzania, was the main celebrant, whose rite was used; many other Bishops con-celebrated and helped in the administration of the Communion to the huge congregation. Donald Coggan's text was from Psalm 85.8: 'I will hearken what the Lord God will say', a reminder of what he saw as one of the purposes of the Conference. During the course of his sermon he remarked, 'We have stopped listening and our spiritual life has died on us,' which was interpreted by the press as a warning to bishops of 'lost belief', *not* his intention.

This is not the place for a lengthy description of the eleventh Lambeth Conference itself, but of Archbishop Coggan's handling of it, as President. The theme of the Conference, 'Today's Church and Today's World', with a special focus on the ministry of bishops, was Donald's own, which he had announced at Trinidad in 1976. Bishop

---

[103] Donald Coggan, *Sure Foundation*, pp. 246-9.

Howe's report to the General Synod on the Conference[104] gave a realistic review of the event, which is a help in the assessment of it and of its leadership. The Conference, he said, faced difficulties in trying to do two things at once: first to act as a Council, seeking solutions to deep and complex problems; a body of 400 was too big and three weeks too short to accomplish this; secondly to be a Congress, sharing experiences. Donald in his planning, veered towards the second type of objective.

He did not possess the sophisticated management skills of some of his North American brethren, with their knowledge of the principles of group dynamics and other modern techniques. But he had skills of his own. He could make instantaneous relationships with people of all nationalities and all walks of life, from Buckingham Palace to a thatched hut. To him everything was personal; his was a very personal religion. He had been everywhere in the Anglican Communion, and had met most of the Bishops on their own terrain; he cared deeply for them and their work. It gave him a unique, empirical view of the member Churches. He had seen the vigour and joy of the younger, rapidly-growing, communities in Africa and the Pacific Islands, as well as the apathetic nature of some of the parishes in his own Province where, however, what did happen was done on time. He longed to see the sharing of gifts. The Archbishop realized that the form of decision-making in many areas had a pattern older than the English parliamentary system upon which synodical government had been based. He therefore set about using his own talents of communication within the context of the problems which he had seen to face individual bishops. His chairmanship at the beginning was low-key, which was his way of responding to the situation before him. He played the piano for Evensong the first evening of the Conference; he and Jean entertained most of the bishops one way or another, and gave each of their guests personal attention. The result was threefold: first, whereas at the 1968 Lambeth Conference it was six days before a bishop from the Third World rose to speak, in 1978 the first speeches from the floor were from the Bishops of Kenya, the West Indies and Polynesia. Secondly, a spirit of cohesion and family relationship was created, what the Report[105] called 'person-to-person, mind-to-mind, soul-to-soul interaction which made "Lambeth 1978" so memorable an

---

[104] *General Synod November Group of Sessions 1978 Report of Proceedings*, Vol. 9, No. 3, pp. 1136-43.
[105] *The Report of the Lambeth Conference 1978*, (CIO Publishing 1978), p. 6.

experience for everyone who took part'. Thirdly, after the first week a certain feeling of ineffectiveness was being expressed because the method of allowing a good deal of domestic (and therefore inevitably repetitive) talk meant that nothing positive was emerging to present to the world. As the Archbishop had called for a maximum of flexibility, it allowed the Conference, as Bishop Howe's Synod Report stated, 'to take hold of the planned programme twice and remake it'; because the Conference was *alive* and things 'were working out in a different way than could have been seen in advance and apart from the living forces which were shaping its work and progress'. It was not Archbishop Coggan's initiative that effected the changes, though he absorbed them into his leadership, but it was he who had given the Conference the life that enabled them to happen.

The problem areas were in the Hearings. The Archbishop had chosen two forms of treatment of subsidiary subjects and topics, under his overall theme. The first consisted of Sections, also announced at Trinidad on: What is the Church for?, the People of God and the Ministry, the Anglican Communion and the World Wide Church, with ten to thirteen groups of twenty or so bishops studying aspects within the range of each Section. Secondly, afternoon plenary sessions were given over to four Hearings; these in some respects turned out a less than satisfactory method of dealing with at least two of the subjects. The first on Training for the Ministry, gave rise to a large number of speeches from the Third World which told of the need for new bishops to be trained for their role, or the shortage of academically excellent and spiritually mature teachers to train people for the ministry and to relate theological education to the local cultural context. A useful purpose had obviously been served by the inclusion of this subject, but it became very repetitive, with no imput of theology on the ministry or sharing of ideas.

In the second case, it seemed even more important to make changes. The last of the four Hearings, that on the Anglican Communion and its future, was removed from full session on the initiative of Bishop John Allin, representing the regional grouping of North America and the West Indies; by a show of hands the Conference agreed to take the subject to discussion in small groups. It would probably be fair to say that discussion was not high up on the Archbishop's list of priorities: preliminary ground-clearing, establishing contiguity and mulling over a subject would have seemed to him generally a waste of time. But he accepted the decision of the bishops, although it involved him in difficulties during the last few days. Resolutions came in later than would otherwise have been expected, and it was a considerable feat of chairmanship, to which he proved more than equal, to secure that the Conference finished on time.

During the last week, Donald Coggan introduced a paper which he thought seemed to be required on 'Authority in the Anglican Communion'.[106] The Conference had not asked for it, but called it from him, which demonstrated a degree of reciprocity at work between President and bishops. There were inevitably some matters imperfectly or only partially resolved; the question of the relationship between bishops and synodical government was one. Archbishop Scott posed seven searching and profound questions[107] as 'a spiritual check list for our Churches in the years that lie ahead', which represented, no doubt, part of what would have been his agenda had he been planning the Lambeth Conference. But most of the bishops felt that useful purposes had been served by their coming together, particularly on account of the time deliberately set aside for common worship. To Donald, and to Jean, who had run a week's conference separately for over two hundred Bishops' wives, went admiration and affection for their tireless efforts.

The Lambeth Conference was the last large event of Donald Coggan's ministry which owed its origin personally to him. His last eighteen months as Archbishop showed no lessening of the pressure of his activities, rather the reverse, but there were fewer initiatives or innovations. He continued rather to press for the causes dear to him that were already underway: an increase of candidates for the sacred ministry, evangelism, partnership in mission, the ordination of women, a growth of the sphere of the Primates in the development of the Anglican Communion. This less innovatory role was not a diminution of his function as Archbishop, for when his ministry at Canterbury came to be viewed as a whole, on his retirement, it was the dedication and faithfulness with which he had fulfilled the daily calls upon him that were considered his main contribution in giving stability and confidence to the Church, not his more spectacular and unique acts.

Among the visits that the Coggans made, the ones they enjoyed most were to geographically isolated territories. With groups of human beings who had come to terms with hardship and privations,

---

[106] ibid., pp. 122-4.
[107] ibid., pp. 112-13.

and who faced the difficulties of their lives with cheerfulness and resolution in their Christian faith, they found deep affinity. So it was with the Eskimo people whom they met on a journey to the North West Territories of Canada, almost directly after the Lambeth Conference, in circumstances of peculiar interest.

In 1578, Martin Frobisher, the renowned Elizabethan seaman, made his third journey to the Canadian Arctic in search of a north-west passage. He got no further than Baffin Island, where his landfall is still known as Frobisher Bay. But this expedition held a special significance for Anglicans, because it began the history of the activities of the Church of England on Canadian territory. On board Frobisher's ship on that journey was an Anglican priest, Master Robert Wolfall, a scholar of King's College, Cambridge, from the diocese of Bath and Wells:

> This Maister Wolfall being well seated and setled at home in his owne Countrey, with a good and large living, having a good honest woman to wife, and verie towardly Children, being of good reputation among the best, refused not to take in hand this paynefull voyage, for the only care he had to save Soules, and to reforme thos Infidels, if it were possible, to Christianitie[108].

Between the days from July 31 to September 1 1578, Robert Wolfall celebrated the Eucharist in the land which is now called Canada; the first in the New World. A record by one of the ship's company survives:

> Maister Wolfall on Winter's Fornace (Baffin Island) preached a godly Sermon, whiche being ended, he celebrated also a Communion vpon the lande, at the partaking whereof, was the Captaine of the Anne Fraunces George Best and manye other Gentlemen & Soldiers, Marrinters & Miners with hym. The celebration of diune mistery was ye first signe, seale, & confirmation of Christes names death & passion euer knowen in all these quarters. The said M. Wolfall made sermons, & celebrated the Communion at sundrie other times, in seueral and sundrie Ships, bicause the whole company could neuer meet togither at any one place[109].

Archbishop Coggan, in August 1978, set foot in Frobisher Bay in the steps of Master Wolfall. Clergy and lay people of various language groups, including Inuit and Cree Indians, assembled from all over the vast diocese of the Arctic. The celebrations included a Training Congress, conducted by the Archbishop of Canterbury, with interpretation by one of the indigenous clergy, Jonas Allooloo.

[108] *The Arctic News*, Fall 1978, pp. 3-5.
[109] ibid.

It was followed by the Third Synod of the Diocese, presided over by the Bishop, John Sperry, with four archdeacons, six canons of St Jude's Cathedral, and twenty-six clergy and representatives of forty-six parishes, most of whom had flown immense distances. The Primate of Canada, Archbishop Scott, the Dean of Greenland, Jeus Christian Chemnitz of the Danish Church were also present.

A flight further north to Pangnirtung, over snow-covered mountain ranges, took the Coggans to a missionary outpost, where from the Eskimo people at a training college for clergy and school for weaving and carving they received a great welcome. In a church service the Archbishop preached to a congregation where many younger members were swaddled in parkas on the backs of their mothers. A precarious visit was also made by helicopter to an ice-breaker. The warm faith of the people of the region made its mark on the Archbishop, while his tireless interest and individual approach impressed them. The happy and constructive visit was a turning point in the history of the diocese.

The death of Pope Paul VI during the course of the Lambeth Conference had been followed by the election and short reign of Pope John Paul I. Archbishop Coggan, who might well have attended Pope Paul's funeral in person had it not been for his own involvement in the Conference, decided to go to Rome for the Inauguration of the ministry of John Paul II, as a sign of ecumenical friendship. He attended the Inaugural Eucharist and together with visiting dignitaries met the new pontiff during his brief visit, in the company of the other Anglicans: Bishop Millard representing the Presiding Bishop of the American Episcopal Church, Bishop Misaeri Kauma of Uganda and Bishop Howe.

Early in October Archbishop Coggan made a further call for more priests, in the form of another Pastoral Letter from himself and the Archbishop of York. He saw, he said, signs of renewed life in many parishes. The People of God were recovering confidence in their mission and ministry.

> If we are to maintain and increase this momentum, our need for a dedicated, well qualified and full-time ordained ministry will be even greater than in the past.

The previous year 301 deacons had been ordained. The Church needed to see this annual figure rise to between 400 and 450, to maintain its present strength.

Because of his strong belief that the ordination of women had much to contribute to the Church, the Archbishop made a last fervent appeal during the Synod debate in November, when Hugh Montefiore[110], Bishop of Birmingham, moved that the Synod should ask the Standing Committee to prepare and bring forward legislation to remove the barriers to the ordination of women[111]; it had in 1976 been left to the bishops to decide when the moment was propitious. The Archbishop deplored that there were those who had tried to determine in advance how members intended to vote; true to his customary thinking, he protested that it was of the essence of synodical debate and dependence on the Holy Spirit to be open to his guiding and come with a measure of fluidity to be persuaded if 'new vistas, new aspects, new light' were recognized. He spoke of the debate on this subject at the Lambeth Conference, and of the absence of sharpness and presence of openness, love and frankness. This was not a matter of women's rights; no one has a *right* to be ordained. Ordination has nothing to do with rights; 'It is due solely to the sovereign mercy and grace of God who calls and then enables.' After a five-hour debate, the motion was lost. Bishops voted in favour by 32 votes to 17; the laity by 120 to 106; the clergy voted against it by 149 Noes to 94 Ayes. Archbishop Coggan's particular disappointment was with attitudes in the Synod; he wrote to John Robinson[112], Dean of Trinity College, Cambridge, 'I sense a resurgence of party spirit of the kind that ever since I became a bishop in 1956 I have tried to avoid'[113].

Some bishops voiced their own anxiety that the discussions lacked theological base; moreover, Roman Catholic and Orthodox official opinion was being used somewhat arbitrarily to support negative views. Archbishop Coggan agreed to a suggestion by Bishop Runcie that tripartite talks should be held with both these Churches, inviting them to join in a theological examination of the matter of women's ordination.

Donald Coggan's last year in office began with some weeks of more than usual diversity. His preliminary talks on the ordination of women with Cardinal Hume took place early in January. The Cardinal gave an assurance that he would discuss the whole question

[110] 1920- ; Fellow and Dean of Gonville and Caius College, Cambridge 1954-63; Bishop of Kingston 1970; of Birmingham 1978-87.

[111] *General Synod November Group of Sessions 1978 Report of Proceedings*, Vol. 9, No. 3, pp. 996-1070.

[112] 1919-83; Bishop of Woolwich 1959-69; Dean of Trinity College, Cambridge 1969-83.

[113] 23 November 1978.

with the Pope. As the Archbishop told the General Synod at their February Session[114], Bishop Runcie in the course of visiting Orthodox Patriarchates in Europe and the Middle and Near East would then discuss the matter of women's ordination. Close touch would be kept with those Churches where women were already ordained.

Feelings on the rising cost of living manifested themselves sharply during that month of January 1979, and culminated in a series of strikes by low-paid ancillary workers, whose regular presence was vital to the continued smooth running of schools and hospitals. Very cold weather and shortage of fuel due to strikes exacerbated the unhappy conditions. Donald Coggan was disturbed by the effect of this withdrawal of labour on the treatment of the sick and the education of children, and made a number of public utterances, the first in Upper Hardres Church during the course of a Sunday sermon.

> The right to strike is a right to be prized. But to use that right irresponsibly, or too readily, is to cause suffering and sometimes even death to innocent people and to helpless animals. It can be a pitiless weapon, and against this pitilessness we Christians must protest. Perhaps our voices have not been loud enough in this respect.

He spoke of support for settlements without resort to strikes, and for keeping inflation under control. He ended with a plea for concern for what was right, more than for rights. 'Duty, and responsibility to the community at large, must be the watchword of management, workers and all of us alike.' Later in February, he returned to the subject during the course of a sermon at St John's Church, Folkestone, when he spoke of the forces of selfishness, 'each man for himself and never mind if someone gets hurt or dies'. He included the higher paid and those whose salary rises were 'out of all proportion to the work done or to the good achieved for the community'. He repeated his words on 'sheer pitilessness which injures the old and the very young . . . which leaves the dead unburied and the sick and dying uncared for'. During the House of Lords debate on the Industrial situation, he made a speech on similar lines:

> Personal and sectional interests were made to appear more important than the welfare of the whole community and the nation at large.[115]

---

[114] *General Synod February Group of Sessions 1979 Report of Proceedings*, Vol. 10, No. 1, pp. 2-3.
[115] 25 January 1979, *Hansard*, Vol. 397, pp. 1577-80.

The Archbishop's intervention, as may be imagined, drew upon him much controversial opinion, including questions in the House of Commons. His case was not strengthened by the almost simultaneous rise in rents charged on property in North London owned by the Church Commissioners, nor by their intention, announced at this period, to increase the salaries of bishops by eighteen per cent. There was an offer made to discuss wage claims and industrial action with the General Secretary of NUPE (the National Union of Public Employees) on Donald's part, but his forthcoming visit to West Africa made the timing difficult, and the talk did not take place.

A more encouraging event was the launching, at last, of the Nationwide Initiative for Evangelism with a service[116] in Lambeth Palace Chapel. It was a unique gathering of those committed to evangelism on a wide ecumenical basis, who had never before worshipped together. Both its fulfilment and comprehensiveness were owed to the Archbishop's leadership. Tom Houston of the Bible Society and Cardinal Hume led the prayers; Donald English preached, and later wrote to Archbishop Coggan:

> I know how close to your heart this work is, but I am most moved by the fact that in the midst of so many other things which you have on your mind, you have given so much care and support to this Initiative.

The Archbishop replied:

> The gestation period of NIE was long and at times difficult and I still feel that the child born on 22 January is a delicate creature, but God has been good and the child is launched into the world.

Literature introducing the NIE was sent to the dioceses, so that each parish should be aware of the National Assembly in September 1980 and the need for prayer and plans 'to make the Good News of Jesus Christ known more effectively throughout the country'.

At the beginning of March Donald Coggan, with David Painter and John Miles, left for West Africa for what was to be, in his own words, 'the most strenuous tour I have ever taken, and that is saying a good deal.' There was little time to prepare, and, worst of all, Jean had been ill for some weeks with an infected gland and her doctor advised her to remain in England. The itinerary covered six countries, the Gambia, Liberia, Sierra Leone, Ghana where a tense political situation made travelling difficult, Guinea and Nigeria. Far too many engagements had been crowded into the programme; the

[116] 22 January 1979.

weather was intensely humid. Although the tour had value because the presence of the Archbishop of Canterbury encouraged local churches, particularly in isolated localities, he felt that his time had not been well used: there were too many formal occasions and speeches, rather than opportunities for the exercise of the teaching and preaching ministry he preferred.

On his return there was a spate of meetings which took him out of England: three days in Belfast for the British Council of Churches, with travel by armoured car and a twenty-four hour guard; the Anglican Consultative Council at Huron College, London, Ontario; and three weeks later he and Jean flew to East Berlin.

The visit to Eastern Europe had been planned to cover Poland also, but since this would have coincided with the first journey back to his homeland by Pope John Paul II, Donald felt it tactful to withdraw from this part of the itinerary. He had continued to involve himself in the matter of personal freedom in Communist dominated countries and had joined in some recent protests. Georgi Vins, whose cause he had championed during his visit to Russia, had been exchanged for two convicted Soviet spies as the result of an arrangement between the USA and USSR, and was now in America. In East Berlin the Archbishop had a meeting of one-and-a-quarter hours with Dr Eric Honecker, Chairman of the German Democratic Republic and Communist Party Secretary, as well as with the leaders of the Churches. In Hungary, likewise, he met the Deputy Prime Minister, members of the Jewish community, and of the Lutheran and Hungarian Reformed Churches, as well as Cardinal Lekai, Archbishop of Esztergom. As usual, Donald Coggan worked hard to encourage Christians living under duress; it was a cause with which he felt a keen personal sympathy.

The public announcement of his resignation came on 5 June 1979, planned earlier but not published. It was a relief that he no longer had to keep up the barrier of secrecy and could openly discuss his future. Retirement would take place on 25 January 1980. From now on he had more engagements than ever: his usual programme, together with many farewells.

The most significant were two Free Church occasions, and a third of a kind where English sensibilities are invariably tender: he spoke at a Methodist Conference for Mission and Unity, and at a Congress of the European Baptist Federation; he had also become President of the Royal Society for the Prevention of Cruelty to Animals, and his address at the annual meeting on the inheritance of Creation and the responsibility it brought was well received.

When the Coggans were about to leave for a visit to the Churches of Sweden and Finland, the violent death occurred in Ireland of Lord Mountbatten and two members of his family. The Archbishop returned early for his funeral in the Abbey on 6 September. The following day, at a village church in his diocese, Donald was required to preach at the burial of Nicholas Knatchbull and his paternal grandmother, Lady Brabourne. Lord Mountbatten had died after a long and full life, his grandson at only fourteen years of age. To Archbishop Coggan fell the interpretation of the meaning and mystery of youthful sudden death. He rose to the challenge with a sermon which was considered one of the most sensitive of his ministry. He recognized that it would be fatal to say too much. After a few words of assurance and confidence in the abiding love of God, he ended: 'That is all for today; and it is ample, for today and for all the tomorrows, however dark they may be'.

A journey across the Atlantic in October was the last overseas as Archbishop of Canterbury. Among other commitments, he gave the Reinicker Lectures[117] at the Episcopal Theological seminary in Virginia, on the Ministry: three talks under the titles Grace, Grind and Glory. Bermuda on the way back home had some difficulties: Donald visited a prison where there were sullen looks and a district where several youths were antagonistic; onlookers remarked that the Primate looked tired. There were still three months left to serve; he confided to his daughter that it was sleep to which he looked forward.

Farewells began to proliferate: a dinner from the Anglican Bishops, one from the Free Church Federal Council, another at Number 10 Downing Street with the Prime Minister; on 8 November, farewell to the General Synod. Archbishop Coggan made a valedictionary Presidential Address of some length, in which he touched on many of the issues that had concerned him most: relationships with other Churches, Roman Catholic, Orthodox, the World Alliance of Reformed Churches, dialogue with Lutherans which had received impetus from his recent visit to Sweden and Finland, the problems that were facing the Churches' Council for Covenanting. He spoke of the Nationwide Initiative for Evangelism and finally of the Synod and its relationship with other bodies, and of synodical government itself. He gave a last warning on the evils of the revival of party spirit.

The Archbishop of York led the Synod's thanks for Donald's

---

[117] Donald Coggan, *Sure Foundation*, pp. 187-218.

'many and distinguished services to the Church and people', pointing out that during thirty years, he had spent 360 days at Sessions, a year of his life. Archbishop Blanch looked forward to the return to bonfires on Donald's part; they had not been possible at Lambeth because of the Clean Air Act. Prolocutors of the Southern and Northern Convocations added their tributes: to particular care of the parochial clergy; a leadership of prayer and gospel had been presented, one in which 'in every sort of way people matter'; steel and humanity had been a rather surprising combination. The Chairman of the House of Laity spoke of 'an intense devotion to the person of our Lord', seen in the Archbishop.

The Anglican Primates met for the last time under Donald's chairmanship at Ely at the end of November. In a spirit of generosity he invited his successor, Bishop Runcie, to join them. 'A fine bunch of men,' he wrote, 'with great experience and some having endured much for Christ's sake'. The Archbishop of Burma was present, allowed to bring only £7 out of his own country; also Bishop Dehqani Tafti who had escaped death in Iran. Finally, there was a large farewell Eucharist[118] in Westminster Abbey in January, and BBC broadcasts[119] early on each morning of the week, in which Donald acknowledged his thanks for the gift of Christ, ministry and friends; he remembered Katie Hazzard in Islington, forty years before, who had 'lived a life of exceptional grace'.

The parting from Canterbury came on 25 January, so significant a day for the Archbishop, marking as it did the Conversion of St Paul, the model for his ministry, and the anniversary of his own consecration as Bishop. His address[120] to an immense congregation at an evening Eucharist spoke of St Paul's towering faith and ended with his words to the leaders of the church at Ephesus:

> Keep watch over yourselves and over all the flock of which the Holy Spirit has given you charge, as shepherds of the Church of the Lord which he has won for himself with his own blood.

The next day Donald Coggan awoke a temporal peer, and a free man.

In his farewell speech to Donald Coggan in the Synod, Archbishop Blanch had remarked that to be Archbishop of Canterbury had become an impossible job. Donald's merit, or perhaps his demerit,

[118] ibid., pp. 21-5.
[119] ibid., pp. 26-30.
[120] ibid., pp. 31-4.

Stuart Blanch went on to say, was that he had made it possible by virtue of his extraordinary energy of body and mind and the self-discipline which he had hammered out over the years. To search for the origins of these qualities is to go to St Paul. During the first years of his retirement, Donald wrote the book[121] about St Paul that had been waiting to emerge throughout his active ministry. His identification with his estimate of the Apostle is so strong that the book is almost autobiographical. Paul made Christ the centre of his existence: 'We have seen a man' Donald wrote,

> whose claim to apostleship brooked no denial, but whose chief delight was to be the slave of Jesus Christ and, for the sake of his fellow-Christians, to be their slave too; a man for whom suffering and the loss of all things were irradiated by the confident hope of being 'in Christ' in an intimacy which would transcend his earthly experience[122].

So, Donald himself made the following of Christ his total preoccupation, not only in faith, but in works too; he set himself what he saw as a Christ-like way of living. 'Everything is hollow if it is not fleshed out in real life'[123]. Donald's hope, his confidence, his faithfulness, likewise, were based on what he had read in Paul's Epistles:

> Meanwhile, in this era of the 'not yet', God has given us, in the person of Christ, a foretaste and a pledge of his triumph over death and of the final consummation of the End.

His marked ability as a teacher derived not only from his innate didactic capacity, but from his assurance that he was passing on priceless gifts.

Even the drive towards preaching was shared with Paul: 'It would be misery not to preach'[124]; as also his sense of the need to be self-effacing. Donald wrote of the Apostle:

> As a man, intimately indebted to Christ, it was his first care 'not to get in the way' . . . the secret – and he learned it the hard way and by no means always at once – was to die daily[125].

Already by nature endowed in this direction, Donald proceeded to develop the principle in his own life. Here was the origin of his oft-repeated phrase: 'God first, others next, self last'.

---

[121] Donald Coggan, *Paul: Portrait of a Revolutionary*, Hodder and Stoughton 1984.
[122] ibid., p. 221.
[123] ibid., p. 114.
[124] ibid., p. 227; 1 Corinthians 9.16.
[125] ibid., p. 224.

The results of this particularly strong personal dedication were several: his confidence, hope and trust he undoubtedly conveyed to the Church which he led; moreover, it was a comprehensible, straightforward leadership which endeared him to many, accompanied as it was by an exceptional capacity for rapport with individuals. One who did not enthuse over some of Donald's causes has written: 'What matter when his heart beats so strongly for the Lord'.

The total commitment, as interpreted by him, was not achieved without cost. Many spheres of life remained unexplored, which, it has been suggested, impoverished what he wrote and said. His good, clear mind and intellect were concentrated upon biblical theology; his Bible studies were legendary. But many of his contemporaries were aware that beyond this compass his intellectual range was limited. He could read Latin and Greek, but the philosophy and literature of the ancients impinged little on his thinking; nor was he greatly interested in patristic writings, or the philosophy of the medieval or modern periods, or politics, or economics. There was little time for the discussion of ideas, for general reading, or entertaining; the enjoyment of culture, art, the theatre, opera, concerts, architecture, and the company of friends, even of his family, were sacrificed to a constant round of official engagements.

These self-imposed restrictions were considered to have affected the range of his written and spoken words in several ways. For example, his writings, it was said, tended to be unimaginative and to lack depth; his illustrations from the Old Testament were regarded as less than apposite in circumstances considered more complex than the days of Jeremiah, Hosea and Amos; and his style of preaching, from a desire to be comprehensible, homely.

In the field of the emotions also, restrictions were seen to have been imposed. A strong sense of self-discipline, training of the will and need to efface self, can lead to a hesitation to recognize the extent of human nature and experience. Men who worked closely with Donald were aware of his defences; communication, as a result, was not from depth to depth, but occupied a plateau which some felt represented his chosen habitat. It may be that his struggle as a boy to master his own sensibilities left him determined, as he grew up, to be less susceptible.

This is not to suggest that his contemporaries found Donald cold; friendliness, humour, compassion, were always near the surface, but underlying reserve was there also. Paradoxically, one of his main characteristics was the value he placed upon spontaneity; it precluded his being a strategist. As already indicated, it was part of his understanding of response to the presence of the Holy Spirit. He never read his sermons, but spoke from notes, because he valued an immediate reaction to those whom he was addressing. Some spontaneous utterances on current events, as we have seen, landed him in hot water, as in the case of the economic crises of 1975, immigration in 1976 and strikes in 1979. He was in their regard, accused of oversimplification. Both his practical experience and his knowledge of affairs outside his own field were more limited than those of many of his contemporaries. But his sensitivity to moral issues was considerable, his aspirations high, his conscience tender; he found it impossible to remain silent.

There were incidents where Donald Coggan was thought to have been mistaken, but his care for the Church and its members was so transparently uppermost and his concern for the coming of the Kingdom so whole-hearted, that these remained the more lasting impressions. It would be imprudent indeed, after such a short interval, to attempt any long-term appraisal, but this much is certain: the Church of England and the Anglican Communion had increased in stability and confidence under his leadership, and were better prepared to enter a new era.

One of Donald's greatest gifts lay in his ability to communicate with young children. It would, therefore, seem appropriate to allow one of them to have the last word. At the time of his enthronement, some pupils in a primary school in Kent sent Donald letters after watching the ceremony on television. One child wrote:

I think you will do well being Archbishop of Canterbury.

Ex ore infantium.[126]

---

[126] Matthew 21.16: 'Out of the mouths of babes and sucklings thou hast perfected praise.'

Epilogue

The first need for Frederick Donald, Baron Coggan of Sissinghurst and Canterbury in the County of Kent, on 26 January 1980, was rest. Three months later, he seemed to have dropped ten years of his age. It must have been borne upon him that he could not have worked harder. He had retired with the gratitude and good wishes of many inside (and outside) the Church. Cardinal Hume had written an open letter of appreciation to the *Times*[1]; the Sovereign had thanked him in person and given him the Royal Victorian Chain, a rare honour. But it was not in his nature to do nothing. It can have been no surprise that he was soon ready for the next burst of activity.

To provide a comprehensive account of Lord Coggan's programme since his retirement would require another biography; such is not the intention. Only the barest outline is possible. The main difference in his engagements in future was the absence of the official round and of heavy responsibility. With the many invitations he received, the decision which he should accept now lay entirely with him. He adopted a policy of priorities: first the training of clergy, deaconesses, and lay workers, quiet days, retreats and diocesan teaching programmes; second came universities, colleges and schools. Parish events, courses of lectures, sermons and Confirmations (as one of the Assistant Bishops in the diocese), help for incumbents in his own locality, appeared frequently in his diary. Visits abroad with heavy commitments continued, including several to the United States (eleven separate journeys between 1980 and 1987); two in Canada, two in India, one to Australia, to Thailand for the United Bible Societies' conference (as Honorary President) at Chiang Mai; other tours took him to Sri Lanka, Gibraltar, Uganda, Turkey, Greece and Italy, Switzerland, Pakistan, France, Egypt, Israel and Holland. Chairmanship of the Council of Christians and Jews involved him in meetings in Germany (twice), Holland, Italy and Spain. During the first seven years of his retirement he wrote three books;[2] acted twice as chaplain to large corporations: to the

[1] 25 January, 1980.
[2] See Appendix 1, Publications.

Merchant Taylors' Company 1980-81 and to St John's College, Cambridge for the Lent term 1983. He was also much in demand to give the address at memorial services.

Jean, who had many speaking engagements during the Canterbury period when she followed her own interests as well as supporting her husband, continued to do so in retirement, exemplified by her painting and three recent publications: the first, completed just before leaving Canterbury, was a series of meditations *Through the day with Jesus*[3]; the second a number of Bible Studies with a selection of prayers, entitled *Welcome Life*;[4] the third *A Pilgrim's Way*[5], a personal spiritual anthology.

There has been less pressure in the Coggans' house at Sissinghurst than in the Palaces of the past, with time to garden, to read and to write, to sew tapestry, to meet old friends and colleagues: to visit Ann in her house in Winchester and to correspond with Ruth; to enjoy the spate of celebrations that accompanied their Golden Wedding on 17 October 1986. Donald and Jean became Joint Presidents of the East Kent Retirement Association in 1983 – in their respect an inept title; for those who know them realize that, having entered, they will finish the race.

[3] Mowbrays 1979.
[4] Mowbrays 1982.
[5] Mowbrays 1986.

Appendix 1: Publications

Story of the English Bible, illustrated in the memorial windows of Wycliffe College Chapel, University of Toronto Press 1942.

A People's Heritage, Church House Toronto 1944.

The Ministry of the Word, Canterbury Press 1945.

The Glory of God, Church Missionary Society 1950.

Stewards of Grace, Hodder and Stoughton 1958.

Five Makers of the New Testament, Hodder and Stoughton 1962.

Christian Priorities, Harper and Row 1963.

The Prayers of the New Testament, Hodder and Stoughton 1967.

Sinews of Faith, Hodder and Stoughton 1969.

Word and World, Hodder and Stoughton 1971.

Convictions, Hodder and Stoughton 1975.

On Preaching, SPCK 1978.

The Heart of the Christian Faith, Abingdon Press 1978.

The Name Above All Names, SPCK 1980.

Sure Foundation, Hodder and Stoughton 1981.

Mission to the World (Chavasse Memorial Lectures), Hodder and Stoughton 1982.

Paul: Portrait of a Revolutionary, Hodder and Stoughton 1984.

The Last Eight Days (with Paul Rooke Ley), Churchman Publishing 1987.

The Sacrament of the Word, Collins 1987.

Appendix 2: Honorary Degrees

DD
Wycliffe College Toronto, Lambeth, Cambridge, Leeds, Aberdeen, Huron, Tokyo, Saskatoon, Manchester, Hull, Moravian Theological Seminary, Virginia Theological Seminary

DHum
Westminster Choir College, Princeton

DLitt
Lancaster

LLD
Liverpool

STD
General Theological Seminary, New York

DUniv
York

DCL
University of Kent at Canterbury

FKC
King's College, London

Index